REEL JEWISH

JOEL SAMBERG

jD JONATHAN DAVID PUBLISHERS, INC.
Middle Village, New York 11379

REEL JEWISH

Copyright © 2000

by Joel Samberg

JONATHAN DAVID PUBLISHERS, INC.
68-22 Eliot Avenue
Middle Village, New York 11379

www.jdbooks.com

2 4 6 8 10 9 7 5 3 1

Library of Congress Cataloging-in-Publication Data

Samberg, Joel.
    Reel Jewish / Joel Samberg.
        p. cm.
    Filmography: p.
    Includes bibliographical references and index.
    ISBN 0-8246-0424-5
    1. Jews in motion pictures. I. Title.
    PN1995.9.J46 S26 2000
    791.43'65203924—dc21   00-064499
                                                                                             CIP

Book design by John Reinhardt Book Design

Printed in the United States of America

For my children, Celia, Kate, and Dan:
joys, inspirations—and critics!

Contents

CONTENTS

Acknowledgments

MAKING BOOKS, LIKE MAKING MOVIES, is a highly collaborative process. Though the initial conception may have been a solitary affair and watching dozens of videocassettes (while one of the coolest ways to build a career) a rather lonely pursuit in itself, everything else, from development to research to production, requires the expertise, support, cooperation, opinions, understanding, and convictions of many people. To an author, they are all superstars.

Rabbi Alfred J. Kolatch and David Kolatch of Jonathan David Publishers deserve my deepest thanks for giving me this opportunity. They became my mentors with the creation of this project, and now I know they are also going to be my friends forever.

I am very fortunate to have had the editorial guidance of Deborah Fogel, who vastly improved upon my effort without leaving too much of it on the cutting room floor. She is a "reel" pro to whom I am grateful.

Among those who made this book possible with their help and special efforts on my behalf are Stacey Freed of the *Jewish Monthly* (Washington, D.C.), Dawn James and the gang at Curry Home Video (Bloomfield, N.J.), Ed Martachi from Blockbuster Video district office #410, the staff of Movie Star News (New York, N.Y.), Steven Schloss and Kerry Bayowitz of *Jewish Week* (New York, N.Y.), Ira Schorr at West Coast Video (Montclair, N.J.), and the staff of the Walder Memorial Library of MetroWest (Whippany, N.J.).

I would also like to thank Robert Alper (the world's only practicing clergyman doing standup comedy… intentionally), Jon Amdursky (the *real* Mr. Saturday Night), Jeff and Jeannie Bass (for a prophetic Chanukah gift), Gloria Bass (for making sure I finished on time), Bill Freytag (a funny friend and honorary *landsman*), Gary Hallingse and Joni Hornidge, Peter Lebovitz, Irene and Steve Levine (for the wedding scene in *The Duchess and the Dirtwater Fox*), Joan Liewant, Jerry and Renée Samberg (for helping out with the renting, taping, and unlimited access to the Exclusive Samberg Video Library), Lynda and Pedro Soriano, Vivian Toporek, Dan Unger, John Wagman, Dave Weiner (who will have to read the introduction to discover why), Linda and Toniann Wright, and Cindy Young (for another Chanukah gift that was enormously helpful).

And my wife, Bonnie, for graciously putting up with computer beeps, pages turning, printers printing, and even Barbra Streisand singing late into the night for a couple of months.

Introduction:
In the Beginning
There Was Tzeitel

He wasn't Jewish, hadn't seen the Broadway show, didn't have the same kind of consuming passion for movies that I had, and it wasn't even raining that day.

Still, I dragged my friend Kevin to the Salisbury Theater to see *Fiddler on the Roof* one weekend afternoon when we were teenagers during a summer rerelease of the 1971 musical. I was certain I could talk him into sharing my enthusiasm for the film, a particularly challenging task, since he was only lukewarm about it to begin with. There's a funny kind of satisfaction in that.

I was wrong.

Not even bribery, which I don't think I actually resorted to at the time, can persuade people to like something when they have different perspectives on life, liberty, and the pursuit of movie matinees. Different cultural backgrounds and personal experiences quite simply give people different likes and dislikes, passions and peeves. Although Kevin said he enjoyed *Fiddler on the Roof* (as did many of the non-Jews who saw it), the movie certainly didn't touch him the way it touched me, and still touches me today. That was easy enough to tell just by discussing it with him afterward as we walked through the neighborhood. There was little eagerness on his part to make believe we were in a Westbury, Long Island, version of the movie, the way we had done with *Planet of the Apes* a few years before. That was one sign. Then, when he didn't even want to try to pronounce Tzeitel correctly, I knew for sure that I had lost.

That's also when I realized, however, that there always were and always will be movies that some people will enjoy, appreciate, adore, admire, or just feel connected to more than other people. For better or worse, in black and white and color, that's just the way it is. And perhaps that's when the idea for this book began to take shape.

When I began to write *Reel Jewish* (twenty-seven years after that momentous event at the Salisbury Theater) I was fortunate to have a brief telephone conversation with a nationally known film critic and media personality. When I told him what I was doing he said, "The question your book should address is not why there are so few so-called Jewish movies, but why there are any at all."

At the time, the apparently sarcastic-rhetorical nature of his comment bothered me because I wasn't quite sure what he meant; I was so thrilled to be starting off the research portion of the project with such a notable source that I didn't bother to get a clarification while I had him on the line. Did he mean it was ironic that there were any Jewish movies at all, considering how small the Jewish population is the world over, or did he mean that since the Jewish population *is* so small, why bother making any in the first place?

If the irony is what he had in mind, on one hand he's right: Jews make up only 2 per cent of the population of the United States (and less than less than a hundredth of 1 per cent of the world population), so even one film every year about Jewish people or Jewish experiences may seem high to some. On the other hand (as *Fiddler on the Roof*'s Tevye in would say), a precedent to the contrary has already been set for decades—as indeed it has for many other eth-

nic and cultural groups—for despite the population statistics, there are thousands upon thousands of books published about Jews and the Jewish experience, hundreds of plays and television shows with major Jewish characters, and dozens of Yiddish words spoken daily even by non-Jews in the media, the entertainment world, and across society at large. Why should the motion picture industry be any different?

And if my source meant why bother making any Jewish movies at all due to the incredibly small numbers of Jews, shouldn't the same be said of movies about other similarly small groups? Why make movies about American Indians (*Little Big Man, Dances with Wolves*), or astronauts (*The Right Stuff, Apollo 13*) or gangsters (*The Godfather, GoodFellas*)? Heaven forbid someone should want to make a movie about an American Indian gangster who becomes an astronaut!

The other obvious question that arises from my telephone conversation is, What constitutes a Jewish movie in the first place? For the purposes of this book I have decided to define as Jewish those motion pictures in which Judaism, a Jewish experience, or simply a character's Jewish background plays a definite role in the development of the story. Indeed, human drama is the stuff of a vast number of motion pictures, and if there is one group nearly defined by human drama, it is the Jews. As has been proven for decades, many novelists and screenwriters have developed quite a skill to turn Jewish human drama into true movie entertainment.

How many of these movies are there? When you weigh the number of Jewish movies against the number of movies produced since the silent days just beyond the turn of the century, it is but a microscopic fraction. But even that microscopic fraction can provide weeks and even months of enjoyment, study, fascination, appreciation, debate, or contemplation. I thought it would be worthwhile, then, to revisit some of the best, most intriguing, most unusual, oddest, silliest, and most honored of these Jewish movies—at least those that are available to the general public—in an effort to recognize their Jewish highlights, share some trivia and anecdotes (which sometimes make motion pictures more enjoyable to discuss than actually watch), and promote their appeal (even of the lousy ones) for those of you who still like to make believe your neighborhoods are movie sets—whether or not you share your flights of fancy with others.

Be assured that you don't have to be Jewish to enjoy Jewish movies, just as you don't have to be dead to enjoy *Poltergeist, Ghost,* or *Genghis Cohn* (which, by the way, is about a Jewish ghost).

It seems that many Jewish movies, particularly those discussed in this book, have all made news in one way or another. Many are Academy Award winners, five having won the award for best picture (*Gentleman's Agreement, Annie Hall, Chariots of Fire, Driving Miss Daisy,* and *Schindler's List*). Several have caused studio executives to buy more than a few boxes of antacid, either because of distribution problems inherent in the subject matter (*Crossfire* was banned by the U.S. Navy because of its depiction of an anti-Semitic soldier) or because of production excesses (*The Ten Commandments* used 12,000 people and 15,000 animals in the exodus scene alone). Some were noted for words

exchanged off camera (Paul Newman and Otto Preminger didn't get along while making *Exodus*) or for action generated off set (Warren Beatty and Annette Bening fell madly in love while making *Bugsy*). A few redefined careers (*Schindler's List* is likely to be Steven Spielberg's crowning lifetime achievement).

Neither the awards, the news, nor the gossip columns, however, are of the greatest consequence—although such choice tidbits *are* fun and interesting to learn and make a major contribution to *Reel Jewish*; what you remember about some of these movies, how they may contribute to your own thoughts or reflections about the ways Jews and Jewish experiences are portrayed, which ones you might want to rent after reading a little about them here . . . those are the things that are important to this endeavor. In fact, I have commented to friends that if just a handful of readers are encouraged to rent a video because of my *Reel Jewish* reflections, I will consider the book to be a real success. (I have since amended that to mean in addition to the number of copies sold.)

These are not in-depth critical reviews—although it will be obvious throughout which films I loved and which ones I did not. In-depth critical reviews are readily available from many other sources (among them books, magazines, newspapers and the Internet) and they will invariably be more penetrating than my own comments and synopses. The task I set myself was simply to determine which of the movies made available for home viewing illuminate Jewish characterizations and situations more than others, and then share my impressions within the framework of Jewish content and general appeal.

All of the movies covered in Chapters 1

through 13, and a majority of those in Chapter 14, are commercially available either at video stores, in special Judaica libraries or media centers, or through various mail-order services. (Some of these services are listed in the back of this book.) Less than a handful were still in theaters or had recently finished their initial theatrical run when the book was being written. Quite a few also turn up on broadcast or cable television from time to time. They cover an incredibly wide array of styles and genres, from a silent horror movie made in 1914 to a Catskill melodrama released in 1999. They include dramas, comedies, biblical films, critical and commercial bombs, blockbusters, the first to use spoken dialogue, and even a cartoon made for children and grownups alike. Most of them are American-made, to an extent reflective of the birth and growth of the medium (and, as will be shown, Jewish movies have been around nearly as long as American movies have been around). Filmmakers outside the United States have certainly added many interesting shades, colors, and emotions to the world of Jewish films, and several of these are included in this book.

There may not be many Jewish movies out there—but those there are certainly embrace just about every motion picture category there is. Not bad for less than 2 per cent.

Even among audiences of similar background there are differences of opinion. What makes one individual cry with joy makes another fall asleep from boredom. What one person thinks is a clever narrative idea might be regarded by another as a clawing plot device. That's why I would prefer readers to make their own decisions. A lot of arguments can be avoided that way.

It's not that I don't expect or even want some arguments based on my choices and my words. After all, even the pros disagree. Roger Ebert called *Crimes and Misdemeanors* "the best kind of suspense," whereas Pauline Kael said it had "no excitement." In fact, sometimes it seems I myself have been having movie arguments ever since my first film class at Hofstra University, back in the days when Barbra Streisand's current husband (James Brolin) was a bona fide movie star. I recall that my professor (who shall remain nameless just in case he can still help my career) suggested that movies can be dissected technically and narratively to determine without question which ones are good and which are bad. I never wanted to believe that. I wanted to believe that a movie was good if you enjoyed it, bad if you fell asleep. I remember discussing a movie with that professor (starring Brolin, incidentally) and saying to him, "It didn't work for me." He practically strangled me as he criticized my use of the phrase. It's not about what works or doesn't work for a person, he chided, but about the way the individual filmic elements come together to produce a desired effect. I've always found that hard to accept.

I would even suggest, although I didn't dare say it in class that day, fearing for my life, that if you *did* enjoy a particular movie, it may be because you were of a certain age when you saw it, that you saw it with a certain friend, or that you had just failed a certain test in a certain class before going to that certain movie theater with that certain friend. And that if *any* one of those elements had been different, you might have had an entirely different reaction to the movie. It would make my dear professor *plotz* (or burst) if he heard me say that. Actually, that's a lot better than almost being strangled by the man.

So, arguments won't be that much of a surprise. Furthermore, I suppose that merely by including some of the movies in this book I am inviting protests from people who think they should not have been included, and some movies that are *not* mentioned, other people will protest, should have been. And there may very well be arguments and criticism about the way the book is categorized: Family stories can easily be thought of instead as comedies, musicals as love stories, and Holocaust dramas as indictments against anti-Semitism.

But arguments can be invigorating, illuminating, and fun. In fact, another vivid movie memory of mine concerns a former colleague, Dave Weiner, with whom I worked when we both reviewed programs for a home video magazine. We argued off and on for years about the casting of Topol

as Tevye in *Fiddler on the Roof.* Dave was adamant in his opinion that the role should have gone to Zero Mostel, who originated it on Broadway. My position was that Mostel's over-the-top personality, vocally and physically, while effective on stage, would have been an intrusion on screen. Topol, I maintained, gave Tevye a strong and reserved authority, an effective quality Mostel may have lacked. Our arguments were long and loud—and full of laughter.

So let the arguments begin. Read and enjoy. Argue and criticize. Laugh. Cry. Scream. *Plotz.* Maybe one or two of you will seek out my old professor and tell him—to his face—which of these films "worked for you" and which didn't. If you do, wear an iron turtleneck. Maybe someone will seek out Dave Weiner and tell him he's entitled to his opinion and to believe he was right all along. By the way, if you do find Dave, please also tell him that if it weren't for Topol, I might not have written this book in the first place, which in some way proves that *I* was right, after all.

1

From Henry Street to Hollywood

The Jazz Singer

The Benny Goodman Story

Funny Girl

Fiddler on the Roof

Yentl

BY THE TIME *The Jazz Singer* was remade for the second time in 1980, the Hollywood musical, with very few exceptions, was all but dead. If it had any life left in it at all, Neil Diamond and company seemed only too pleased to say "Toot, toot, tootsie goodbye."

Once upon a time, the Hollywood musical was as common as the nickel matinee. Between *The Jazz Singer* of 1927 and *The Jazz Singer* of 1980 more than 250 musicals were produced for the American cinema, both imports from Broadway and originals

written directly for the screen. Very few of them concerned the Jewish experience or celebrated its inimitable joys and daily challenges—and many of those that did have a certain Jewish flavor almost never made it to the screen. The first *Jazz Singer*, for example, ran into trouble right away when George Jessel, who played the role on Broadway and was signed to reprise it on film, had a major disagreement with the studio, Warner Brothers. *Yentl*, Barbra Streisand's personal film crusade about a young yeshiva student, was turned down so many times that the actress-director could almost have made a movie about Yentl as a grandmother instead.

That's why a bomb (by most critical accounts) like the Neil Diamond version of *The Jazz Singer* is especially troublesome. With that Jewish-flavored failure forever looming in the marketing minds of American filmmakers, we can almost be assured that there is unlikely to be a major movie musical in the future from which Jewish audiences might *shep* a little *nachas*, that is, to derive some special pride from the story.

Still, it's nice to know that in 1927, the original *Jazz Singer*, which featured Jewish characters with Jewish hearts and conflicts (and even a few Hebrew prayers) not only made a lot of money for its studio but made history as well. As the first motion picture to use several sequences of synchronized dialogue and music (it was otherwise a silent film), *The Jazz Singer* is generally considered both the first talkie *and* the first movie musical. That a movie of such importance is also in some respects a love letter to Judaism is certainly reason enough for Jewish audiences to *shep* a little *nachas* of their own.

A strong central love story has been the unifying force in movie musicals for generations. *The Jazz Singer* didn't settle for just one. It actually had four of them—almost as if Warner Brothers was trying to break the rules of the movie musical game before the game even started. *The Jazz Singer* was a love story to a young man's mother, sweetheart, chosen profession, and religion.

The story, of course, didn't originate with the studio; it was based on a play by Samson Raphaelson, which in turn was based on his own short story, "The Day of Atonement." George Jessel starred in the Broadway version but it was Al Jolson who ultimately won the role in Warner's movie, starring as Jakie Rabinowitz, a young singer and cantor's son who changes his name to Jack Robin when the footlights start to call out to him. Not only does Jack love his Jewish heritage, he also loves show business (which in his father's eyes is an evil interloper), his devoted mother (who is troubled by the division in their family), and a pretty girl named Mary Dale (who is not Jewish). Maybe *that's* what Jolson meant when he said, "You ain't seen nothing yet."

The movie, adapted by Jack Jarmuth and directed by Alan Crosland, introduced to wider audiences than ever before such Jolson classics as "Mammy," "Blue Skies," "My Gal Sal," and "Waiting for the Robert E. Lee" through the new Vitaphone sound-on-disc process that Warner Brothers had purchased from Western Electric. In addition, *The Jazz Singer* is noted for introducing one of the earliest quintessential Jewish mothers on screen, played by Eugenie Besserer, a leading character actress of the day who had appeared in more than thirty films by the time she played Mama Rabinowitz.

Mama knows how much her Jakie loves her, but little by little she and Papa Rabinowitz (Warner Oland) discover that there are many other influences in their boy's life, a fact that sits about as well with both of them as a large stuffed cabbage.

"Maybe our boy doesn't want to be a cantor, Papa," Mama laments.

"What has *he* got to say?" Papa rebuffs. "For five generations a Rabinowitz has been a cantor. He must be one."

Still, Jakie hits the road, as Jewish boys do from time to time, and almost at once finds enthusiastic audiences for his special brand of music. Meanwhile, Mary, the young ingenue (May McAvoy), hangs on fast to her rising star with the boyish grin (even in blackface) and man-size ego. It isn't long before Jakie feels the need to write to his beloved mother about all that's happening to him on the road.

"Read me what he says about the girl," a family friend says to Mama after she receives a letter from Jakie.

"Maybe he's fallen in love with a *shikse*," she realizes, painfully re-reading the words on the page, using that sometimes wicked-sounding Yiddish word for a non-Jewish woman.

"Maybe not," the friend says, trying desperately to alleviate her concern. "You know Rose Levy on the theayter is Rosemarie Lee!"

But Mary Dale ain't no Rose Levy, and between the showbiz and the *shikse*, Cantor Rabinowitz has little to be proud of.

"I told you never to open his letters," he warns his sullen wife. "We have no son."

Later, however, Jakie scores a point for conciliation when he says to Papa, "You taught me that music is the voice of God! It is as honorable to sing in the theater as in the synagogue." If only it were as easy in real life to come up with the right things to say so quickly.

Not surprisingly, some of *The Jazz Singer*'s primitive technical values and flat dialogue make it difficult for modern audiences to take seriously. But there is no denying its importance to movie history, and to the his-

tory of popular music. At the first Academy Awards presentation in May 1929, Warner Brothers was given a statuette (not yet called an Oscar) "for producing *The Jazz Singer*,

---

The Jazz Saga

Imagine *The Jessel Story*, or *Jessel Sings Again*.

While that may never have happened, actor and comedian George Jessel, who played the lead in *The Jazz Singer* for over nine months on Broadway, was signed to reprise the role on film for Warner Brothers. That, too, never happened, and there are a few variations on the story that attempt to explain why.

When Jessel discovered that Warner Brothers wanted to add songs using a new process called Vitaphone, he held out for a higher salary than the one offered—reportedly $10,000 more. It is said that he knew how much hope Warners had for the new process and that it was their anticipation of a blockbuster that made Jessel ask for more money.

However, Jessel himself stated that he did not like the screenplay's ending, which was different from the ending of the play, in which Jakie Rabinowitz gives up the stage and embraces the pulpit for good. In the movie, he doesn't.

Still another theory, posed by Neal Gabler in *An Empire of Their Own: How the Jews Invented Hollywood*, says it was Jessel's ethnicity that ultimately got him replaced. Jessel, Gabler writes, may have been "too Jewish for the kind of assimilationist fable Jack Warner had in mind." Although Al Jolson was Jewish, too, he was nationally regarded as a completely assimilated Jew.

---

the pioneer talking picture, which has revolutionized the industry." Even today, *The Jazz Singer* gives audiences the chance to hear the biggest musical superstar of his day sing in the biggest movie blockbuster of that decade. Not only to hear him sing, but to hear him talk, too! It was Sam Warner himself, one of the founders of the studio that made the film, who suggested adding a few lines of dialogue between choruses of "Blue

With a style of his own, Al Jolson ushers in a new era of motion pictures as The Jazz Singer.

Jolson Speaks Again

At work, Harry Cohn was the powerful, very involved and often despised head of Columbia Pictures. But after hours (as limited as they were) he was an enormous Al Jolson fan who simply kept quiet whenever the great entertainer sang. When casting *The Jolson Story*, the last thing Cohn was prepared to do was make a quick decision as to who would play his favorite performer. He also wanted to make Jolson happy.

Cohn's first choice was James Cagney, who was spectacular in the 1942 film *Yankee Doodle Dandy*, but Cagney had no interest in playing another showbiz legend. Cohn's next choice was Danny Thomas, who was on his way up the entertainment ranks. But the studio wanted Thomas to have an operation to reduce the size of his nose, and Thomas refused to do so.

José Ferrer and Richard Conte were also on Columbia's list of potential leads.

The first actor to actually make a screen test as Jolson was Larry Parks, a Columbia contract player. Cohn and other members of the production team were confident enough to let him test a second time—at the end of the entire search process. Before that final test, Parks watched all the films in which Jolson had appeared, listened to all his records, and was even coached in the Jolson style by Columbia music directors.

At the final screen test, Jolson was present and couldn't believe how much like himself Parks appeared to be. He was pleased, and so was Cohn. But later, when Jolson went to New York's Winter Garden Theater, where a sequence was being shot, he watched Parks on stage and commented, "The kid just doesn't move like me."

Skies." So in the middle of the song, performed in his parents' apartment, Jakie tells Mama to shut her eyes, and when she does he kisses her on the cheek and tells her that if his new Broadway show is a hit, he is going to buy her a better place in which to live. By the expression on Eugenie Besserer's face, audiences knew that she was as surprised as they were to hear him speak.

Thanks in part to Sam Warner's suggestion, the studio, after several years of struggle, regained its hold on tremendous profits. And one of the first Jewish mothers on screen renewed her faith in the love of a successful son.

The phrase "lip-synch" didn't exist when *The Jazz Singer* was made. No one knew that there would ever be a need for it. But when Hollywood finally got around to producing Al Jolson's biography almost twenty years later, it was commonplace.

Jolson, as he did in *The Jazz Singer*, sang his own songs in the biopic *The Jolson Story* (1946) and in the 1949 sequel *Jolson Sings Again*, but it was actor Larry Parks, who played Jolson in both films, who did the lip-synching. It was a gimmick that worked very well for audiences.

In 1955, Valentine Davies wrote and directed a movie biography of famed Jewish bandleader and clarinetist Benny Goodman, and lip-synching of a different kind was necessary—Steve Allen made believe it was his lips producing the sounds that came out of Goodman's clarinet when in fact it was really Goodman's lips that did the job.

The Benny Goodman Story did a respectable amount of box office business despite its being a woefully abridged version of Goodman's life, with a rather one-dimensional portrayal by Allen. As with *The Jazz Singer* before it and many movie musicals thereafter, it was beset with preproduction conflicts. Music producer, and Goodman associate, John Hammond made the initial waves. Hammond's efforts to be allowed to see the script of *The Benny Goodman Story* before filming began were successful, but he was greatly disappointed in the way he and

Steve Allen makes the right moves in The Benny Goodman Story, *while Goodman himself plays the right notes.*

his sister Alice (who would later become Mrs. Benny Goodman) were portrayed. When he fought the studio executives about the issue, they tried to pacify him with money. Ultimately, the Hammond character's role in the movie (he was played by Herbert Anderson) was significantly reduced.

Then some of Goodman's original instrumentalists who were not asked to play on the movie's soundtrack made more waves, especially since many others *were* asked, including Harry James, Hymie Schertzer, Babe Russin, Gene Krupa, and Martha Tilton.

With that many waves, it's amazing *The Benny Goodman Story* didn't drown before Davies' first call for action.

Without the novelty of having real music provided by real swing band musicians, *The Benny Goodman Story* might very well have been considered an unintentional comedy, particularly in its opening scenes. In 1919, in hopes of steering them clear of trouble in the tough Chicago neighborhood in which they live, Benny's father (Robert F. Simon) takes his three nice Jewish boys to a music teacher. Benny is given a clarinet, which he mistakenly calls a flute, and learns to play it so quickly that you wonder if his mother gave him a woodwind in the crib instead of a pacifier. Incidentally, Steve Allen's fingers often move slower than Benny Goodman's playing, proving that it is much easier to lip-synch than to finger-synch.

The gentile girl in the story, Alice Hammond, is played with typical geniality by Donna Reed. Alice is a cultural snob who likes only classical music, but when she hears Benny play she feels the emotion pouring out of him. And while he may feel a trill in his heart for the beautiful Alice, he is far too busy building his band to play any of the right notes with her.

True to twentieth-century Jewish motherhood, Benny's outward lack of interest does not lessen Mama Goodman's heartburn over the situation. Bertha Gersten as his mother continues the tradition of the sweet yet suffering Jewish mama who ultimately learns to accept fate with humility.

"Harry," she says to one of her other sons, "I have a horrible sinking feeling in my stomach. It's Alice. I'm afraid she's falling in love with my Benny."

"Mom," a surprised Harry responds, "I thought you liked her."

"I might like the Queen of England too if I met her," Mama says, "but God forbid she should marry my Benny."

Later, confronting Alice directly, she tells her she'll make some man a good wife, "but not my Benny," and when Alice asks why not, Mama says, "Because you don't mix caviar with bagels."

But even Mama cannot deny the effect Alice is having on her Benny and his outlook on life, and before long she calls Alice at her Vermont hideaway and asks her to come to New York to see Benny in his Carnegie Hall debut.

Most critics acknowledged that *The Benny Goodman Story* took enormous liberties with the facts of Goodman's life, but most also agreed that the score, which includes such Goodman swing era classics as "Sing, Sing Sing," "And the Angels Sing," and "Shine," makes it almost as easy to accept as a late-night talk show on a snowy evening. The movie was shot in just eight weeks, and Allen, who was hosting *The Tonight Show* on live television at the time, did not miss a single performance of the program even after shooting all day long. Still, he was tired and admitted to having trouble remembering his lines. Fortunately, his mouth was occupied through much of the movie on a clarinet mouthpiece. If only his fingers had been able to keep up. . . .

Steve Allen isn't Jewish but was passable as a Jew. Nobody could ever make a statement like that about Barbra Streisand; she *is* Jewish and will always *appear* Jewish even if she plays Doris Day.

There have been many movie biographies of famous Jewish entertainers—*Till the*

Omar Sharif sees more than a Funny Girl *in Barbra Streisand as the comedienne-singer Fanny Brice.*

Clouds Roll By in 1946 with Robert Walker as Jerome Kern, *The Eddie Cantor Story* in 1953 starring Keefe Brasselle, *Lenny* in 1974 with Dustin Hoffman—but for the most part these films all but ignore the Jewishness (or lack of it) of their celebrated subjects. But in *Funny Girl* (1968), the musical biography of comedienne Fanny Brice, written by Isobel Lennart and directed by William Wyler, Streisand won an Academy Award as best actress and almost overnight became an international superstar playing a legend whose Jewishness was actually part of her act and her success.

The difficulty in getting *Funny Girl* made had less to do with the complaints of the real people portrayed in it (since most of them were dead) than with who was chosen to portray one of those people. As far as Fanny herself was concerned, there was never any question that Streisand would repeat her stage role, having already become famous on the basis of the Broadway show, television specials, and records. But the role of Fanny's gambler husband, Nicky Arnstein, was quite another story.

Several actors were considered for the part, including Tony Curtis and Sean Connery, but

Wyler spotted Egyptian actor Omar Sharif one day at the studio and thought he would be perfect. The Six-Day War in Israel was recent history, and pro-Israeli organizations raised a fuss about a Jew and an Arab playing lovers. Despite Wyler's choice, some Colum-

All or Nothing at All

Producer Ray Stark once had to rain on Barbra Streisand's parade.

While it had been assumed that Streisand would be asked to reprise her sensational stage role as Fanny Brice for the screen version of *Funny Girl*, there were few assumptions about who would play Nicky Arnstein, although everyone, including Streisand, had opinions.

Not one of the actors who played the role of Brice's gambler husband on Broadway was seriously considered for the movie, none of them being hot box office properties. By contrast, Omar Sharif had already appeared in *Lawrence of Arabia* and *Doctor Zhivago*. Among those who were initially considered for their marquee value and good looks were Tony Curtis, Sean Connery, Gregory Peck, David Janssen, and James Garner.

Streisand's dream, however, was to cast Marlon Brando in the role, but producer Ray Stark uttered a resounding no. Then composer Jule Styne suggested Frank Sinatra, anticipating lines around the block with such superstar billing. Styne even went so far as to contact Sinatra about it and Sinatra said he might consider it if the salary was acceptable to him, if a few new songs were composed for him, if a few new scenes were written for him, and if top billing was reserved for him.

This time Stark and Streisand agreed. The answer was no.

bia Pictures executives suggested removing Sharif, but Wyler fumed, threatening to walk off the project if the actor were let go. When production ended, Wyler commented that if all Jews and Arabs got along like Streisand and Sharif, the Middle East would be a Garden of Eden. You don't hear sentiments like *that* every day of the week.

Funny Girl captured the praise of both the critics and the public with its likable characters, memorable score, effective balance of humor and drama, and show-stopping performance by Streisand, who even a harsh critic like Pauline Kael acknowledged has "the gift of making mere dialogue sound like natural improvisation." Kael even likened her to great screen comediennes of the past such as Jean Arthur, Claudette Colbert, and Carole Lombard.

Funny Girl was one of the most successful musicals of the 1960s, a decade that also produced *West Side Story, The Music Man, Bye Bye Birdie, Mary Poppins, My Fair Lady,* and *The Sound of Music.* While it was Barbra's show all the way, the screenplay had enough good old-fashioned backstage melodrama to make it a lot more than just a Streisand lovefest. After all, when a star like Fanny Brice walks out onto an empty stage, points an invisible machine gun at the audience, and fires away, you know we're peeking into a public person's private angst.

Nicky Arnstein is her angst.

Handsome, suave, and sophisticated—"You're Park Avenue and I'm Lower East Side," Fanny says to him—the proud, stubborn, and somewhat shady gambler becomes a gigantic cloud on Fanny's otherwise bright horizon. What do you say about a husband who would rather play a poker game than go to his wife's opening night on Broadway? Fanny may finally become the "Sadie, Sadie, married lady" of her lifelong dream, but then what? When the chips are down, Nicky can't even keep up the charade. As one of his gambling associates points out to him, "That big spotlight on your wife lights you up, too."

Still, following Fanny's exploits as she *kvetches* her way into the Ziegfeld Follies is a bundle of fun. Legendary producer Florenz Ziegfeld (Walter Pidgeon) usually hires only graceful beauties to be in his shows, but Fanny is a klutz, she's funny, she's different, she's just a plain old kid from Henry Street. As she says, "I'm a bagel on a plate full of onion rolls." That's why Ziegfeld wants her. She has the *chutzpah* to do or say almost anything she wants, and most of the time it's a riot. Even at the very first rehearsal of her first show, after arguing with Ziegfeld and being reminded she is in *his* theater, Fanny looks at him and says, "So? Nobody argues with the landlord?"

Like most movie biographies it is a rather sketchy account of her life, but the songs, both those written for the show by Jule Styne and Bob Merrill as well as Brice originals, give a certain amount of depth to Fanny by explaining who she is, how she feels, and what she wants. Styne and Merrill's score includes "I'm the Greatest Star," "People," "You Are Woman, I Am Man" and "Don't Rain on My Parade." Brice classics include "I'd Rather Be Blue Over You," "Second Hand Rose" and "My Man."

Indeed, it is an ethnically flavored score that reminds audiences just who Fanny Brice was: one of America's foremost Jewish-American comediennes. After all, "What a beast to ruin such a pearl—would a convent take a Jewish girl?" isn't a lyric you hear every day of the week.

The Jewish musical of all Jewish musicals hit the screen in 1971, three years after *Funny Girl* and with the same kind of anticipation. Actually anticipation was even greater since the stage version of *Fiddler on the Roof* was a bigger hit than *Funny Girl,* and the curiosity about how well the screen's Topol would measure up against the stage's Zero Mostel developed into an American-Jewish version of "Who shot J.R.?"

A story of Jewish traditions tenaciously clung to in the face of adversity, *Fiddler on the Roof,* written by Joseph Stein and directed by Norman Jewison, was blessed with a versatile, enthusiastic ensemble. It also boasted a marvelous Broadway score and an old world reality found and replicated by the production crew in realistic Yugoslavian locations and filmed with shades, tones, and colors specifically chosen to resemble a Marc Chagall painting.

In terms of production problems, why should *Fiddler on the Roof* be different from any other movie musical? First, of course, there was the Tevye tribulation, and then the director dilemma. Many actors, including Mostel and Danny Thomas, lobbied hard for the part of the poor milkman with five daughters. But it was the Israeli actor Topol, who had played Tevye for many years on the London stage, who won the coveted role. Many thought his more muted approach to the character (compared with Mostel's) would hurt the film. Topol, in turn, raised concerns that the studio's choice for director, the non-Jewish Jewison, might not be able to interpret the emotions or characters of the story properly.

Topol and Jewison, as it turned out, were both excellent choices.

Even with a lame horse, Topol uses a sense of humor in Fiddler on the Roof *to help him get through each day's tribulations.*

The townsfolk of Anatevka, a Russian *shtetl*, or poor, tiny village, try to "scratch out a simple little tune without breaking their necks." Tevye's horse, though, breaks its leg, his daughters begin to break tradition—and his wife, Golde, would like to break his neck when he gives in to his daughters' marital whims.

But Tevye is not a broken man—a poor man, yes, but not a broken one. He has faith in his faith, and everything he does, including the songs he sings, speaks to that faith. He dreams of being a rich man so that he would have more time to sit in the syna-

gogue and pray. He talks and even argues with God, coming to some very special realizations along the way. When his eldest daughter, Tzeitel, and her beau, Motel the tailor, tell him that they have given each other a pledge to marry without using a matchmaker, Tevye suddenly realizes that they are indeed using a matchmaker—the same one used by Adam and Eve—and he takes comfort in that.

Tevye may be the story's central character (Joseph Stein's libretto and screenplay are based on a collection of Sholom Aleichem short stories called "Tevye and His Daughters") but *Fiddler on the Roof* is peopled with a cast of likable characters played by talented pros, which gives the movie much of its charm. Leonard Frey plays the tailor with an infectious innocence, goodness and earnestness that won him an Academy Award nomination as best supporting actor. Norma Crane is a tough and effective Golde. Yiddish stage star Molly Picon is an adorable and quirky Yente the Matchmaker.

But Tevye is the one who holds it all together more than anyone else. Stoic, warm, and wise, he is the only one who can get away with jabbing his finger at God and saying, "I'm not really complaining. After all, with your help, I'm starving to death."

The score, by Sheldon Harnick and Jerry Bock, effectively evokes the daily struggles of these life-loving Jews. Beginning with the opening ensemble number, "Tradition," through "Matchmaker, Matchmaker," "Sabbath Prayer," "To Life," "Miracle of Miracles," "Do You Love Me?" "Far from the Home I Love" and others, each one seems hand-sewn to the characters to tell the story of their lives and their little village. (Thanks to the success of *Fiddler on the Roof* on stage and screen, every wedding band in the world knows "Sunrise, Sunset" backward and forward.) The dances by Tom Abbott, who was Jerome Robbins's assistant on the original Broadway production, are based on the stage play's choreography.

Jewison, whose body of work includes *The Cincinnati Kid, In the Heat of the Night*, and *Moonstruck*, is one of the most serious and insightful directors around, and as much as

Long Island Tradition

The poor people of Anatevka didn't always sing. Twenty-five years before Sheldon Harnick and Jerry Bock gave them a musical score with which to tell their story, there was *Tevye*, a 1939 movie based on one of the Sholom Aleichem stories about the poor milkman trying to hold on to Jewish tradition in an ever-changing world.

The movie was written and directed by renowned Yiddish stage star Maurice Schwartz, who also starred in it. *Tevye* is like its tuneful descendant, *Fiddler on the Roof*, in the heartfelt manner in which it treats its subject and in the colorful ways (despite its being in black and white) in which its actors inhabit their roles. The major differences between the two, besides the obvious musical one, are strictly a function of the times in which they were made: The 1939 film was shot entirely in Jericho, on New York's Long Island, whereas the 1971 musical was filmed in Yugoslavia. Long Island would be a difficult location for such a film today. The story takes place in a small, poor Jewish village commonly known as a *shtetl*, but not many modern Jerichos or Levittowns could pass for a *shtetl* at the end of the nineteenth century.

drama, musical comedy always benefits from insightful direction. So when Motel feels like a king for standing up to Tevye, the angle Jewison chooses, unlike any other angle in the film, almost literally shows how he feels ten feet tall. And when Golde tells Tevye that their third daughter, Chava (Neva Small), has run away to marry the gentile Fyedka (Raymond Lovelock), the scene is set in a vast expanse of cold, barren landscape, as if all the beauty and familial comforts of their lives have been ripped mercilessly away from them. It's a chilling scene in more ways than one.

Fiddler on the Roof was the third most successful movie musical of the 1970s, the last decade in which movie musicals were brought to life to any great degree (among them were *Cabaret, Funny Lady, A Star Is Born, Grease, Hair* and *The Rose*). In addition to Frey's Academy Award nomination

That Goy!

American television audiences made room for Danny Thomas every week for eighteen years. But before he became famous as a TV daddy (and as *That Girl* Marlo Thomas's father), he wanted to become famous as a cantor's son by playing Al Jolson in *The Jolson Story*. Thomas greatly desired the role and was, in fact, one of several actors considered, although Larry Parks eventually got the job in the 1946 film.

Thomas, however, was pleased to walk in similar territory a few years later in the 1948 film *Big City*, a family drama about a priest (Robert Preston), an Irish policeman (George Murphy), and a cantor (Thomas), all bachelors, who "adopt" young Margaret O'Brien and then become more attached to her than they had anticipated they would.

Big City wasn't a very successful film, but Thomas revisited the cantorial domain once more in 1953, with a remake of the motion picture that in many ways started it all, *The Jazz Singer*. Many critics cited its solid direction by Michael Curtiz and the supporting cast led by Peggy Lee and Mildred Dunnock, but Thomas's version of the famous story received only a lukewarm reception from the public.

Of course, right after that he found his true calling on weekly television in the enormously popular *Make Room for Daddy*, which ran from 1953 to 1971.

---

for best supporting actor, *Fiddler on the Roof* also received nominations for best picture and best actor, and though it lost both (to *The French Connection* and Gene Hackman), it won over many audiences that might otherwise never have learned how to make a toast "to life" by shouting *l'chaim*!

While Tevye was *schlepping* a milk cart across Anatevka's dusty roads, somewhere in the same corner of the world a young girl named Yentl was bouncing around a bookseller's cart

desperately trying to buy sacred Hebrew texts reserved only for men. The two never met (being fictional characters in separate stories) but share a similar genesis as enchanting characters created by two treasured Yiddish writers.

Yentl, a highly diverting tale based on the short story "Yentl the Yeshiva Boy" by Isaac Bashevis Singer, was a pet project of Barbra Streisand's for over a dozen years before she was able to turn it into a movie musical—as director, star, and cowriter with Jack Rosenthal. Nobody in Hollywood wanted to take a chance on such an ethnic and esoteric movie that would also be very costly to produce. But when it was completed, many people in and out of the industry were pleased with the results of Streisand's tireless efforts—with the notable exception of Mr. Singer himself. Upon seeing it, the writer said that "Miss Streisand was exceedingly kind to herself. The result is that Miss Streisand is always present, while poor Yentl is absent." True—but on the other hand, millions go to a Barbra Streisand movie precisely to see Barbra Streisand, no matter who she's pretending to be.

Playing a young girl who disguises herself as a boy in order to attend a *yeshiva* (a learning academy for Orthodox young Jewish men) could have been an insurmountable challenge even for an actress of Streisand's talent and nerve (she was forty at the time). In the movie, however, the character was made a little older than in the original story, and the unflinching earnestness of all the

Mandy Patinkin and Barbra Streisand share some unique secrets and passions in the musical Yentl.

supporting players further helps surmount the challenge. Of course, Yentl does have the cleanest complexion and highest voice of any man since Wayne Newton, but there is such devotion in every scene that it is almost impossible not to appreciate the results.

Streisand wanted with all her heart and soul to tell this story, and she did it with a certain amount of cinematic poetry, even though she had never directed a movie before (and didn't direct another one for eight years).

Yentl wants to study in a *yeshiva* because she longs to study Torah, a privilege forbidden to women in her world. At intervals throughout the picture birds are seen flying in the open sky, a gentle counterpoint to the freedom Yentl does *not* have in the world

of learned men. When her father (Nehemiah Persoff) passes away, she realizes that, despite missing him terribly, she now has an opportunity to do something radical in pursuit of her dream. She cuts her hair, leaves town, calls herself Anshel, applies to and is accepted at a *yeshiva*, and soon meets the handsome Avigdor, a fellow student with whom she soon falls in love. But Avigdor, sincerely played by Mandy Patinkin, is in love with, and is waiting to marry, the beautiful Hadass (Amy Irving).

Yentl cannot share her secret, her thoughts, her desires, or her agony with Avigdor—but she *can* share them with the audience through song, which is why *Yentl* became a musical in the first place. As lyricist Marilyn Bergman said, it is Yentl's "rich

It took over twelve years for Barbra Streisand to get behind the camera—and in front of it—to create the musical Yentl.

Oh Boy!

In the twenty-eight seconds Barbra Streisand had to spare between making *Funny Girl* and *Hello, Dolly!*, she first began to think about turning Isaac Bashevis Singer's "Yentl the Yeshiva Boy" into a movie. In 1971, it was announced that a movie based on the Singer tale would star Streisand and be directed by someone else. But Streisand was unhappy with the early drafts of the screenplay, and the project stalled.

Throughout the 1970s, one studio executive after another turned it down for fear of its potentially limited appeal. Streisand made a super-8 film of herself dressed as a boy, singing a song written for her by Michel Legrand and Alan and Marilyn Bergman, which she played for Sherry Lansing, then president of Twentieth Century Fox. Lansing, too, turned it down. Streisand was crushed. "I couldn't believe that a woman wouldn't understand how universal this story was," she said.

In 1979 Orion Pictures announced a *Yentl* project with Streisand starring and directing, and her then boyfriend Jon Peters coproducing. But Peters, who favored light comedy for his lover, opposed the project and stood in its way.

Orion finally did give the go-ahead. But then, when the notorious failure of *Heaven's Gate* sank United Artists, Orion began to fear that a project as big as *Yentl*, which was to be filmed overseas, would not be a wise investment and dropped out.

It took another three years for Streisand to get *Yentl* made.

inner life," especially after her father dies, that becomes the score. Soliloquies all, the songs enable the story to be told through Yentl's eyes—and voice. When she thinks about Hadass's devotion to Avigdor, Yentl croons about her as one "whose only aim in life is to serve you and make you think she

doesn't deserve you. No wonder he loves her, what else could he do. If I were a man, I would too."

The Academy Award-winning score, with lyrics by Alan and Marilyn Bergman and music by Michel Legrand, includes over half a dozen songs, all sung by Streisand. They

Choice Roles

No one knows for sure if actors who play rabbis on screen have to answer to an even higher authority than the director. But it is certain that their performances are usually full of conviction—in addition to quite a lot of zest and humor.

Zvee Scooler, who was a member of the Yiddish Art Theatre for twenty-five years, played a rabbi twice on screen, in *Fiddler on the Roof* and *Hester Street*. He also appeared in the Broadway version of *Fiddler* as the innkeeper, and in regional theater has played Mr. Frank in *The Diary of Anne Frank*.

Among other renowned thespians who have assumed cinematic pulpits are Hugh Griffith in *The Abominable Dr. Philbes*, Jeff Corey in *Oh, God!*, Eli Wallach in *Girlfriends*, Kenneth Mars in *Radio Days*, and Nehemiah Persoff—who played Barbra Streisand's father in *Yentl*—in *The Last Temptation of Christ*.

Of course, even a higher authority might be embarrassed by such screen fare as *Everything You Always Wanted to Know About Sex (But Were Afraid to Ask)*, in which Baruch Lumet, father of director Sidney Lumet, played Rabbi Baumel, and *Robin Hood: Men in Tights,* in which Mel Brooks played a version of Friar Tuck named Rabbi Tuchman.

Zvee Scooler

also become a way of seamlessly bridging different times and places throughout the fanciful tale. Among the numbers are "Papa, Can You Hear Me?" "The Way He Makes Me Feel" and "Where Is It Written?"

Hadass's parents insist that the engagement between their daughter and Avigdor be broken when a horrible family secret in Avigdor's past is discovered. So Avigdor insists that his new best friend, Anshel, marry Hadass instead, because it would be the closest thing to marrying her himself. Tevye never had a problem like this!

Anshel and Hadass do marry. It is Yentl's cleverness (thanks to the imagination of Isaac Bashevis Singer) and the audience's willingness to suspend disbelief (thanks to the sincerity of Streisand, Patinkin and Irving) that keep the gender bomb from exploding on their wedding night, and many subsequent nights. When Yentl's secret is finally revealed, Avigdor calls her "a devil, a demon, a defiler of the Torah," and then wails, "Why why why?" Yentl, weeping, says, "Because I love you." Yentl's spiritual pursuit has turned almost entirely to an amorous one, and *Yentl* becomes almost entirely a love story, although a bittersweet one. At the end of the movie she is on a boat on her way to America (singing, of course, in a scene eerily reminiscent of the "Don't Rain on My Parade" number from *Funny Girl*). It is to be presumed that in America she will continue her religious studies as the woman God wanted her to be.

Hello, Molly!

She got around even more than her most famous character, Yenta the Matchmaker, thanks to the longevity of her career.

Molly Picon, who played Yenta in the movie version of *Fiddler on the Roof*, began in Yiddish theater in the early 1920s, in such shows as *Tzipke*, a Cinderella story in which she sang, danced, and scampered about like a imp. It ran for four years. Then she moved to Broadway in the 1930s, winning enough attention to get her own revue called *Hello, Molly.* Among her later films are *Come Blow Your Horn* and *For Pete's Sake*. She also appeared in regional theater well into her seventies.

A career like that invariably has interesting stories behind it, and one of hers concerns her role as Yente in *Fiddler on the Roof.* Apparently, Norma Crane, who played Golde, had a speaking voice very similar to Molly's. Director Norman Jewison was worried that it might confuse the audience, especially if one of the characters had to speak off camera. Molly had a solution. She pointed out to Jewison that while Bea Arthur, who originated the role on Broadway, had played Yente as a "big, buxom woman with a loud, brassy voice," she, Molly, could do it differently. "I offered to play her, instead, as a whining old crone who could speak in a higher, more frightening voice. Since Yenta was the woman responsible for making—or breaking—people's lives with her matchmaking, I saw her more as a little old witch."

Jewison bought the idea, and it was a match made in heaven.

Streisand reportedly immersed herself in Jewish studies prior to making *Yentl* to help her better interpret the story and the characters on film. At one point she declared her rediscovered pride in being Jewish. Her efforts and her convictions show in the inherent goodness of everyone in the story, and the passion with which it's told. The director and the author must share the credit for the goodness and the passion. Streisand would probably accept all of it for herself, and Singer would probably tell her to go ruin someone else's story.

2

License to *Kvell*

Portnoy's Complaint

Brighton Beach Memoirs

Avalon

Lost in Yonkers

A Walk on the Moon

JEWISH GRANDSONS are not supposed to view their grandmothers as Nazi commandants, and Jewish daughters are not supposed to see their mothers dancing topless at Woodstock.

Welcome to the movies.

In real life, Jewish parents and grandparents typically *kvell*—or swell with pride—at even the slightest accomplishments of their children or grandchildren. In literature, on stage, and on screen, however, that is sometimes a more difficult task, because for years Jewish writers have been using creative license to make points, settle scores, or simply entertain audiences with tales of Jewish family life that are often less than dignified. Without such creative license, these movies would be as boring as family circle cemetery meetings.

"I called the first draft *The War of the Rosens*, and as I approached page thirty-five, I hit a snag," recalls Neil Simon about his play, *Brighton Beach Memoirs*, which was later made into a motion picture. "As funny as it might be, I realized it was only about family bickering. I saw no drama in it, and more than anything, it was drama I was searching for."

Drama *is* what drives most Jewish family dynamics—even in comedies by Neil Simon and satires by Philip Roth. Once the writer finds the drama, however, there is always the possibility that a semiautobiographical mother, father, cousin, uncle, or aunt will turn out not to be among the most exemplary members of the family circle. That's a chance every writer takes—usually with little concern.

But there are also a lot of love and a lot of pride in most Jewish family dramas—although in some cases you have to search for it with a microscope. "Although the Jew has for centuries been surrounded by bitter enemies who sought to destroy him, he has always found renewed strength in his home," writes Morris Golomb in *Know Jewish Living and Enjoy It.* The love and pride are there, innately perhaps, though they may be camouflaged by the tensions, struggles and secrets of everyday life. That's what makes some of these movies rather accurate reflections of real life. After all, most of us have a skeleton or two we'd rather leave in the closet, not to mention a relative or two we wouldn't bring in for show and tell. Sometimes the *only* difference between our family lives and the lives of the Jewish families on screen is that our skeletons aren't viewed by millions of people.

We all talk about our families. Right? Of course right—and usually to everyone *but* our families. If water fountains could talk, they'd be experts on the wit, wisdom, and

occasional absurdities of Jewish families around the world. Nothing wrong with that; the more we share our laughter and pain, the easier it becomes to deal with it.

But when a tormented and potently creative mind like Philip Roth's is the one beside the water fountain, the results can be devastating.

Roth says that as a young author he used to talk freely about his family with friends in New York City and that his based-on-fact impressions became the spirit of his 1969 book, *Portnoy's Complaint.* Roth and his friends enjoyed turning what he called their "irreducible Jewishness" into "boisterous comic mythology." Three years after the book came out, in 1972, a boisterously comic movie was made, written and directed by Ernest Lehman, and by most critical accounts it was an irreducible mess. Critics hated *Portnoy's Complaint,* calling it unfunny, vulgar, and a lethal stereotype of Jewish families. Even director Lehman expressed his disappointment in the results and called himself naïve and unprepared for the Jewish response. Eventually, he even labeled the film anti-Semitic.

Can a fictionalized Jewish family, even a caricature of one, be *so* horrendous? Just searching for that answer can make *Portnoy's Complaint* rather fun to watch.

The movie is one long psychoanalytical joke, literally and figuratively, in which Alexander Portnoy, played diligently by Richard Benjamin, sits on a psychiatrist's couch and flashes back to the family, friends, addictions, and intrusions that forced him there in the first place. There's no real story in *Portnoy's Complaint*—just sketches that add up to one sordid portrait of the artist (Roth) as a fictional young man.

Alex's mother and father (Lee Grant and

Jack Somack) take *kvetching* to entirely new cinematic levels. "Did you eat french fries after school?" his mother badgers him when he goes to the bathroom repeatedly, ostensibly because of diarrhea. To her husband, who spends too much time in that same poor room with constipation, she yells, "You eat like a pig, someone should tell you the truth!"

Alex is addicted to sex, masturbation, and a girlfriend named Monkey (Karen Black), who is really nothing more than a willing collection of choice body parts. Judaism to him is an intrusion. He feels it has evolved into nothing more than daily doses of guilt and panic. And as if all that weren't enough, he continues to ask for trouble simply by telling his parents what he's up to. He even mentions to his father that he's dating a non-Jewish girl. Had he told his mother, she'd have thrown herself out of the window and then come back to hit him with a frying pan. But his father, a helpless, hapless *schlemiel*, simply says, "What's so new about that? Did you ever go with a Jewish girl?"

In one of Alex's daytime nightmares he tells everyone at his bar mitzvah that he's sick of hearing about Jews and Gentiles. "Take it and stick it up your ass," he screams. Another nightmare features a big Star of David on top of his refrigerator and, in front of it, a noose hanging from the ceiling. It's hard to decide who deserves more sympathy: Lehman for picking *Portnoy's Complaint* as a movie project, Benjamin for agreeing to be in it, or Roth for having these ideas in the first place.

For Alexander Portnoy, Jewish family life

isn't satisfying, sex isn't satisfying enough, and religion was never satisfying. So he does the only thing a boy in his situation can do. He runs away.

To Israel!

Lying in bed one morning, he hears what he thinks are machine guns outside. That would be the irony of ironies—for a mixed-up, self-hating Jew to be killed by anti-Semitic terrorists in the Holy Land. As it turns out, it's just a jackhammer on the street below that he hears.

As he tells his analyst, "This is my only life, and I'm living it in the middle of a Jewish joke."

It should have stayed a joke in New York and left Hollywood alone.

The war of the Rosens was not really a war at all. It wasn't even the Rosens who weren't warring. The Rosens became the Jeromes as

A happy family portrait, for the moment, in Brighton Beach Memoirs: *Stacey Glick, Brian Drillinger, Blythe Danner, Bob Dishy, Judith Ivey, Lisa Waltz, and Jonathan Silverman.*

Neil Simon revised his original play, and the war became a battle of quick wits and personal snits among its personable, anxiety-ridden family members.

Brighton Beach Memoirs (1986) was the first play in Simon's semiautobiographical stage trilogy, and the first to make it to Hollywood. It was followed by *Biloxi Blues* in 1988 and *Broadway Bound,* produced as a television movie, in 1992.

The screen version of the introductory story in the trilogy is a pleasant enough stroll down memory lane in Brooklyn's Brighton Beach neighborhood of 1937, thanks to Simon's screenplay and the competent direction of Gene Saks, a Simon movie veteran. The problem is that some of the characters don't seem to have come from that part of the neighborhood. In fact, Blythe Danner as Kate Jerome, the long-suffering mother and wife, and Judith Ivey as her widowed sister, Blanche, don't even seem Jewish. (They're not.)

And those who *do* seem Jewish aren't as

strong in their roles as those who don't. Brian Drillinger as the older brother Stanley, who yearns to break away from the claustrophobic Jerome household, does not have the manic sarcasm and seething energy that Jason Alexander brought to the role on Broadway. Alexander, by the way, shows up for about a minute in a poolroom scene. Jonathan Silverman, as the teenage Eugene, through whose eyes we see the story unfold, sounds as if he's auditioning for the part at the Brighton Beach Community Playhouse. This is the role that made Matthew Broderick a star on Broadway. Silverman did go on to succeed in films and on television despite his affected style and delivery, but his Eugene is more a young Jewish caricature than a young Jewish character. Only Bob Dishy as Jack, the father whose battery is definitely down, builds a believable and approachable character.

In *Brighton Beach Memoirs* we are treated to a few days in the distracted lives of the two families living in Jack Jerome's apartment. Jack has lost his part-time job, which he needs because of his extended household, and soon suffers a heart attack. Stanley hates his job in the hat store and is thinking about joining the army. Blanche sees spinsterhood right around the corner. Her daughter Laurie has medical problems. Kate worries about everyone.

And worst of all, Eugene can't believe he's never seen a naked girl.

Almost as much as he wants to see real,

Chai Hopes

Most of Neil Simon's plays and movies are family dramas, even when they are comedies. More specifically, they are usually about Jewish families, even when the families are not described as Jewish. That's because the characters Simon develops are based on many of the Jewish people he grew up with, lived with, and worked with throughout his life. But that doesn't mean they are always played by Jews.

In 1963, a movie was made of Simon's play, *Come Blow Your Horn*, and the Jewish character of Alan Baker is played by none other than Frank Sinatra. Alan is a swinger with family problems. Paramount executives wanted to—and tried to—de-emphasize the movie's Jewishness, but both the screenwriter, Norman Lear, and director, Bud Yorkin, urged the studio to keep the play's Jewish content intact on screen. With Lee J. Cobb and Molly Picon cast as Alan's parents, Lear and Yorkin were assured that much of the Jewish content would be there when the movie opened.

Alan Baker wasn't the first Jewish character Ol' Blue Eyes played on screen. In *A Hole in the Head*, directed by Frank Capra in 1959, Sinatra plays a devil-may-care bachelor father at odds with his conventional businessman brother (Edward G. Robinson). In the original play the character's name is Sidney; in the movie it is Tony. Still, many script and story elements, such as Jewish phrases and family values, suggest that Tony *is* Jewish. Apparently, though, it wasn't the Sinatra character that prompted Columbia executives, particularly Harry Cohn, to play down the Jewish angle; Robinson's character, Mario, is a very miserly man, and it was that trait that Cohn didn't want to be too closely associated with Jewishness.

live breasts, Eugene wants to be a real, live writer, and he therefore takes a strange delight in everyone else's problems as raw material for stories to come. "I love tense moments," he says when his cousin Nora breaks the news that she wants to cut school to audition for a Broadway show, "especially when I'm not the one everyone's tense about."

What works best in *Brighton Beach Memoirs* is the occasional tenderness, which may actually be part of the drama Simon was after. When Stanley speaks with his father about his problems at work, including his impertinent confrontation with his boss and how he gambled away his paycheck in a pool hall, it's almost as if they were making up in this scene for all the blandness that came before it.

"Pop, I have problems," Stanley tells him.

"If you didn't, you wouldn't live in this house," Jack replies.

In one long scene inside the apartment, a sad, ethnic-sounding clarinet plays in the background, perhaps to remind us that this is a Jewish family in crisis. There is a crisis on the outside as well, overseas, but Jack's radio doesn't play as well as it should and he accuses Eugene of fooling around with it.

"Guess who's gonna be blamed for the war in Europe," Eugene laments.

That's when we're reminded why Eugene is telling us the story in the first place: He wants us to know that this is a dramatic family with a comedy writer in its future. One can only hope that when he gets there, he'll work with a better casting director.

"If I knew things would no longer be, I would have tried to remember better."

Sometimes a great line of dialogue can pop into your head without warning. That's a terrific thing, particularly if you happen to be a writer and director with a production deal. Otherwise, it might stay in your head forever.

Fortunately, it happened to Barry Levinson, whose previous efforts included *Diner* and *Tin Men* as writer and director, and *Good Morning, Vietnam* and *Rain Man* as director. So he didn't have to keep it in his head.

He used it in *Avalon*, which he wrote and directed in 1990.

The line more or less summed up for Levinson the end of an era—the immigrant era of the 1940s when his grandparents, who had emigrated from Russia, and his first-generation American parents lived in a small town outside Baltimore. Years later, Levinson realized that on behalf of his parents and grandparents, *he* could remember best by making a movie about that era.

Once he decided to do it, he went back to Baltimore, interviewed relatives, and constructed a story that is on one level about the Russian-Jewish Krichinsky family in their adopted Avalon, and on another level about an America in which Jews grow more dependent on assimilation and less dependent on each other.

Levinson is a poetic filmmaker who takes great care with regard to period detail, realistic characters, and the artistic composition of every shot—yet his films do not seem overly designed or overly crafted at all; they seem natural. *Avalon* is a natural film, with natural charm. By the way, Levinson also directed *The Natural.*

The story unfolds through the collective eyes of three Krichinskys: Grandpa Sam, beautifully played by Armin Mueller-Stahl, a leading German actor who had come to the United States a year or two before; his son, Jules, given a strong, touching portrayal by Aidan Quinn; and Jules's little son Michael, innocently rendered by Elijah Wood. Their story is full of love, tenderness, and hope—even though Levinson has plenty of criticism to dish out, particularly about stubbornness and the isolation of the television age. What family doesn't have a stubborn mule or two within its ranks, and what family doesn't have meals interrupted by a television show everyone has to watch? In Levinson's hands the stubbornness is funny, the isolation chilling.

Avalon is a world of family circle meetings, holiday gatherings, tenuous business opportunities, financial struggles, crowded living rooms, loving parents, dependable grandparents, impetuousness, traditions, and more.

Little by little Levinson and company break down the starry-eyed vision of the new land in which Sam Krichinsky and his four violin-playing, wallpaper-hanging brothers now find themselves. "It was a celebration of light," Sam says, remembering his first night in the festively-decorated, turn-of-the-century Baltimore. But before long, celebrations are no longer so festive, particularly family gatherings with so many uncles, aunts, and cousins who have agendas of their own. With the growing number of children the rooms get smaller, the tables longer, the tempers shorter—and it gets harder to wait for all the latecomers to arrive.

Jules and his cousin Izzy (a great performance by Kevin Pollak) go into business but change their names from Krichinsky to Kaye and Kirk, which doesn't sit well with Sam. It's a fairly common American Jewish story, but as played by Quinn, Pollak, and Mueller-Stahl, it's almost as if being told for the first time.

It is also a tribute to Levinson's skill that he packs so much into the story without making it feel rushed or overloaded. Grandma Eva (Joan Plowright) discovers she has a brother, once presumed dead, who will be coming over

Royal Bubbes

Joan Plowright started out in England and Irene Worth started out in Nebraska, but both ended up in Jewish homes on the East Coast.

Plowright, Grandma Eva in *Avalon*, has a classical theater repertory that equals and often surpasses that of the finest and busiest stage actresses on both sides of the Atlantic. Born in Brigg, England, in 1929, Plowright has been as active on screen as she has on stage, appearing in such films as *The Entertainer*, *Equus*, *The Scarlet Letter*, and *Jane Eyre*. She was married to Laurence Olivier.

Irene Worth, the central figure in *Lost in Yonkers*, made a reverse classical trek, from New York to London. Born in Nebraska in 1916, she relocated to England in 1944 and appeared regularly with the Old Vic Theater Company and the Royal Shakespeare Company with such intriguing costars as Laurence Olivier, Alec Guinness, and Noel Coward. Back in the United States she won several Tony Awards and appeared in such plays as *Tiny Alice* and *Sweet Bird of Youth*. She played Grandma Kurnitz in the Broadway version of *Lost in Yonkers*.

Joan Plowright gives a quiet but strong presence to Grandma Eva in Avalon.

from Europe. The house will become even more crowded, a prospect that doesn't make Jules's wife, Ann (Elizabeth Perkins), any happier. There is already tension between Ann and Eva, but when the news of the rediscovered brother is followed by the news of Ann's pregnancy, Grandma and Grandpa must finally get a place of their own.

Then Jules and Izzy open a television

Avalon, *a place of surprises for the Krichinskys. Joan Plowright, Armin Mueller-Stahl, Elizabeth Perkins, Aidan Quinn, and Kevin Pollak watch a parade go by.*

store. It's not successful. So they open a department store but are rather quickly forced out of business due to an unfortunate accident. Finally, Jules becomes a television advertising salesman. Their new house shapes up. Their family grows. Everyone gets older.

"In the end you spend everything you earn just to end up in a place like this," Sam says years later in a nursing home, when little Michael is grown and visits with his own son (named Sam, breaking yet another tradition).

Critics have called *Avalon* an American tragedy, a cinematic dream of a mythical past, a tale of empathy and heartbreak. It's all that—and very lifelike, too. At the frac-

tious Krichinsky family circle meetings it doesn't even seem as if there's any acting going on; rather, it seems as if Levinson decided to film an actual family circle meeting. Lou Jacobi as the irascible Gabriel, the uncle who's always late, is particularly instinctive.

Unfortunately, if the Krichinskys were real (and in a way, of course, they were), there would probably be no remnant of their precious family circle today. But at least Levinson gave us a moving, colorful, live-action photo album to help us remember why family circles were so darn fractious in the first place.

Neil Simon returned to the screen in 1993 with another family story and in the process created a strange new world that took two Jewish boys where no grandsons have gone before.

Lost in Yonkers, written by Simon and directed by Martha Coolidge, provides as much of a dramatic punch as any of the latter Simon tales, and it does so without sacrificing the comedy at all. Eugene Jerome in *Brighton Beach Memoirs* may have been tripping down mammary lane, but fifteen- and thirteen-year-old Jay and Artie Kurnitz crawl through monster alley, with their paternal grandmother at the other end glaring at them with suspicion. Perhaps it's a good thing the film didn't connect with audiences; we don't need a slew of copycat characters to tarnish the precious world of the Jewish grandmother.

Recreating their roles from Simon's Pulitzer Prize-winning play, Irene Worth and Mercedes Ruehl as Grandma Kurnitz and her daughter Bella respectively provide a magnetic field that both pulls and repels the rest of the family during the course of the story. They are indeed magnetic performers—and polar opposites—who give *Lost in Yonkers* its solid emotional core.

In the summer of 1942, Jay and Artie are told that they must stay with their grandmother in Yonkers while their widowed dad, Eddie (Jack Laufer), goes out of state to look for work. But as Jay says in a voice-over, "Even though it was 98 degrees, you could feel a chill in the air as we approached the house where Grandma lived."

Grandma is a German immigrant who has seen more than her share of torture, pain, suffering, and heartbreak—including the deaths of two infant children—in her younger years. The result is a Jewish grandma unlike most Jewish grandmas on stage and screen over the last seventy-five years. She's one tough cookie, the owner of a soda shop who won't even allow her grandsons a grain of salt from a pretzel in a jar. Nor will she allow Jay or Artie to joke around, which Neil Simon characters *have* to do to stay sane.

The boys haven't seen their grandmother in two years because their father never got along with her. "Evelyn never turned me against you," Eddie says to his mother during an argument about his departed wife, "she turned me towards *her*, towards loving, towards caring."

While staying with Grandma, the boys must also deal with their crazy Aunt Bella, a confused, needful person with a woman's body but a child's mind; their nervous Aunt Gert (Susan Merson), who can't speak about her mother without wheezing like Felix Unger; and their mysterious Uncle Louis (Richard Dreyfuss), who wears fedoras and peeks out of windows at the street below.

"Did you ever notice," Jay says to Artie, "that there's something wrong with everyone on Pop's side of the family?"

Bella is by turns ebullient and morose, goofy and compassionate, spirited and resigned. Like her brothers Eddie and Louis—although Louis sees it more as a game—Bella does not get on well with the old woman. Her mother calls her dreams stupid, derides her love of movies as wasteful, and is forever short with her. It is hinted in the story that the mother used to hit Bella in the head and severely punish Louis, and this detail is intended to explain at least par-

Little Arty and big Louis—Mike Damus and Richard Dreyfuss—find each other, for a while, in Lost in Yonkers.

Lost in Yonkers was directed in a straightforward, unpretentious way by one of Hollywood's few women directors, Martha Coolidge, who began as a documentarian and independent filmmaker and eventually went on to direct the highly acclaimed *Rambling Rose* in 1991. And like a documentary, *Lost in Yonkers* doesn't really tie up all loose ends about its subjects. After the boys are picked up by their dad, we are left to wonder just what will happen to Grandma, Bella, and Louis, and whether any of them will ever be touched by love. That we care is a testament to the skilled creation of the characters and the effective telling of their stories.

When she sees Bella mindlessly hanging clothes on the line behind the candy store while dark thunderclouds threaten in the distance, the old woman shakes her head in pitiful resignation. That must be how Neil Simon, Martha Coolidge, and producer Ray Stark felt when *Lost in Yonkers* did so poorly at the box office. It was a financial failure, which only proves that even scary Jewish grandmas deserve a second chance.

tially why Bella is a loon and Louis a no-goodnik.

"I'm as strong as an ox," Bella yells to her mother during a climactic confrontation. "I'm like steel. . . . Only my babies won't die. I will love them. . . . My babies will be happy because I will teach them to be happy. . . . You never had anyone around you who loved you enough to want to touch you because you made it so clear that you didn't want to be touched with love."

Jay and Artie hear it all. What an educational summer they're having up in Yonkers! They learn that taking a stand and speaking up builds character. Brad Stoll as Jay and Mike Damus as Artie, though young and unknown, have what it takes to play against Worth and Ruehl. They are both believable and very funny and help us follow the action without getting drowned in it. They are anchors in a sea of rather muddy goings-on.

"Oy!" exclaimed *Premiere* magazine when *A Walk on the Moon* was about to open in early 1999. "The Catskills haven't simmered with this much sex since *Dirty Dancing.*"

Borscht and Found

Adirondack chairs, duck ponds, screen doors, fleeting romances, talent shows, lots of food . . . The once vibrant world of the Catskill Mountain resort is all but gone, kept alive only in books, memories, and movies like *A Walk on the Moon*.

Catskill movies actually go back to 1935, when Henry Lynn filmed a movie version of Yiddish radio star Herman Yablokoff's play, *Papirosn*, at the Catskill's Parkside Hotel. The silent movie featured future director Sidney Lumet (*The Pawnbroker*, *A Stranger Among Us*) as an eleven-year-old cigarette vendor at the hotel (*papirosn* means cigarette) observing summer romances blossoming and falling apart.

In 1938, *Having a Wonderful Time* was adapted for the screen from Arthur Kober's Broadway play, which was heavy with satire about Jewish New Yorkers at a Catskill resort hotel. But in the movie version, starring Ginger Rogers, Douglas Fairbanks, Jr., Eve Arden, Lucille Ball, and Red Skelton, virtually nothing Jewish survives. The play's Stern became the movie's Shaw, while Kessler became Kirkland, Aaronson became Armbruster, and Rappaport became Beatty.

Sweet Lorraine (1987) is about the Lorraine Hotel owned by Lillian Garber (Maureen Stapleton) that is facing obsolescence. Lillian's granddaughter Molly (Trini Alvarado) works in the kitchen trying to think of ways to keep it open, while the head chef yells "Livestock! Livestock!" each time he requires meat to be brought in. And in *Dirty Dancing*, also made in 1987, Baby (Jennifer Grey) finds her summer romance with dance instructor Johnny Castle (Patrick Swayze), while hotel owner Max Kellerman (Jack Weston) is pleased still to be standing despite all the crazy goings-on around him. "I want you know," he says to Baby about her father, who's a doctor, "that if it were not for your dad, I'd be standing here dead."

Jennifer Grey and Patrick Swayze star in Dirty Dancing.

Oy! is right. Is this what we want our children to think went on in the Jewish Alps back in the good old days?

In addition to the sex, which is a key element in this otherwise conventional drama of a Jewish family in crisis, *A Walk on the Moon* touches upon a predicament many people decide they have from time to time, summed up by actress Diane Lane, playing thirty-one-year-old Pearl Kantrowitz. "The most important decision I made all week," she says, "was whether to

Diane Lane takes A Walk on the Moon *and tries to rebuild her marriage with Liev Schreiber.*

go to the A&P or Waldbaums. Did you ever feel trapped by your life?"

Pearl indeed feels trapped. A "walk on the moon," figuratively speaking, might untrap her. The movie was written by first-time screenwriter Pamela Gray, based on a script that won the Samuel Goldwyn Award at UCLA, an award designed to nurture new talent. It was directed by Samuel Goldwyn's grandson, Tony Goldwyn.

The Kantrowitzes—Pearl; her devoted though conservative husband, Marty (Liev Schreiber); blossoming teenage daughter, Alison (Anna Paquin); little son, Danny (Bobby Boriello); and mother-in-law, Lilian (Tovah Feldshuh)—spend their summers at Dr. Folger's Bungalow Colony, where the loudspeaker constantly announces the showing of someone's bar mitzvah pictures, the arrival of the *knish* man, or the start of a morning stretch. Dr. Folger's is a place where tentative friendships can develop between Conservative Jewish girls who know just a little about love and sex, and Orthodox girls who may know even a little more. It's a place where time passes quickly or slowly for the guests, depending on how much tolerance they have for seeing the same people do the same things day after day. Jewish families live there for weeks or months each summer, often without their husbands and fathers, except on weekends, because the men have to go back to the city during the week to earn a living.

But this isn't an ordinary Catskill summer. It's the summer of 1969, the summer of love, of Woodstock, of sowing wild oats, and letting spontaneity rule. It's the summer when everyone gets caught up in the excitement of Neil Armstrong's first steps on the lunar surface.

Marty, a television repairman, has to spend some extra time away from Dr. Folger's because everybody wants to watch Armstrong take those first steps on perfectly tuned television sets, and Marty's services are needed overtime back at the shop. Suddenly, the blouse man (Viggo Mortensen), a gentle and modern salesman of ladies' summer clothes, appears at the bungalow colony and gives Pearl a chance to walk out of her trap and into his own. His is a trap of sexual liberation that has nothing going for it but the sex, although that's all she seems to need at the moment.

Who but the wise, worldly, and somewhat mystically oriented Lilian can sense something terribly wrong? "You're *shtupping* someone," she tells her daughter-in-law, using a Yiddish word Jewish mothers-in-law typically do not say to their daughters-in-law—a vulgar reference to the act of fornication. "You're *shtupping* the goddamn blouse man. I'm right. I'm always right. It's a curse."

And as if that's not enough, Alison runs off to spend the day at Woodstock and sees her mother lost in a sexual dance with that very blouse man in the middle of all those happy, emancipated hippies.

This is not the way young Jewish women in the Catskills, or anywhere for that matter, are supposed to behave. Not even in the movies. Marjorie Morgenstern hankered after Neal Airman in *Marjorie Morningstar*, but he was Jewish and they were both single. "Baby" Houseman danced dirty with Johnny Castle in *Dirty Dancing* but remained a dutiful daughter. Screenwriter Gray's intentions here were a little more severe. Fortunately, she made Lilian understand the forces that drove Pearl insane, and she also made her the type of family matriarch *not* to let the family be torn apart, thereby making Tovah Feldshuh's role somewhat more important than her screen time might imply. "Marty, get your *tuchas* up here," she commands her son over the phone, this time using a Yiddish word Jewish mothers typically *do* say to their children—a not at all vulgar reference to the rear end.

Eventually, Pearl and Marty reach a delicate understanding about what went wrong, and possibly even why, and together they

Small Consolation

Coproducing the first movie that he didn't act in, Dustin Hoffman chose a project that he knew held dim commercial prospects. But Hoffman loved the story and decided to produce it anyway. When told that *A Walk on the Moon* was too small and too ethnic to be a major motion picture, the Academy Award-winning actor casually retorted that *he* was small and ethnic too.

All through the movie's preparation and production, Hoffman maintained that although it didn't have much of a chance to make a lot of money, as long as the people who see it enjoy it, making it would be worth the effort.

When *A Walk on the Moon* was shown at the Sundance Film Festival, it received a standing ovation. Hoffman was there along with the film's star, Diane Lane. He turned to Lane and told her to enjoy the feeling while she could, because *Ishtar* had also once received a standing ovation. (*Ishtar*, starring Hoffman and Warren Beatty, was one of the most colossal flops in Hollywood history.)

Shvitzing in the Rain

In its jump from book to screen, Herman Wouk's *Marjorie Morningstar*, the story of an ambitious Jewish American princess seeking fame and romance at a Jewish Catskill resort, lost most of its Jewishness.

Sidney Lumet (*The Pawnbroker*, *A Stranger Among Us*), who was very anxious to direct it, flew to Los Angeles to meet with Jack Warner, who had already put the film into preproduction. Lumet noticed sketches of the production design and didn't think the set looked at all like a Catskill resort. When he complained, Warner said he didn't want the movie to have a narrow appeal—which meant that all ethnicity would be toned down. Lumet walked off the project and flew back to New York before Jack Warner could say *Oy vey*.

Natalie Wood wanted to play Marjorie so much that she personally appealed both to Warner and Wouk. The actor chosen to play her romantic interest was Gene Kelly (after Montgomery Clift, Paul Newman and William Holden were passed over). But on screen Wood and Kelly had no chemistry between them—nor anything particularly Jewish about them, either.

Nevertheless, *Marjorie Morningstar* broke all of Radio City Music Hall's opening day attendance records, but that was due to the immense popularity of the book (it sold over four-and-a-half million copies in its initial release). After that, it died a horrible box office death. Many industry observers said that it wasn't only because of the odd casting that the film did so poorly; by one estimate, ninety-five percent of the story's Jewish flavor was left out of the screenplay, and word of mouth apparently eliminated ninety-five percent of the Jewish moviegoers who would otherwise have flocked to see it.

look tentatively into the near future, believing that as a family they can remain intact.

While the Folger Bungalow Colony scenes ring true, *A Walk on the Moon* isn't the most realistic movie in the world. The Woodstock episode in particular is highly improbable, and Pearl's devotion to the blouse man, however brief, lacks plausibility. But it is full of memorable performances by the entire cast and highly evocative moments, particularly for those who spent any time at all in the Jewish Alps during its heyday.

While it is too early to tell if *A Walk on the Moon*'s director, Tony Goldwyn, inherited the kind of genes that will pave the way for him to have a long and exciting career, he does do something very admirable with this movie that his father, independent producer Sam Goldwyn, Jr., and grandfather did regularly, partly as products of their times: He relied not upon outlandish special effects, not on high concept, not on an audiovisual assault on the senses to make the movie soar, but simply upon real characters telling an interesting story.

And, of course, a couple of games of mah-jongg.

3

In the Face
of Insanity

The Great Dictator

Me and the Colonel

The Frisco Kid

Leon the Pig Farmer

Life Is Beautiful

IT'S BEEN A PRETTY ROUGH five thousand years for the Jews. So Jews in turn have cultivated a very distinctive way of dealing with all that mayhem and misfortune: comedy.

There are almost as many theories about why Jews and comedy have such a unique relationship as there are Jewish comics. Milton Berle once said that you don't need to look any further than the Jews for proof that humor can insulate almost an entire people against everything life can dump on them. Comedy used to help Jewish immigrants better deal with the often difficult challenges of assimilation. Humor has been used to show the rest of the world that Jews have some of the same needs and share the same frustrations as people everywhere.

With humor, Jews, who often resemble fish out of water in an alien world, are put smack dab into the thick of things, often with admirable results.

Hollywood loves comedy, too, and the motion picture industry has always had many Jewish writers, so it is really no great surprise that a Jewish-flavored comedy sneaks in every once in a while. Quite a few of them over the last sixty years have been tied in one way or another to the Holocaust.

But Jewish movie comedy is certainly not single-minded. As has been proved many times, Jewish comedies are capable of embracing subjects far beyond a single period of insanity. It's a big world out there, and Jews are only a small fraction of it, but there are countless comic variations on the basic fish-out-of-water story. And while fish-out-of-water stories are not that unique in motion pictures, it's quite refreshing when, figuratively speaking, it is a gefilte fish in the central role.

The Little Tramp was not a Jew. Charlie Chaplin, despite a widespread belief to the contrary, did not come from a Jewish family, but by 1940, when he made *The Great Dictator*, he had decided never to contradict any statement that said he was. The sharp satire of the film was Chaplin's answer to Germany's Third Reich, and of the film he said, "I did this film for the Jews of the world."

The Great Dictator, which Chaplin wrote and directed, concerns an inept Jewish barber in 1918 (Chaplin) who is mistaken for the Jew-hating dictator of a country called Tomania, whose name is Hynkel (also Chaplin). The mistaken identity ultimately gives the barber the opportunity to speak out to the world against greed, hate, and intolerance. In many ways, at the end of the movie the nameless barber finally gets a name, and it is Charlie Chaplin.

It is interesting to note that in the movie,

As Adenoid Hynkel, leader of the Double Cross, Charles Chaplin is a triple threat in The Great Dictator *as writer, director, and star.*

although the Third Reich becomes the Double Cross, Hitler becomes Hynkel, Mussolini becomes Napolini, and Italy becomes Bacteria, Jews nevertheless remain Jews. Some things, even in satire, must never change.

Jews remain Jews—and brunettes remain brunettes. "Brunettes are troublemakers," Hynkel tells an underling while discussing women. "They're worse than the Jews. But they're too small. So, first the Jews, then the brunettes."

When the story begins, Tomania is at war, and the barber is a Tomanian soldier in the thick of battle. While these opening scenes look as deadly serious as any war film, what follows is infectious lunacy. The barber, suffering from amnesia, goes back home, and Hynkel, to deflect economic concerns, promotes anti-Semitism, and that's when the story moves ahead with enough comic devices to fill the Catskill Mountains—with bits borrowed by subsequent movie comics from Jerry Lewis to Roberto Benigni. Grenades are dropped down pants, bad guys are bopped in the head with frying pans, airplanes are flown upside down, speeches are translated without a smidgen of sensibility. And it's all served up in an agreeable soufflé in condemnation of Nazism. In fact, *The Great Dictator* was the first major Hollywood movie to respond directly to German anti-Semitism and Nazi policies.

Tucked in between the comic bits are some serious sentiments. The barber's lady friend, Hannah, played by Paulette Goddard, makes a case for the need to rise up against aggression. After the barber is attacked by anti-Semites, she says, "You sure got nerve the way you fought back. That's what we should all do, fight back. We can't fight alone. But we can lick them together."

Finally, Hynkel falls from a boat while duck shooting, swims ashore, is thought to be the Jewish barber, and is hit on the head. The look-alike barber, meanwhile, is thought to be Hynkel. Chaplin's final speech, as the barber-cum-dictator, is a six-minute sermon that has been hotly debated in critical circles since the movie's release. In it, Chaplin speaks

---

Lust for Garbitsch

If Hynkel had wanted an egg cream, he wouldn't have had to go too far.

Making the first of nearly fifty screen appearances in a small role in *The Great Dictator* was Bernard Gorcey, known to thousands of Sunday morning movie buffs as Louis Dumbrowski, the sweet shop owner on the *East Side Kids* and *Bowery Boys* movie serials. Gorcey was the father of serial star Leo Gorcey, otherwise known as Slip Mahoney, and it was Bernard who first suggested that Leo try out for the Broadway play *Dead End*, which in turn led to Hollywood and the long-running serials.

The Great Dictator also featured an actor not typically associated with comedy classics. His name was Henry Daniell, the debonair stage and screen star of many serious dramas and melodramas including *Camille*, *The Philadelphia Story*, *The Man in the Gray Flannel Suit*, and *Lust for Life*. The English-born actor's appearance in Chaplin's film was a rare comedic departure, but as propaganda minister Garbitsch, Daniell was hilarious.

One person who was *not* featured in *The Great Dictator* was Fanny Brice, although Chaplin had intended to cast her as the wife of the nefarious Hynkel. But as the story and screenplay continued to develop, Chaplin abandoned the idea.

---

of people in power thinking too much and feeling too little. "Only the unloved hate," he says. "The kingdom of God is within man. Not one man, but all men . . . You have the power to make this world a wonderful adventure." The speech has been called, among other things, a grave mistake, inappropriate in its sermonizing to the spirit of movie comedy and satire.

Later, Chaplin said, "Had I known of the actual horrors of the German concentration camps, I would not have made *The Great Dictator*. I could not have made fun of the homicidal insanity of the Nazis." Still, the movie was a powerful enough satire to become an almost instant classic. Although

A Change of Plans, Part I

The Great Dictator was great, but the dictator himself wasn't great. Why, then, should it be called *The Great Dictator*?

When Charlie Chaplin was planning to turn Hitler and the Nazis into mindless buffoons in 1940 for United Artists, his working title for the movie was simply *The Dictator*, but he soon discovered that Paramount already owned that title. So Chaplin quickly registered the name *The Great Dictator*, although he was never particularly happy with the choice. In order to have plenty of options to play with once the release date came near, he also registered *Ptomania* (a variation on the spelling of the fictional country in which the story takes place), *The Two Dictators*, *Dictamania*, and *Dictator of Ptomania*.

Mel Brooks had dictator problems of his own when trying to interest producers and studios in his first screenplay, which he called *Springtime for Hitler*. No one was interested. Finally, producer Sidney Glazier agreed to work with Brooks to try to get the movie made, but too many executives involved in the project, many of whom were Jewish, believed that Jews would be offended by the title and stay away from the theaters. So the name was changed to *The Producers*. The movie was released in 1968 and won Brooks an Academy Award for best original screenplay. Glazier continued to insist that if *Springtime for Hitler* had been kept as its title, the movie would have been a monster hit. *The Producers* did only modest business in its initial run.

nominated for the Academy Award as best picture of the year, *The Great Dictator* lost to *Rebecca*, a haunting romance starring Laurence Olivier and Joan Fontaine. Perhaps in 1940 people did not yet realize just how important it is to put anti-Semitic and anti-brunette dictators in their place.

In real life, Danny Kaye was at home on stage, on screen, in an airplane cockpit and in front of a symphony orchestra. In *Me and the Colonel* he had no home, which may be why he looked a little lost.

The real Hynkels of the world created millions of refugees—displaced persons, Jewish and otherwise, forced to seek places throughout Europe and elsewhere to call home. Cinematically, they also created hundreds of fictional refugees. Kaye played one of them, an intriguing Jewish refugee by the name of S. I. Jacobowsky in this 1958 comedy written by S. N. Behrman and George Froeschel and directed by Peter Glenville.

"I've spent most of my life trying to become a citizen of some country," Jacobowsky says as he enters a Paris hotel at the beginning of the story. An introduction like that gives Kaye the opportunity to be a nobody and everyman at the same time. It is the kind of complex and sophisticated characterization he loved to tackle—as cunning as he is courteous, as bitter as he is resilient. It is a role that was tailor-made for him, but the film lacks vitality, which ultimately makes it seem like a poor fit.

Based on a Broadway play by Franz Werfel called *Jacobowsky and the Colonel*, the movie is actually what is now called a buddy picture, with a World War II backdrop much like Kaye's more successful *White Christmas*, made with Bing Crosby four years earlier. In *Me and the Colonel*, the buddy—an unwilling one at that—is Colonel Prokoszny, a pompous Polish anti-Semite on a mission to deliver Allied papers to the French coast before the Germans catch him. The colonel, played with amusing bombast by Curt Jürgens, is an inveterate womanizer who says to his many paramours, "In the cathedral of my heart, a candle has always been lit for you." No one is fooled by his phoney sincerity, except perhaps the paramours themselves.

The colonel bumps into Jacobowsky in the Paris hotel and immediately takes a dislike to him because of his craftiness and impudent remarks, not to mention his faith, and he makes his hostility abundantly clear.

"I understand," Jacobowsky says to him sympathetically, "the colonel does not like Jews. He can't help that. That's the way he was brought up."

But the colonel tolerates him because Jacobowsky knows how to get a car when there are no cars to be found, how to get gas when there is none available, and how to elude Germans when Germans work very hard at not being eluded.

The two join forces. That unlikely partnership provides most of the comedy, as the two bicker and negotiate, and as Jacobowsky observes the ways of the obstinate colonel. Can a pesky Jew and an overblown anti-Semite really get along? Kaye and company seem to be saying yes, they can, when it's necessary, when you work at it, when you're Danny Kaye, and when even the anti-Semite is likable, in a pitiful sort of way.

Neither Jacobowsky nor the Colonel really changes all that much throughout the story. Prokoszny still yells and threatens and spends too much time in his romantic pur-

Nobody's Fool

Just four years after dreaming of a *White Christmas*, Danny Kaye became very picky about the film roles he accepted, and he accepted very few. But he liked the script for *Me and the Colonel* very much and decided to sign on as the inimitable S. I. Jacobowsky.

"I don't know how it will do as a picture," he said, shortly after shooting was completed. "There's no great violence in it, no love story. It's really just the story of two vastly different men thrown together, and of how people can get along with others when they must."

But as Martin Gottfried says in his biography of Kaye, *Nobody's Fool*, *Me and the Colonel* had dim commercial prospects from the beginning, "being a black and white movie about not the top four on a list of moviegoer interests—a Jew, a Pole, the Nazis, and compassion. With the picture's failure, the Danny Kaye Hollywood career was all but over."

Kaye made only five movies after *Me and the Colonel*, none of them very notable, and most of which were labeled "silly" or "misfires" by the critics. He did, however, win the film industry's prestigious Jean Hersholt Humanitarian Award in 1981, which was the same year he made a stunning television movie dramatic debut as a Holocaust survivor in *Skokie*, about the controversy surrounding a neo-Nazi march in Illinois in 1977.

suits. Even in the midst of a dangerous episode he manages once again to tell a woman that in his heart's cathedral a candle burns for her. (Jacobowsky replies, "That must be the best-lit cathedral in Europe.") But this time, Jacobowsky himself feels a certain warmth toward the woman (Nicole Maurey) and tells her, "In the synagogue of my heart, a candle will always burn for you."

The colonel, ever mindful that he is a man with power and authority, and the clever Jew, ever mindful that he is more resourceful than most others, determine to use their skills—and a borrowed bicycle—to get to the coast on time to deliver the papers, although the

Germans are hot on their trail. It is quite likely that in no other movie in history have two grown men, an anti-Semite and a Jew, amicably ridden a bicycle together through the French countryside. It is a rare spectacle, and one of the handful of odd pleasures in this well-intentioned comedy.

Although it followed many of Danny Kaye's motion picture successes, *Me and the Colonel* is a slight, even unenergetic comedy. Sometimes, even in skilled hands, anti-Semitism isn't funny. Kaye may actually have felt that before the lovely bicycle ride through the French countryside.

Getting robbed isn't funny either, but it is practically the first thing that happens to Rabbi Avram Belinski when he arrives in America. *The Frisco Kid*, an offbeat 1979 western comedy written by Michael Elias and Frank Shaw and directed by Robert Aldrich, is another buddy movie, this time about a rabbi traveling across the country in 1859 with a bank robber. It is not one of Gene Wilder's more successful efforts, but it certainly adds another odd and affable character to his comedy repertoire.

"Out of eighty-eight students," says the chief rabbi at Belinski's Polish *yeshiva*, "you came in a close eighty-seven." So the newly ordained Rabbi Belinski leaves Poland to take over the pulpit of a synagogue in San Francisco. But on his way from New York to California he is almost immediately conned out of money, stripped of everything but his long johns, and robbed of all other worldly possessions

Welcome to the New World.

Then he meets the softhearted outlaw named Tommy, played by Harrison Ford (two years before he became a superstar in *Raiders of the Lost Ark*), and Tommy, a bank robber by trade, becomes Rabbi Belinski's partner in survival as they continue their trek through the untamed land.

"What a beautiful country," the rabbi says, seeing the miles and miles of beautiful land that lie ahead of them at the beginning of their journey. He can barely find the words to describe it—although before long, "*oy vey!*" will work very well indeed.

Tommy may be as good with a gun and a horse as Indiana Jones, but the wild west is a little too wild even for him, and soon the rabbi and the bank robber run into more trouble than they can handle.

"Why is this Saturday different from all other Saturdays?" Rabbi Belinski asks when Tommy insists they move on despite the rabbi's need to rest on the Sabbath.

"Because there's a hanging posse right behind us," Tommy urges.

Captured by Indians who have found the Torah stolen and trashed by thieves earlier on, the rabbi is asked if would trade his horse, knife, and clothes for the Torah; without flinching, Belinski says yes. It is a rare serious moment in an otherwise crazy, frivolous plot. There's even some vaudevillian slapstick when Belinski, working on the railroad, accidentally smashes a burly fellow worker several times on the foot with his hammer and then calms him down by grabbing his face just as an old Jewish grandmother would do and willing the pain away.

When the con men from an earlier scene reappear, Tommy saves the rabbi's life. Though it is an unlikely alliance, Belinski is willing to accept the bank robber's friendship because America is too tough a place in

Gene Wilder and Harrison Ford sometimes don't have a prayer as they make their way west in The Frisco Kid.

which to go it alone. Besides, as Tommy himself says in almost rabbinical tones, "I am what I am," and nothing can change that.

But just who is Rabbi Belinski? Certainly not one cut out to be a frontiersman. "When those men were shooting at you," he laments to Tommy, "I ran and saved the Torah... I care more about a book than I do for my best friend."

"If I am what I am," Tommy says, "why can't you be what you are?"

With Tommy's help, Belinski finally makes it to San Francisco, where he finds not only his congregation, but also a beautiful woman who becomes his wife.

"How many rabbis," he says, "can say they had a bank robber as a best man?"

The biggest problem with *The Frisco Kid* is that it wants to be more than it is. It strives to be a broad comedy, a message film, and a western satire all rolled into one. Like many movies, there were a lot of changes from conception to completion. John Wayne was originally supposed to play Tommy, and many of Ford's scenes were cut from the final print. Movies are often improved by changes. In this case, however, as good-natured as it is, the momentum simply dissipates somewhere between the rabbi losing his clothes and finding his Torah.

Unlike S. I. Jacobowsky and Rabbi Belinski, Leon in *Leon the Pig Farmer* has no buddies. In fact he's quite the loner, a handsome, dour, and serious young Jewish Londoner with a sardonic sense of humor and a couple of problems. First of all, Leon has no love life. Second of all, he hates his job. Third of all, he finds out he's not the nice Jewish son he thought he was.

A 1993 British film written by Michael

Normand and Gary Sinyor and directed by Vadim Jean, *Leon the Pig Farmer* has a plot as unique as its title. Leon, played by Mark Frankel, is a real estate agent, but real estate agents must lie, and Leon loathes lying. His occasional girlfriend Lisa (Gina Bellman), whom Leon would love to love on more than just a few occasions, doesn't find him interesting enough for her tastes; a conventional man in a conservative position is just not her cup of tea. All of which makes poor Leon very sad, so sad that he feels like screaming. But Leon would never scream. He's too reserved.

That is, until he finds out something very interesting about his parents. *Then* he can be heard shouting from London to Liverpool.

Right after he quits his job he joins his mother's catering company, Geller Kosher Katering, and makes a delivery to a sex clinic ("First floor, marriage counseling . . . second floor, premature ejaculation . . .") where he inadvertently finds out he's the product of artificial insemination. But that's not what makes him yell. On his next visit, he is told that, due to an administrative mixup, the sperm with which his mother was inseminated was not from her husband Sidney Geller, but from Brian Chadwick, a pig farmer.

"You mixed them up?" Leon squeals to the technologist who spills the beans.

"One day you'll laugh," she answers quietly.

Like many comedies, *Leon the Pig Farmer* has a much bigger message to explore, about the power and resilience of faith. Leon's Jewish heritage is as much a part of him as his personality. He doesn't even think about it, and that's fine with him. Even when he discovers that his real father is a pig farmer, his

Until Mark Frankel becomes Leon the Pig Farmer, *Gina Bellman has little use for him.*

faith in the faith he grew up with remains unshaken.

There are little bits of physical, verbal, emotional and even "decoration" comedy in *Leon the Pig Farmer*; for example, at the Chadwick farm, where Leon goes to live for a while, there are pig *chotchkees* everywhere—on the front door, over the fireplace, on the walls, on the headboards, on the furniture. Brian Chadwick (Brian Glover) is virtually England's godfather of pork. It's a culture shock the likes of which even Rabbi Belinski, a century and a continent away, could never imagine. It's hard for Leon to decide if he really belongs there, or with his real mother and Sidney.

Leon's new family, which includes Brian's wife and son Keith, try to make Leon feel at home by saying "Oy!," and reading *Portnoy's Complaint*. And they make a concerted effort to surround him with the kind of care and concern for which they understand Jews are known.

"I've always admired the way Jews believe in family," Brian says, effectively turning the godfather of pork into the godfather of compassion.

But Leon cannot quite come to grips with all his porcine surroundings, nor with the enthusiasm with which Brian goes about his work. He would love somehow to bridge the two worlds—and an unusual mishap may very well do the trick for him. Having learned the ropes of artificial insemination in the barnyard, Leon accidentally crossbreeds a pig with a sheep, and thinks he may have just developed the world's first kosher pig. He even asks two rabbis to stop by to investigate.

Back in London, Leon meets up with his old girlfriend Lisa once again. In Leon's absence she hasn't had much luck with the conventional and conservative accountants, bankers, management consultants, or dentists she has dated. Good old Leon has a surprise for her.

"Can you imagine," he smiles, "Leon the pig farmer?"

By the look on her face, that just might be an offer even Lisa can't refuse.

The world couldn't refuse *Life Is Beautiful*, an Italian film first released in 1997 that won an Academy Award for best foreign language film in 1999. An English-dubbed version was released to theaters in the summer of 1999. Its star, Roberto Benigni, who cowrote it with Vincenzo Cerami, and also directed it, won an Academy Award for best actor as Guido, which he accepted by saying it must be a mistake because he had already used up all his English accepting the first award for best foreign language film. The movie also won the Grand Jury Prize at the Cannes Film Festival, and eight David Di Donatello awards, which are the Oscars of Italy. For Benigni's career, the movie was aptly titled.

It could almost have won *two* Academy Awards—one for comedy and one for tragedy. One for laughter and one for tears. One for anger and one for hope. The story of a silly and devoted father who shields his son from the nightmare of a German concentration camp, *Life Is Beautiful* is, in a way, two movies in one: The first part is a brilliantly colorful celebration of slapstick during which a Jewish waiter, Guido (Benigni), meets and pursues a beautiful schoolteacher, Dora; the second is a grim and gray reminder

Roberto Benigni is incapable of letting a moment go by when he doesn't amuse his son, Giorgio Cantarini, in Life Is Beautiful.

sight (Nicoletta Braschi)—he realizes yet another by having a child with her, Giosué, pronounced Joshua (Giorgio Cantarini), and then still another by opening up a bookstore. But then the dreams end abruptly when the Germans advance, and Guido decides to inoculate his beloved boy against the horrors by turning life in the concentration camp to which they are all sent into a giant game. His rubber face, short-circuited arms and legs, and quick thinking succeed in making little Giosué accept that everything happening to him and his family is a fun-filled contest, and that the prize is a big green tank.

Benigni is a skilled storyteller, for even through the slapstick it can be felt that trouble lurks around the corner. In one scene, for example, Guido is working at a restaurant when a government official, there to dine, salutes a portrait of Hitler on the wall. It's brief, but it's telling.

And then the trains come.

"I don't like the train," Giosué says to his father.

But with Guido as his father—a man who can make marching look like a parade of clowns, a man who can make German officers seem like camp counselors—even trains are no longer scary to the innocent boy.

Benigni brings Guido to life with unfettered enthusiasm. Known in the United States primarily for the comedies *Johnny Stecchino*, *The Monster*, *Down by Law*, and *Night on Earth*, Benigni is comfortable enough with his material to be as effective as a loving husband and devoted father as

of how love and resilience are absolutely necessary in the face of insanity.

Benigni has been called an Italian Woody Allen, Charlie Chaplin, and Groucho Marx. His Guido, even in the midst of a slapstick routine, is entirely believable. After he makes his first dream come true—marrying the woman he fell in love with at first

Wilder Tongues

Hollywood may be in the city of angels, but when some movie people are jealous or skeptical of other people's projects, they have a devil of a time keeping a straight face.

When Robert Aldrich decided to make *The Frisco Kid*, a western comedy about a Polish rabbi starring Gene Wilder, the inside buzz was quick to label the project "Blazing Bagels" and "Fiddler on the Range."

When it was announced that Barbra Streisand had finally signed a deal to write, direct, produce, and star in the movie musical version of Isaac Bashevis Singer's "Yentl the Yeshiva Boy," industry wags started secretly calling it "Funny Boy."

Sidney Lumet's *A Stranger Among Us*, about a gentile detective who must infiltrate a Hasidic community to solve a crime, drew comparisons to *Witness*, an earlier film in which Harrison Ford had played a detective hiding out with an Amish family. Before long, Lumet's project was being called "Vitness."

After mogul Jeffrey Katzenberg left Walt Disney to found a new studio, DreamWorks SKG, with Steven Spielberg and David Geffen, one of his first projects was *The Prince of Egypt*. It didn't take long before Katzenberg and company were hearing their biblical cartoon epic being referred to as "The Zion King."

Vats in a name? Sidney Lumet, here directing A Stranger Among Us, *is no stranger to the words of industry wags.*

he is a clown and a cut-up. He also had the good sense to cast his real-life wife as Dora, because the love and affection Braschi and Benigni have for each other is as honest on screen as it must be in real life.

Dora had been engaged to a Fascist official, but Guido wins her in ways only Guido can. When their lives are shattered, their son never even realizes it. Throughout their internment, Guido perpetuates the game, which includes a hilarious scene in which he "translates" a German officer's instruc-

The Nutty Director

Long before Steve Martin was a jerk and Jim Carrey a pet detective, Jerry Lewis was Hollywood's most successful clown. After breaking up with Dean Martin, Lewis was involved as actor, writer, producer, and director on over thirty movie comedies, providing audiences with enjoyable escapism through slapstick, buck teeth, funny voices, and general lunacy.

But by the early 1970s Lewis had an urge for a change of pace. He was looking to do something a little more serious in film when he came across a screenplay called *The Day the Clown Cried*, about a failed German clown named Karl Schmidt, captured by the Nazis for making fun of Hitler. Once at Auschwitz, the gentile clown is forced to use his meager yet serviceable talent to lead Jewish children to the gas chamber.

Talk about a change of pace.

A Belgian producer agreed to option the script, and Lewis was set to star and direct. Lewis immediately began to alter the script to his liking, changing the character from a second class clown to a successful one and making him a Jew named Helmut Doork. Once he started performing the role in front of the cameras, the portrayal, according to several accounts, was more like Jerry in the 1970s than a German in the 1940s.

Not long after production began in Europe, the producer disappeared among reports of troubled finances. Lewis used his own money to continue. Meanwhile, the option on the script expired. Lewis continued anyway, editing it on the road while performing in clubs. But the original writers refused to sell the rights, and to this day *The Day the Clown Cried* sits on a shelf, unfinished and unreleased. There are many who say that's just where a depressing story like that should stay.

tions as if they were additional rules for the game. Although conceptually it has been done before in the movies, Benigni handles it so well, and with such comic skill, that it will be remembered, discussed, and imitated for generations to come.

"They said all of us kids have to take a shower today," Giosué says. It's a painful moment reminiscent of a scene in *Schindler's List* when a group of women is forced to take a shower which turns out to be just that, a shower. Both the *Schindler* scene and this one are frightening, but *Life Is Beautiful* ends with poignant optimism when an Ameri-

can tank suddenly pulls up to the camp, now liberated.

"It's true!" Giosué shouts, realizing the game has been won, just as his father promised.

Benigni, who is not Jewish but whose father was imprisoned in a German work camp for two years, said he developed the story over many years in his head before committing it to paper. It was worth the wait. Besides, we all need a little time between comedies to catch our breath. Especially Holocaust comedies.

4

So It Was Written, So It Shall Be Filmed

David and Bathsheba

The Ten Commandments

Solomon and Sheba

The Bible

The Prince of Egypt

IT ISN'T EASY TO KEEP a straight face when a voluptuous and pouting Anne Baxter forcibly grabs a half-naked Charlton Heston and wails, "Oh Moses, Moses, you splendid adorable fool."

But then again, no one ever said that biblical movies were supposed to be taken seriously. They exist more or less for the purpose of entertainment, and in many cases titillation, which means a big take at the box office.

When Cecil B. De Mille first suggested making *Samson and Delilah* in the late

1940s, studio executives balked, saying that a Sunday school story would barely attract enough of an audience to warrant the expense. De Mille asked a studio artist to draw a picture of a muscular athlete wrapped around a seductive vixen. He showed the picture to the executives. They changed their minds and bankrolled the picture.

Several years later, Gregory Peck was offered the leading role in *David and Bathsheba*, but Peck was not comfortable with studio head Darryl Zanuck's decision to cast him as David and shared his concern with

Zanuck. Zanuck in turn showed Peck some paperwork that indicated the hundreds of millions of dollars the handsome, popular actor had made for the studio over the years. "I'm not giving you good roles because I like you, although I do," Zanuck told him. "The reason is, you're box office."

David and Bathsheba was the top-grossing movie of 1951.

Biblical movies have been around almost as long as movies have. As early as 1909, filmmaker J. Stuart Blackton made a five-reel silent film for the Vitagraph company called *The Life of Moses,* which was released to theaters one reel per week, and in 1928 Warner Brothers produced *Noah's Ark,* which at two hours and fifteen minutes was at that time the studio's longest picture.

But through the years there really haven't been as many major biblical movie epics produced as one might imagine. Perhaps the lack is attributable, at least in part, to the difficulty in matching the spectacle to the story in ways that excite without offending, that moralize without preaching, that are accurate without being literal. After all, being literal can be a problem. For instance, Noah was six hundred years old when the rains began. That would require a hell of a makeup job. And when God made his covenant with Abraham, Abraham took all the males in his household and had them circumcised. Try showing *that* on screen. The censors would go crazy, and the actors probably wouldn't be too happy either.

That's why most filmmakers forgo the biblical details and stick to busts and biceps. It's always been a lot easier.

David and Bathsheba is one of the most intriguing of the biblical spectacles, simply because spectacle is the last word you would use to describe it.

As King David of Israel, one of the most complex personalities in all the biblical books of the prophets, Gregory Peck uses much more of an inner strength than other actors do when portraying biblical legends. He cuts quite a clear, pensive, and enigmatic character in the process. Also, where other biblical films play up the glamour, grandeur, blood, and guts, *David and Bathsheba,* written by Philip Dunne and directed by Henry King, offers a far tamer and more subdued version of the story. Some critics called it maudlin, dull, even lifeless, in part alluding to David's brooding and introspective behavior. Hamlet was equally brooding and introspective, but rarely is he called dull and lifeless.

The story of David, from the book of Samuel, *is* in fact an almost Shakespearean morality tale of lechery, treachery, and atonement, the chronicle of a king who sins, wrangles with God, realizes the errors of his ways, and finally begs forgiveness. In this production, the emphasis is on the words and emotions, not the special effects and costumes.

Determining that going into battle after a long time away will put some life back into his soul, David says, "It's been a long time since I've shed any blood. It's good to know it still runs through me." But a little blood is not enough to solve all of his personal problems, one of which is his first wife, Michal (Jayne Meadows), with whom he is no longer in love. When David sees her for the first time after a long absence, he tells her to leave him alone.

"Yet you have time for your other wives," Michal says. "A shepherd's son is dismissing the daughter of Saul? You have never loved anyone but yourself."

Brooding once more, and stung by her words, although he wishes not to be, David suddenly sees a woman bathing in the distance. The wife of a soldier named Uriah, Bathsheba, as played by Susan Hayward, is a sultry beauty with a quiet, husky voice that begs for attention, almost as if every word is an invitation to make love.

"We Hebrews are of the desert," David tells her. "Our emotions are fierce, like the desert wind. We worship our God fiercely, we love fiercely, we feel sorrow fiercely."

"If the law of Moses is to be broken," she says, "let us break it with full understanding of what we want from each other."

And so the stage is set for a little fierce lovemaking and law breaking.

But the story doesn't center only on the unholy triangle of David, Bathsheba, and Uriah—a triangle broken by David when he arranges for Uriah to die in battle. There are also elements of the brotherly discord between David's sons Amnon and Absalom, and of the power of the Ark of the Covenant, for which David is responsible. Of course, there is also a flashback to David's youth and his cunning victory over the mighty Goliath, without which it would hardly be the story of David.

True to the sober spirit of *David and Bathsheba*, there are no astonishing sets or scenes of sweaty masses. But as it *is* a Bible movie, there are plenty of sheep, torches, and enclosed stone chambers, which gives it much more the aura of a stage production than of a wide-screen spectacular.

The brooding star of David and Bathsheba, *Gregory Peck.*

Also true to the film's spirit is the amount of time it spends on David's relationship with God. Could it be that the power of love that consumes him is extinguishing his devotion to the Almighty?

"David is no longer David," onlookers comment. "He is often not in the city. The king himself forgets that he is a servant of the Lord. The history of David's house is a history written in blood."

Even the lovers know the measure of

Casting God

How do you cast God?

An ancient biblical legend made it easy for Cecil B. De Mille. According to the legend, when God spoke to Moses from the burning bush, the voice Moses heard was that of his own father, which served to allay his mortal fears. So De Mille had Charlton Heston record God's lines, which were then played back a little slower and deeper, sounding much like an older Heston. De Mille was certain audiences would accept the effect.

De Mille knew he could no longer use Heston's voice in the scene when Moses is given the Ten Commandments because it had to be much more powerful and revered. Several men's voices were recorded for De Mille's review. The one he chose belonged to a friend and associate named Donald Hayne, who was not an actor.

The Prince of Egypt used the same method and reasoning as *The Ten Commandments* in its burning bush scene. Val Kilmer, who provided the voice of Moses, also provided the voice of God.

Those movie Gods are unseen. But the makers of *Oh, God!* (1977) had a much more daunting task—casting Him in the flesh. George Burns got the part. In the movie, Burns comes down to Earth to guide grocery clerk John Denver in a quest to spread the message that He's still around and expecting everyone to act accordingly. In the sequel, *Oh, God! Book Two*, George's messenger was a little girl, and in *Oh, God, You Devil*, George had a dual role—the good guy and the bad guy.

George Burns, comedian, storyteller, and author, added quite an impressive new position to his resume, thanks to a series of films beginning with Oh, God!

their sins. Bathsheba, after seeing a woman stoned to death for betraying her husband, realizes she must die as well. David will not hear of it. He remembers that God is mercy, goodness, and forgiveness, and asks to be taken in her place. So he touches the Ark of the Covenant, which under normal circumstances would mean instant death.

But David lives. After all, these are not normal circumstances.

David and Bathsheba received many Academy Award nominations—for Alfred Newman's score, Dunne's screenplay, art and set decoration, cinematography, and costumes. It won nothing. That's what happens to biblical epics with too many soliloquies and not enough blood.

Hams

Not all of the children of Israel in the 1923 epic *The Ten Commandments* were actors, extras, or friends of studio workers. Several hundred were Orthodox Jews from Los Angeles, hired by the studio under the hopeful assumption that their authentic looks and inherent emotions in filming the exodus from slavery to freedom would translate particularly well on film.

What crew members did not take into consideration, however, was that kosher meals would be required. On the first evening of shooting, the dinner included ham. De Mille went into action immediately, giving orders for a kosher kitchen to be set up for the remainder of the shoot.

As it turned out, De Mille was more than pleased with the casting decision. The voices of the Orthodox extras rang with sheer joy, De Mille later stated, and their faces shone with the light of freedom. It was, after all, *their* exodus.

Cecil B. De Mille's cinematic vision for *The Ten Commandments* was in some ways the antithesis of *David and Bathsheba*. Bold and bodacious, long and panoramic, *The Ten Commandments* was, in 1956, the biggest biblical blockbuster ever to hit the silver screen. Almost as if bribing us to accept it all without quarrel, De Mille promised this in the opening credits: "Those who see this motion picture will make a pilgrimage over the very ground that Moses trod more than three thousand years ago." A wonderful notion, but slightly beyond even his control.

What was *not* beyond his control, however, was the duplication of the ancient pyramids (because the real ones weren't white enough for him) and the restaging of the exodus of thousands of Hebrew slaves as they cross the Red Sea to freedom. To produce a motion picture of such scale, with so many people, in so many locations, took the strength of Samson and the wisdom of Solomon. De Mille, who produced and directed it at seventy-three years of age, had both.

So seriously did he take the project that he spared no expense with regard to the actors or production staff he hired, the sets he built, or how long it took. He had four writers work on the screenplay (Aeneas MacKenzie, Jesse Lasky, Jr., Jack Gariss, and Fredric M. Frank); researched biblical history to help the writers fill in the missing pieces of Moses' life; hired the well-trained Egyptian army to play the chariot soldiers in pursuit of the children of Israel; and employed twenty assistant directors who spoke both English and Arabic.

De Mille and his writers took some liberties with the story, but at three hours and forty minutes, *The Ten Commandments* probably benefits from such liberties. In the actual Bible text, the young girl Miriam follows the basket carrying her baby brother on the Nile to the place where Pharaoh's daughter finds it. She asks the princess if she should find a Hebrew woman to nurse the child. The princess says yes. So Moses goes back to live with his own mother for a time, only later returning to the palace to grow up as a young prince.

But in *The Ten Commandments*, the infant Moses is kept by Pharaoh's daughter, Bithiah, played by Nina Foch, from the very beginning. That way, the drama can unfold right away:

Charlton Heston was always regarded as a strong enough screen presence to carry The Ten Commandments.

"Do you know the pattern of that cloth?" Bithiah's maidservant asks her, pointing to the Hebrew design of the swaddling blanket.

"If my son is covered in it, it is a royal robe," Bithiah snaps.

Years pass, and Moses, now in the muscular, stone-jawed person of Charlton Heston, is finally discovered to be the son of Hebrew slaves. That is good news for his half brother Ramases (Yul Brynner), who is jealous of Moses' skill as a leader and his love affair with the beautiful Nefretiri.

"No pretend brother shall ever have my crown, or Nefretiri," Ramses scowls.

It is clearly a biblical soap opera, although cleaner than television soap operas of today. Even when the children of Israel become defilers while waiting for Moses to return from the mountain, the debauchery is virtually pantomimed while a voice-over says, "They were viler than the earth. They became servants of sin." Oddly enough, De Mille himself was a known debaucher, having had mistresses and affairs throughout his life. He was roundly criticized in some circles for making *The Ten Commandments*.

The ten plagues, too, occur without a repulsive frame among them. The Angel of Death is effectively spooky but not unseemly (based on the long, thin clouds one of the movie's art directors saw out of her window one morning). The parting of the Red Sea, though crude by modern special effect standards, was a highlight then and remains one today. It was accomplished by photographing 300,000 gallons of water pouring into a tank and then playing it backwards.

There are also little touches of narrative grace. In one such vignette, barely noticed and rarely discussed, Moses, now a slave, happens upon an old, broken man lying in the mud on the verge of death. He laments that his lifelong prayer to look into the eyes of the Deliverer before he dies will go unanswered. Then he dies—his dream fulfilled, albeit without his knowledge.

Like many epics before it, and only a few since, *The Ten Commandments* fills its scenes with endless gold and towering stone statues, fields of mud and armies of muscle, shameless, unrealistic costumes and endless glistening skin. To its credit, the story basically stays on track with the principal events that brought the Jewish nation into being. Although there are minor subplots involving the troublemaker Dathan (Edward G. Robinson) and the love between Joshua and Lilia (John Derek and Debra Paget), it is the story of Moses first, as he discovers that he is God's messenger, chosen to free His people from slavery and deliver His laws as a gift to the Jewish people and all of mankind.

The Ten Commandments was De Mille's last film. Although it was difficult for critics *not* to find fault with his final epic—*Time* magazine compared it to "an eight foot chorus girl: pretty well put together, but much too big, and much too fleshy"—most respected the effort and acknowledged its place in movie history. De Mille probably cared little about the criticism anyway, believing to the end that *The Ten Commandments* was good enough and important enough, and that if there were a directors' hall of fame in heaven, he'd soon be on its throne.

And if by some chance there were no throne, he'd probably have one built.

Ben-Hur killed King Solomon, and King Vidor left Hollywood because of it.

In 1959, the biblical epic *Solomon and Sheba* opened to a tepid response from the public primarily because *Ben-Hur*, which came out at the same time, garnered far more attention and buried *Solomon and Sheba*, directed by Vidor, in the dust of its chariot races. After putting so much energy into the film, Vidor made an unceremonious exodus from the motion picture industry, never to return.

Solomon and Sheba can claim neither an

Delivering the Message

There's no doubt about it: God *has* been on Earth.

Cecil B. De Mille was a strict, daring, gutsy, exacting director—a genius to some, a tyrant to others. Actors and even crew members sometimes feared approaching the great man to ask the simplest of questions or, worse, make the tiniest of suggestions. Future filmmaker Mervyn LeRoy, portraying one of the many freed Hebrew slaves in the 1923 version of *The Ten Commandments*, absorbed all he could on the set as a budding director. He recalls seeing De Mille high up on his official chair while two of the leading actors—Theodore Roberts as the Deliverer and James Neill as his brother—stood nervously off to the edge of the set. Roberts took an assistant director aside and whispered, "Tell God that Moses and Aaron would like to have words with him."

---

audience nor a style of its own; rather, it fuses several styles from many biblical films. It combines the Shakespearean staginess of *David and Bathsheba* with the decadence and orgies of *The Ten Commandments*. It also has Yul Brynner, but here he is Jewish and has hair.

It is not, however, without some distinctive characteristics, particularly a sibling rivalry that makes Cain and Abel seem like the Smothers Brothers, and more international accents in its cast than the bridge of the *Starship Enterprise*.

Taken from the Book of Kings, Solomon's story, written for the screen by Anthony Veiller, Paul Dudley, and George Bruce, is one of a man given great wisdom by a God who is pleased to have been asked only for guidance. Israel, under King David's rule, grew and prospered, and Solomon's great wisdom prolonged its good fortune. But his wisdom is misplaced when a certain foreign queen

Plagued

Even biblical movies need insurance policies.

Dozens of movie productions each year are affected by inclement weather, cast and crew illnesses, accidents, acts of God, and sometimes even deaths. Biblical films are no exception.

In 1928, three extras from Central Casting (and several animals) drowned during the shooting of the flood scene in *Noah's Ark*. In 1956, Cecil B. De Mille climbed to the top of a 103-foot ladder to inspect a camera and suffered a heart attack. He collapsed when he reached the bottom, called it a day, visited his doctor, and returned to work the following morning. In 1958, Tyrone Power died of a heart attack while filming *Solomon and Sheba* in Madrid. (Yul Brynner refilmed his footage, although it is Power who is still seen in some long shots.) Power was only forty-five at the time.

comes his way. That the queen glows with sensuality and looks like Gina Lollobrigida is certainly a key factor in its misplacement.

At the end of his reign, King David has two surviving sons: Solomon (Brynner), the result of his union with Bathsheba, and Adonijah (George Sanders), who has a pathological desire to be the next king. On his deathbed, David says that the friction between his sons is making his last days unbearable. "I leave but one monument to my name: the unity of Israel," David says tentatively, setting the stage for the tension that is to come. "Only in peace can Israel prosper and be made great, not in strife."

When the queen of Sheba (Lollobrigida) and her vast entourage come by on a diplomatic mission, both brothers recognize their opportunities. Since the queen is an ally of Egypt, Solomon, newly crowned as king,

wishes to befriend her and turn *her* into an ally, which would give him leverage against the pharaoh. Adonijah also wants to befriend the pharaoh—but only so that he can one day lead the Egyptian army against his brother.

The queen has motives of her own. "We enjoy life, and pleasure," she tells Solomon upon meeting him—and liking what she sees. What the queen wants is to enjoy Solomon himself, and drink of the power that will be hers once King Solomon is hers.

"Real wisdom," Solomon says, his sexy, cool-steel eyes burning into her, "lies in the ability to decide between the true and the false." But Solomon, for all his worldly wisdom, cannot tell if the seductive queen of Sheba wants him entwined or entombed. Nevertheless, before long the two are locked in an embrace that could melt the pyramids.

But *Solomon and Sheba* is as much a political thriller as it is a biblical saga, and Solomon's dalliance, no secret to the populace, becomes a royal liability.

"His association with the Sheban queen has developed into an open scandal," Adonijah's right-hand man reports to him.

"You and your Sheban slut have defiled the name of Israel," Adonijah promptly reports to his brother.

While the movie holds up well as a political drama, it rather falls apart as a character study, because it is never clear whether the queen is a fearless leader who wants to bring her opponent to death or simply a lonely woman who wants to love him to death. Still, Lollobrigida is very energetic in the role, Brynner cuts quite a virile character, and Sanders is one of the most joyously acrimonious brothers on screen.

Ultimately, the queen's respect for Solomon persuades her to return to Sheba,

Gina Lollobrigida and Yul Brynner wisely keep their distance, at least for the time being, in Solomon and Sheba.

Immature

He looked the part—until he took off his shirt.

Victor Mature was one of director Cecil B. De Mille's first choices to play Samson in *Samson and Delilah* (1949). He thought Mature could look appropriately biblical and impart a pious sincerity to the hairy hulk's character. But when the actor did a screen test, De Mille almost swallowed his eyepiece. Mature's body was out of shape, flabby, and untoned. Furthermore, as De Mille was soon to find out, Mature was also afraid of water, swords, and large animals.

But the famed director kept him on the picture anyway. The Paramount gymnasium, an expert trainer, stunt doubles, and trick photography did what Mature could not do on his own—perform miracles.

where she promises to build a tabernacle for Israel. Meanwhile, Solomon has been driven from the city by the angry Israelites. He and a handful of followers must face thousands of Pharaoh's well-armed soldiers, marching in from the east. They have nothing but their metal shields, which happen to be badly in need of polishing. So Solomon tells his men to polish their shields until they shine like mirrors. An odd request in the middle of what even General Patton would say looks like a no-win situation.

Solomon may have lost the woman after whom he lusted, but at least he has his wisdom, several loyal men with blinding shields—and the bright morning sun behind the advancing Egyptians.

God took six days to create the heaven and earth. John Huston took a year and a half to do it again on screen.

The famed director of *The African Queen* and *The Maltese Falcon* went to great lengths to put his own indelible stamp on the world of biblical movies in 1966 with *The Bible*. With a screenplay by Christopher Fry, the result is both impressive and disappointing at the same time, with moments of inspiration interspersed with moments of banality. Originally, the plan was to make *The Bible* fourteen hours long, with stories both from the Old and New Testaments, helmed by several directors, among them Orson Welles and Federico Fellini. As ultimately produced, it covers only the first twenty-two chapters of Genesis and is 174 minutes long.

Fourteen hours would have been a chore; three hours is merely a challenge.

The long opening creation sequence was actually the work of photographer Ernst Haas who traveled the world with a ten-man film crew shooting landscapes, seascapes, and other examples of nature's fury and nature's beauty in search of images that could represent the earliest days of the planet. Haas had intended to produce a book of photographs to support his theory that the earth is in a continuous state of creation. Instead, he filmed the *first* creation for Huston's ambitious project.

Once man and woman are created, however, Huston takes over the show. And when Michael Parks and Ulla Bergryd as Adam and Eve frolic freely about, *The Bible* is at its most gracious, being as simple and tasteful as a film about Adam and Eve can be. Bergryd, a student in Sweden at the time, was chosen to play Eve after one of Huston's production assistants spotted her at an art exhibit.

Things become a little less idyllic when

John Huston made many friends while directing The Bible *and playing Noah. Most of them had four legs.*

the human-headed serpent appears in a tree and tempts Eve with the forbidden fruit. The sweep and momentum are gone, lost along with the potency of the storytelling. The Tower of Babel episode builds to a rather quick and unenthusiastic climax, almost as if Huston were recreating storybook Bible pictures without the proper text to try to explain them.

The story of the flood and the ark is one of the most enjoyable in the movie, partially due to Huston's performance as Noah, a be-

fuddled simpleton who finds true happiness and meaning in being a pied piper to God's lower creatures. Huston had asked Charlie Chaplin to play Noah, and Chaplin considered it but finally decided he couldn't act in someone else's picture. As Abraham, George C. Scott shepherds much-needed life into the movie, particularly when he reacts to God's command to sacrifice his son Isaac. The destruction of Sodom is of some interest because of its resemblance to an atomic blast.

Huston and company tried to pack so

much into *The Bible*, perhaps trying to hold on to remnants of the original idea of including dozens of stories in a 14-hour epic, that even the more artistic elements are shortchanged—and Huston certainly did not skimp on artistic elements. Sodom was built on the slopes of an active volcano in Sicily, and the dancer Katherine Dunham was hired to choreograph dances that coincided with its destruction. Composer Toshiro Mayuzumi was brought in from Japan to create a score that rises and falls with the drama and humor of the story.

What humor is there in *The Bible*? Huston himself provides some in the Noah sequence, which generally is the most favored portion of the film. Huston visited the animals each morning before shooting began. There was one elephant that loved being scratched behind its upper foreleg, and whenever Huston walked away the elephant would grab his arm with its trunk and pull him back. Huston enjoyed the ritual so much that he put it in the movie.

Animals were flown in from all over the world for the scene, and Huston seemed to love them all. He spent more than five months (and $2 million) on that one sequence alone. By some accounts, the animals thought he was God. And in a way, for about a year and a half, he was.

The final biblical big screen epic of the twentieth century is unlike all the others in one very important way: It doesn't have any real people in it.

DreamWorks SKG, the newest movie studio in the land, used two-dimensional drawings and three-dimensional computer graphics to reacquaint moviegoers one more time with the timeless story of Moses and the exodus of the children of Israel from Egypt. But it wasn't necessarily a new generation of moviegoers the studio was after, for *The Prince of Egypt* (1998) purposely lacked the slapstick humor, cute talking animals, and rollicking score generally associated with animated features designed to attract mostly children. This *Prince of Egypt* is as much for adults as the biblical films starring Gregory Peck or Gina Lollobrigida.

Instead of Disneyesque merchandising tie-ins beginning in fast-food restaurants weeks before the film opened, *The Prince of Egypt* relies on stunning visuals, gentle humor, and a streamlined story.

The brainchild of two of DreamWorks' founders, Jeffrey Katzenberg and Steven Spielberg, *The Prince of Egypt*, despite its modest intentions, goes all the way on the production end. It employed three directors (Brenda Chapman, Steve Hickner, and Simon Wells—although multiple directors are not uncommon in animated pictures), two skilled composers (Hans Zimmer and Stephen Schwartz), hundreds of artists, and the vocal talents of Val Kilmer as Moses, Ralph Fiennes as Ramses, Patrick Stewart as Seti, Sandra Bullock as Miriam, Jeff Goldblum as Aaron, and Danny Glover as Jethro.

Unlike *The Ten Commandments*, *The Prince of Egypt* portrays Moses and Ramses as friends rather than rival half brothers, and that is what provides most of the humor in the early scenes.

"Moses, you always looked up to me," Ramses says as they race their chariots around a mammoth construction site, creating havoc every step of the way.

To agree on what happened is one thing, to agree on what one person said to another is something else. Many advisers are used to create biblical films such as The Prince of Egypt.

Towers of Babble

Many critics joke that even though producers and directors have a pretty divine writing partner when making biblical movies, they *still* get it wrong!

To try to get it right—or, more important, to satisfy everyone—many filmmakers have employed experts of one kind or another to bless the script, in a manner of speaking.

For *The Bible*, John Huston engaged the services of Professor Reverend W. M. Merchant and Monsignor Salvatore Garofalo. For *King David*, a 1985 film starring Richard Gere, Dr. Jonathan Magonet, head of the Bible Department at London's Leo Baeck College, was designated to give Gere as David, Edward Woodward as Saul, and Alice Krige as Bathsheba tips on how their characters might behave.

But the king of all is *The Prince of Egypt*, with over sixty official advisers and, depending on which account you believe, between five hundred and seven hundred academic and religious consultants. Among the advisers were the Reverend Billy Graham, the Reverend Jesse Jackson, Jerry Falwell, Pat Robertson, Rabbi Marvin Hier, Everett Fox, Dr. Burton Visotzky, Rabbi Stephen Robbins, and Shoshanna Gershenzon.

One common criticism of the DreamWorks animated epic was that it was too short. But with all those experts from every side of the aisle, it's a miracle that it got made at all.

A work of dreams and imagination: The Prince of Egypt *told one of the oldest Jewish stories using some of the newest digital methods.*

"Not a very good view," Moses chuckles, looking up to where Ramses rides, his skirt blowing in the breeze.

Soon Moses is forced to flee Egypt after he slays an Egyptian taskmaster who is whipping a Hebrew slave. He stumbles into the camp of Jethro, the Bedouin priest, where he meets his future wife, and God (in the form of a burning bush). God tells him to deliver His people from bondage.

"But I was their enemy," he says, "the son of the man who slaughtered their children. You've chosen the wrong messenger."

But God would never make a mistake like that. As Moses soon discovers, he is indeed the right messenger.

As an animated film, *The Prince of Egypt* employs more visual storytelling tricks than those of De Mille and Huston combined. The perilous journey of the basket in which the baby Moses sails upon the Nile is filled with cliffhanger tension, as the basket weaves and bobs around dangerous obstacles. When Moses as a young prince sees a hidden wall

of hieroglyphics depicting some of his adopted father's nefarious deeds, his mind's eye brings the wall to life as he painfully recalls the very slaughtering to which he later refers in his argument with God. When the Angel of Death visits the Egyptian homes, accompanied by a chilling whisper (a final breath), the helpless shame of the village is palpable. And when the Red Sea opens, a whale can be seen gracefully swimming on the other side of the parted passageway. These are all scenes that add a bit of magic to an already magical fable.

Into the movie's ninety-three minutes also are packed scenes of celebration and joy, as well as a seven-minute musical prologue that is an animated indictment against slavery.

Although *The Prince of Egypt* sets out to portray Moses only as a young man, its abrupt end is somehow unsatisfying. Perhaps ninety-three minutes weren't enough. Perhaps the filmmakers were mindful of keeping their younger audiences interested. Perhaps with a dozen artists spending thousands of hours just to illustrate the parting of the Red Sea, it simply was not feasible to do more.

At the end of the movie, Moses looks longingly into the distance, in the direction of Egypt, and says softy, "My brother . . . ," as if making the subtle point that we are all brothers and should find ways of living together peacefully on this small planet.

Odd that it takes a cartoon character to do that even better than most real people.

5

Mixed Doubles

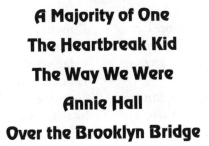

A Majority of One
The Heartbreak Kid
The Way We Were
Annie Hall
Over the Brooklyn Bridge

"Loudmouth Jewish girl from New York moves to Malibu, California, with her gorgeous *goyishe* guy, tells him that she's pregnant," and lives happily ever after.

Right?

Well, maybe half the time. At least in the movies—and if we are to believe the national statistics, in real life, too.

Mixed love—that is, marriages and love affairs between Jews and Gentiles—is a delicate affair and has provided the basis for several interesting if not always terribly successful motion pictures—a rather mixed bag of movie romance and box office results.

That "loudmouth Jewish girl" is Katie Morosky, the female lead in *The Way We Were*, played to type by Barbra Streisand, who falls in love with a "gorgeous goyishe guy" named Hubbell Gardiner, played equally to type by Robert Redford. The pairing was box office heaven; the relationship on film was a hell of a good try. But for Katie and Hubbell, in the end it just didn't work out.

It is no secret that throughout the decades

many Hollywood Jews were married to or had love affairs with non-Jews; as well as anyone, they know the highs and lows, challenges and triumphs that such relationships can produce. Why, then, don't they make more movies about it?

One reason may be traced to one of Warner Brothers' first feature projects, a melodrama called *Your Best Friend* about a Jewish mother who doesn't get along with her gentile daughter-in-law. It bombed.

In the 1940s, Sam Goldwyn, who had divorced his Jewish wife and married a Gentile, hired screenwriter Ring Lardner, Jr., to adapt a novel about the marriage of a Jew and a Catholic. Lardner's draft was rejected, ostensibly because it had portions that could be construed as anti-Semitic, but more likely because Goldwyn felt uncomfortable with the material. In fact, after several more drafts by other writers, he said he was "too mixed up, too torn" to pursue the project any further.

Fortunately, there are some who don't really mind being mixed up and torn. For them, it's just another day at work.

One of the most difficult to swallow of all mixed-up movie romances ever made is *A Majority of One*—difficult not because the story has an elderly American Jewish mother sparking the interest of a dapper Japanese businessman, but because it's just a little too hard to accept Rosalind Russell as the Jewish mother and Alec Guinness as the Japanese businessman.

If not for that lapse of believability, this 1962 film, written by Leonard Spiegelgass

and directed by Mervyn LeRoy, could have been quite a nice little love story in which the spark leads to some serious and intriguing intercultural sizzle.

Based on Spiegelgass's play which starred Gertrude Berg on Broadway, *A Majority of One* suffers in its journey to the screen because, unlike a stage play, the characters are up close and personal. Audiences can hear loud and clear just how hard Russell tries to sound Jewish—she must say "dahlink" to her daughter at least a hundred times and, stereotypically, makes every statement sound like a question. Audiences also see how hard Guinness tries to look Japanese. If he had had any more makeup on his eyes, he could have played his own daughter-in-law; years later even Guinness made fun of it.

The romance is made possible when Russell, as Bertha Jacoby, a widow, is asked to travel to Japan with her daughter Alice (Madlyn Rhue) and son-in-law Jerry (Ray Danton) when Jerry is given a U.S. embassy assignment in Toyko. At first Bertha doesn't like the idea. "Then you'll be living with the people who killed your brother," she laments, referring to World War II. Alice and Jerry proclaim themselves much more liberal and open-minded and implore her to reconsider. "Don't hate the Japanese anymore," Bertha responds rhetorically, "they're our friends. And don't hate the Germans anymore, they're our friends. I don't know where to go to get such lessons. To me it's like yesterday afternoon."

But she does change her mind and then meets Guinness, as the widower Koichi Asano, on the passenger liner from California to Japan. After a shaky start, he begins to enjoy her chatter, and her Yiddish, while she enjoys his honesty and integrity—not to mention his interest in her. Of even greater

Oyl and Water

Why does Rosalind Russell's friend in *A Majority of One* sound like Betty Boop and Barbra Streisand's neighbor in *Funny Girl* sound like Olive Oyl? Because they were both played by Mae Questel, who provided the cartoon voices of Betty from 1932 to 1939 and Olive from 1933 to 1967.

But if Mrs. Rubin in *A Majority of One* and Mrs. Strakosh in *Funny Girl* were somewhat stereotypical sweet old Jewish women, they pale by comparison to the one Questel played in *New York Stories* in 1989. Questel, born in 1908, played Woody Allen's overbearing mother in a segment of the movie called "Oedipus Wrecks." In the segment, directed by Allen, lawyer Sheldon Mills (Allen) wants to get his mother out of his life entirely by marrying a Gentile (Mia Farrow), but even then he is quite literally haunted by his mother, who appears as a giant nagging apparition in the streets of Manhattan.

Mae Questel, a live-action Jewish mama in several films, provided the voice for two famous cartoon heroines. Here she is seen in New York Stories *with Woody Allen.*

Worlds apart, Rosalind Russell and Alec Guinness make the most of their attraction in A Majority of One.

significance, they have one very important thing in common: Asano's son, too, was killed in the war. Bertha and Mr. Asano are, in effect, neighbors in a sometimes perplexing humankind. (The title of the movie comes from the proverb, "Any man more right than his neighbors constitutes a majority of one.")

"All we wished for was a happy and peaceful existence with the flowers and the moon and the sunshine," Asano tells her, refuting her claim that the Japanese and the Germans wanted to run the world. "Is that so different from what you wished for, Mrs. Jacoby?"

Later, during a kosher meal he has prepared in his home, Asano hints at marriage. Alice and Jerry are against it, despite their professed liberalism. Ultimately, Bertha herself discourages the notion because she understands that her Japanese gentleman simply misses his wife, much as she still mourns for her beloved husband.

At the end, Asano visits Bertha once she has returned to her New York apartment. She prepares a Sabbath meal, lights the candles, and says a prayer as the lights go down and the dialogue fades. Their true friendship is frozen in time. It is one of the nicest and most honest moments in the film—but perhaps only because as it gets quieter and darker in the fadeout, it is no longer so easy to hear Bertha talk or to see Mr. Asano's makeup.

Twist of the Nose

Fourteen years before putting on more makeup than a Kabuki dancer in *A Majority of One*, Alec Guinness, as Fagin in *Oliver Twist*, had a fake nose that made Karl Malden look like Nanette Fabray.

The 1948 film classic, directed by David Lean, was banned in the United States for three years because of what Jewish groups considered an anti-Semitic characterization of the notorious Dickens character. Fagin is, of course, Jewish—as well as dishonest and miserly—but Guinness's fake nose was too much for some, and seven minutes of various close-ups and profiles were edited out. It finally opened in the United States in 1951.

There is nothing hidden about Kelly Corcoran's intentions in *The Heartbreak Kid*. In fact, she stands right in the path of Lenny Kantrow's sun while he stretches out on the beach during his honeymoon, just so that she can drive him crazy by blinding him with her beauty.

In *The Heartbreak Kid*, a 1972 Neil Simon comedy adapted from a Bruce Jay Friedman short story and directed by Elaine May, Charles Grodin plays Lenny, a sporting goods salesman who, weeks before seeing Kelly, meets a "nice Jewish girl" named Lila Kolodny. Lila is played to annoying perfection by May's real-life daughter, Jeannie Berlin, who won an Academy Award nomination as best supporting actress for her whiney efforts. Why is Lila a nice Jewish girl? Simply because she seems nice and she's defi-

nitely Jewish. Beyond that, Lenny doesn't know all that much about her, other than the fact that she laughs easily and has a *zaftig*, or robust, physique.

But Lenny soon finds out that giggling and *zaftig*ness do not necessarily make for a fun and sensuous relationship. Lila is not a robust lover. Although she wants to make him happy, she does it in the most annoying of ways, like tracing little circles on his chest. Before long, Lila becomes the nice Jewish girl from hell. As a stereotype it's pitiful, but as comedy it's almost priceless. *The Heartbreak Kid* never pretends to be more than it is—a blistering satire of love, lust, and blisters.

Not insignificantly, Lenny and Lila are married in a small, cramped, stifling room where all the guests are packed in like pickled herrings. Then they hit the open road for their Miami Beach honeymoon. Everything Lila does annoys Lenny, from her incessant stupid questions, to the way she eats her egg salad sandwiches ("I'm an egg salad nut," she tells him), to the way she yells "pee pee" whenever she has to go to the bathroom.

When he finally snaps in Miami, he screams at the top of his lungs, "It's not a question of not appreciating you. It's that I don't like one goddamn thing about you!"

With Lila laid up in their hotel room with a nasty sunburn that puffs her up even more than she's naturally puffed, Lenny goes to the beach alone and meets the gorgeous Kelly, played by the young and winsome Cybill Shepherd. Kelly is vacationing with her wealthy parents. She uses her eyes, her smile and her wit to play with Lenny's head. "You're in my spot," she says to him seductively, although he has yards of empty sand around him. Lenny instantly falls in love. Or so he thinks.

A Star Is Made, Part I

Jewish directors Mervyn LeRoy, Elaine May, and Sydney Pollack all have one thing in common beside making motion pictures featuring Jewish-gentile relationships. At various times in their careers they have all been bitten by the acting bug.

Between 1920 and 1924, LeRoy (*A Majority of One*) acted in nine silent films. Only twenty years old when he made his debut in *Double Speed*, he worked tirelessly in front of the camera in *The Call of the Canyon*, *Little Johnny Jones*, *The Chorus Lady*, and others before beginning an illustrious career *behind* the camera.

Elaine May (*The Heartbreak Kid*) was one half of the comedy team Nichols and May with her husband at the time, Mike Nichols, before she entered the movie acting arena in *Enter Laughing*. Although primarily a writer and director, May also had starring roles in *Luv*, *A New Leaf* (which she also directed), and *California Suite*, in which she had a hilarious role as the suspicious wife of almost-philanderer Walter Matthau.

Sydney Pollack (*The Way We Were*), who won an Academy Award as best director in 1985 for *Out of Africa*, began his career as an actor and, once his directing career was firmly under way, gleefully took on a few more acting jobs. Pollack had a scathingly funny cameo as Dustin Hoffman's agent in *Tootsie* (which he also directed) and then a featured dramatic role in Woody Allen's *Husbands and Wives*. He also appeared in *Death Becomes Her* and *The Player*.

But you have to go back several decades to find one of the oddest cases of directors acting—odd because this Jew almost always played someone who despises Jews. In 1942 Otto Preminger, who later directed *Exodus,* played a Nazi in *Pied Piper*; in 1943 he reprised a role he had performed six years earlier on Broadway, playing a German consul in New York during World War II in *Margin for Error* in which, incidentally, Milton Berle plays a Jewish police officer assigned to guard him; and in 1953, he played the commander of the Nazi camp in Billy Wilder's *Stalag 17*.

Can an aggressive Jewish boy from New York find happiness with an equally aggressive *shikse* from Minnesota?

Lenny meets Kelly several times after that, and to hide the truth from Lila, he lies. And lies and lies. Lies beget more lies, as Lenny becomes a veritable one-man orgy of fabrication. In the process he becomes a very unlikable character—certainly not a member of the nice Jewish boys' club to which many characters in other films have belonged.

Kelly's father (Eddie Albert, in an Academy Award-nominated performance as best supporting actor) makes it known that he hates Lenny and decides to leave the hotel. "Daddy doesn't like this place," Kelly tells Lenny. "He doesn't like the element you get here." Lenny doesn't want to be an element, an easily pigeonholed member of some annoying group, but rather a winner, a possessor of something people like him don't usually get to possess. So he follows Kelly to her new hotel, and then to Minnesota.

Once there, Lenny continues to lie to Kelly's friends and family while pursuing her. At one point Kelly brings him to a cabin in the woods and says she wants them both to take off their clothes and sit as close to each other as they can without touching.

"All my life," Lenny says, "I wanted to be in a place like this, with a girl like you, playing a game like this." But he mentions nothing of love. For him, it's all perception and possession.

Lenny doesn't touch Kelly, which prompts her to say, "I think my father misjudged you. You're the most decent, honorable man I ever met . . . I'll sleep with you tomorrow night." But neither does she mention anything of love. For her, it's all plans and provisos.

Ultimately, Lenny and Kelly marry. But what does he know about his new bride? That she's a beautiful, sexy college student with a rich daddy? If that's all he wants out of life, fine. And what does Kelly know about her new husband? That he's decent and honorable? (That's debatable.) That he's a fast talker? Maybe—although he has absolutely nothing to say to anybody at their sumptuous wedding. Fortunately there's a lot of food to keep him occupied. Even egg salad.

Charles Grodin has some heartbreaking news for Jeannie Berlin, his new soon-to-be ex-wife, in The Heartbreak Kid.

From all appearances, Lenny and Kelly's relationship was empty. By contrast, Katie and Hubbell's relationship was full—full of audiences who, in turn, were full of tears.

But instead of a nice Jewish boy falling for a glamorous *shikse*, In *The Way We Were* a smart and determined Jewish girl falls for a gorgeous *goyishe* guy.

The Way We Were capitalized on the star appeal of Streisand and Redford, together for the first and only time. Warren Beatty was initially offered the role but turned it down. At first, Redford didn't think audiences would accept the relationship. "I just can't see her and me in the same movie," he commented to studio executive Julia Phillips prior to signing on.

But Redford relented—and audiences were pleased. In fact, the Streisand-Redford love story far overshadowed and outmaneuvered the political story that shared its nucleus. Nobody wanted to see these two all fired up in a Senate chamber. Instead, people wanted to see them all fired up in the bedroom.

Katie Morosky is an angry, driven, self-assured and ultrasensitive activist in the late 1930s, a volunteer with the Young Communist League at college, when she meets Hubbell. He's at the same school, but he's a laid-back athlete who just wants to have a good time doing whatever comes easiest to him—mostly hanging around, partying, talking, and writing.

The two meet, fall in love, get married,

The Way We Worked

Although Robert Redford and Barbra Streisand were as dissimilar as the characters they played in *The Way We Were*, once filming began there were the inevitable rumors about a romance between the two stars, especially when they began shooting love scenes.

Director Sydney Pollack had strong feelings about love scenes being as discreet as they were emotional, so when Katie and Hubbell had to be shown in bed together after making love, Pollack made sure they were both under the covers at all times, that there was as much privacy on the set as possible, and that only one camera angle was used, both for effect and expediency.

Redford was dissatisfied with the outline his underpants made beneath the covers. It didn't look real, he said. So he took them off while he was under the covers, shot the scene, and then put them back on again.

Later, when asked how their mother reacted to Daddy's love scene with Streisand, Redford's children told a reporter that their parents had had a fight and that Mommy had thrown a glass of milk at Daddy. Lola Redford was then approached and asked what her husband was wearing during that famous love scene. She replied, "Aramis."

The roles being somewhat reversed, Katie is the moody, never-satisfied boss of the family, while Hubbell is the trophy Gentile. But he isn't just a dumb blonde; he speaks up, time and again, virtually forcing Katie to face their differences. "Why are you always so angry?" he says to her. And, "Are you always so sure of everything?" And, "Everything that happens in the world doesn't happen to you personally."

He may be critical to the point of distraction, but, as Katie knows, he's so damn good to look at, and he has so much potential as a writer, that it's hard for her to leave.

At least for a while.

For her part, Katie has a certain charisma of her own that keeps Hubbell around, even though, as they both admit, she doesn't have quite the right style to be his wife.

A few years after they break up, in the 1950s, Katie sees Hubbell in New York. He has a new blonde wife and is working at one of the networks, and she's married to a man named David Cohen who, she says, is a good father to the daughter she had with Hubbell. Katie is handing out ban-the-bomb pamphlets, and Hubbell is still writing, even though it's just for television. Maybe they're both a little happier now. Who knows for sure? What *is* for sure is that because of their chemistry and charisma, audiences *wanted* them to have a happy ending (although they also reveled in their own tears). What is also sure is that despite the fact that Katie and Hubbell do not end up together—or more likely *because* they don't—hardly a year goes by when someone in the Hollywood community doesn't mention the possibility of a sequel.

and move to Hollywood, where Hubbell becomes a screenwriter.

Arthur Laurents, Alvin Sargent, and David Rayfiel, basing their screenplay on Laurents' novella, had a lot more material in the original script on events surrounding the House Un-American Activities Committee hearings, which gave Katie and Hubbell more reasons to fight and focus on their differences. Director Sydney Pollack admitted, though, that *The Way We Were* was destined to be basically a love story. "I hope audiences also ponder some of the movie's serious undertones," he mused out loud shortly after its release.

Despite the ultimate outcome, Barbra Streisand and Robert Redford created a box office romance that was made in heaven in The Way We Were.

On Oscar night in 1977, Woody Allen was three thousand miles east of Los Angeles, playing clarinet at a Manhattan jazz club, something Alvy Singer, his character in *Annie Hall*, might have done in a similar situation. That's partially what makes the movie so fascinating: Audiences see a fanciful reflection of the real-life love affair between Woody Allen and Diane Keaton.

Like *The Heartbreak Kid* and *The Way We Were*, *Annie Hall* garnered many Academy Award nominations. Unlike those other films, though, this one walked away with several statuettes: best picture, best actress (Keaton), best director (Allen), and best screenplay (Allen and Marshall Brickman).

Alvy is a neurotic Jewish comic looking for love and hoping to live a long and meaningful life without ever having to leave Manhattan. One day, would-be nightclub singer Annie Hall, whose family background Alvy sees as being lifted right out of a Norman Rockwell painting, walks into his life. Both Alvy and Annie are incredibly insecure, and it is their insecurities, not necessarily their cultural or religious differences, that get in the way of a lasting relationship.

Poor Alvy. He's afraid the world is really full of fools and hypocrites—and then you die. As he and Annie go through their stages

The Way We Were won only two of its six Academy Award nominations—for Marvin Hamlisch's score and the title song he wrote with Alan and Marilyn Bergman—but the careers of the principals on both sides of the camera continued to skyrocket. As for Katie and Hubbell, theirs was a heavenly romance that just couldn't stay aloft for too long.

Neurosis, anyone? Diane Keaton (best actress) and Woody Allen (best director) helped make Annie Hall *the most honored picture of the year.*

flits from one personal episode to the next. Then Annie meets a record tycoon named Tony Lacey (Paul Simon), who invites her to follow him to Los Angeles, a prospect far more tempting to Annie than staying in New York.

Apparently it is Alvy's and Annie's similar anxieties that initially attract them to each other. Author Foster Hersch, in *Love, Sex, Death and the Meaning of Life* (which could be the title of Woody Allen's biography), suggests that Annie is the "composite, idealized *shikse* who haunts the fantasies of avid Jewish boys." Jewish boys, Hersch says, "search for the perfect *shikse*, a girl who will not berate, cajole, henpeck, or emote."

But Annie *does* emote, and grandly, and although she herself may haunt Alvy's fantasies, her family haunts his nightmares. In fact, to Alvy, in some ways the Halls in Chippewa Falls are worse than the Singers in Brooklyn. "I can't believe this family," Alvy narrates. "They're talking swap meets and boat basins, and the old lady at the end of the table is a classic Jew hater. And they really look American, very healthy, like they never get sick or anything." Is there anything worse for a guy like Alvy?

Annie also berates and cajoles—but only because of her own insecurities. "You're the

of courtship, Alvy sinks deeper into the realization that he's an incurable neurotic and an incurable romantic at the same time, a lethal combination. As for Annie, she's so afraid she'll never hold her own in any artistic or intellectual endeavor that she simply

one who never wanted to make a real commitment," she says to Alvy, bitterly. "You don't think I'm smart enough."

In the end, of course, it is obvious that Alvy and Annie must go the way of Katie and Hubbell, *schlepping* and flitting to a bittersweet ending. Alvy's still in love, but fortunately for him he can depend on more than just the memory of Annie Hall to sustain him in his wonderful misery. He also depends on New York City and a satchel full of neuroses for sustenance. As for Annie, she still has a career to pursue, which she can do without neglecting many sweet memories of her favorite neurotic. At least Alvy Singer and Annie Hall have a lot more style and substance than Lenny Kantrow and Kelly Corcoran. That's why it's bittersweet instead of just bitter.

Almost universally acclaimed, *Annie Hall* was hailed by many critics as Woody Allen's *8½*, a comparison with Federico Fellini's landmark 1963 film that presented a personal vision of the director's life and work. Allen's oft-repeated and quite characteristic response was, "It's more like my *2½*."

Manhattan is strictly Woody Allen's territory, which may be why the characters in an odd 1984 romantic comedy, fearful of *too* many comparisons to *Annie Hall*, stayed primarily over the bridge on the Brooklyn side.

Over the Brooklyn Bridge was directed by Menahem Golan, the Israeli who has done everything from action (*Operation Thunderbolt*) to crime (*Lepke*) to myth (*The Magician of Lublin*) to war (*Hanna's War*). Comedy is one of his least frequent genres, and in this case the studio apparently just took the money and ran, for the film was little seen, is little known, and is almost never rerun. But its eagerness and ambition to be another *Annie Hall* beg for it to be watched. At least on a night when you have absolutely nothing else to do.

Instead of Alvy Singer there is Alby Sherman, played to neurotic excess by Elliot Gould. Instead of a Rockwellian girl from Chippewa Falls named Annie, there's a blonde Irish princess from Philadelphia named Elizabeth, played by Margaux Hemingway. Instead of a small Singer family dinner where everyone tries to outtalk everyone else, there's a big Sherman family dinner where everyone screams at one another. There are even flashbacks at the end, a device used to much better effect in *Annie Hall*.

As the frustrated and diabetic Alby, Gould is not entirely likable and certainly neither as cute nor as insightful as Woody Allen was as Alvy Singer. And Hemingway is just too annoying to be anything like Annie Hall. Clawing and shrieky, she sets the cause for fantasy *shikses* back a hundred years.

Alby owns a luncheonette in Brooklyn but dreams of owning a fancy eatery in Manhattan. "Look at this place," he says to his Uncle Ben when he shows him the restaurant he wants to buy. "It makes the luncheonette look like a toilet."

But Uncle Ben has his doubts. "From that toilet you make a good living," he says.

Uncle Ben is played by television comic legend Sid Caesar. Although he has since proved himself to be quite a capable dramatic actor, in *Over the Brooklyn Bridge* his facial mannerisms and vocal style eliminate any possibility of adding a level of serious-

A Change of Plans, Part II

Anhedonia? Me and My Goy? Annie Hall, *with Woody Allen, Tony Roberts, and Diane Keaton.*

Talk about anxiety: Woody Allen tossed as many as a dozen titles around before deciding on *Annie Hall*.

Woody Allen had long intended *Annie Hall* to be called "Anhedonia," a Greek medical term meaning the inability to experience pleasure. His cowriter, Marshall Brickman, suggested "A Rollercoaster Named Desire" and "Me and My Goy." Close to its release date, Allen tossed around "Anxiety" and "Annie and Alvy" before settling on *Annie Hall*.

Had Elaine May and Neil Simon stuck to the title "A Change of Plan," the Bruce Jay Friedman short story on which *The Heartbreak Kid* is based, audiences would have known well before meeting Lenny and Lila what they were in for.

And while it is debatable to which direction *Over the Brooklyn Bridge* refers (going away from, or coming back to), had the working title stuck, audiences would have come knowing much more about what to expect when the lights went down. For quite some time during its production, the movie was known as "My Darling Shikse."

ness to the proceedings when called for. It's *shtick* all the way. Uncle Ben has plenty of money to lend to Alby to buy the restaurant, but he's against his nephew's relationship with the Philadelphia princess, which is what Uncle Ben always calls her, and holds it over Alby's head.

"I want a little peace and quiet," Uncle Ben says to Elizabeth. "I'm going to ask my nephew not to see you anymore. You're a complication in his life."

That's not Alby's only complication. First there's a loan shark who gets in the way, and then there's that most nefarious of characters—his mother. Mama Sherman is played by the mother of all Jewish mothers, Shelley Winters, and she lays on the guilt thicker than Rosalind Russell's fake Jewish accent.

"Alby," she cries, "you want to leave here? You already made up your mind. Go. Don't be afraid. I'll be plenty afraid for both of us. . . . You're still hungry. Want a little soup?"

Unlike Alvy and Annie (and Katie and Hubbell, and Mrs. Jacoby and Mr. Asano), love does win out for Alby and Elizabeth.

They profess their love for each other and stay together. But the journey to get there is far less intriguing. Perhaps director Golan thought a love story sprinkled with enough Yiddish expressions to drown out an overcrowded Seder would make a good enough Jewish comedy for a change of pace in his long career. Instead, he ended up with a silly Jewish joke. On the other hand, maybe in another dimension the neurotic deli owner and the Philadelphia princess are still together, living happily ever after. Then the joke's on us.

Biting Professions

In the movies, not every Nice Jewish Boy can grow up to be a doctor or lawyer, no matter how much their mothers wish for it. A sporting goods salesman like Lenny Kantrow in *The Heartbreak Kid* is also n honorable profession—unless, of course, you happen to be less than an honorable person. And owning a little sandwich shop, like Alby Sherman in *Over the Brooklyn Bridge*, also has a measure of distinction—as long as you can at least pretend to be a little happy about it. To be sure, there are some professions that are a lot worse.

For instance, in a 1967 British parody called *Fearless Vampire Killers, or Pardon Me, But Your Teeth Are in My Neck*, Alfie Bass plays an Hasidic vampire named Yoine Shagal who has one big advantage (in addition to big teeth): no one knows how to ward off a Jewish vampire, because crosses don't work.

Neither does every Nice Jewish Boy in the movies grow up to be a black musician or a Nazi soldier—unless he happens to be a human chameleon, as Woody Allen was in 1983's *Zelig*. He also became a boxer, a statesman, and whatever else fit the times and places in which he found himself craving for attention.

6

Enduring the Darkness

The Diary of Anne Frank

The Hiding Place

Voyage of the Damned

Au Revoir, les Enfants

Schindler's List

IT IS ANOTHER ONE OF LIFE'S lousy ironies: the most insidious and repelling event in human history has spawned some of the most intriguing and eminently watchable motion pictures.

As painful as it may be to accept, the Holocaust has given countless writers and directors fantastic tales of courage and terror, personal drama and international intrigue, heroism and evil, to put onto film. Many Holocaust movies are based on fact, diaries, or memories. Certainly not all have Jewish characters in central roles; one true

story is even told from the perspective of a Christian evangelist. Several tell their stories in lyrical, poetic, even hauntingly beautiful ways.

The topic has been the stuff of drama, and even comedy, for over five decades, and audiences have been in the millions. That, of course, brings us to another of life's little ironies: Holocaust movies also make some of us as angry as hell, and yet we watch. It is not always easy to sit comfortably in a dark theater when it's almost a given that the death toll at the end of the picture will be

Frank Casting

Although she was thirty-six at the time, Shelley Winters wondered if George Stevens wanted her to test for the part of thirteen-year-old Anne when he called her after announcing that he would direct the movie version of *The Diary of Anne Frank*. Then, realizing she was too old, she wondered if Stevens's intention was to cast her as Mrs. Van Daan instead, even though Van Daan was fifty years old.

Stevens, who had directed Winters to an Academy Award nomination in 1951 for *A Place in the Sun*, in which she played a seventeen-year-old girl when she was actually in her mid-twenties, thought she *could* play a fifty-year-old with the same conviction. And Mrs. Van Daan is the role that Stevens gave her.

Anne, however, was still to be cast.

At a party given one evening by Lee Strasberg, Winters went over to Strasberg's twenty-year-old daughter Susan, who had played the part on Broadway, and begged her to try out for the role, believing she would be perfect for it. But Susan didn't want to leave New York and her current lover, Richard Burton.

Stevens put a nationwide search in motion to find an unknown to play the part, thinking it would give the movie a more realistic aura. Millie Perkins, a seventeen-year-old model, won the role but confided in Winters that, being Catholic, she worried that her lack of knowledge of Jewish tradition and history would mar her performance. Winters, who *is* Jewish, took it upon herself to help the young woman as much as she could. Ultimately, though, it was Winters herself who took home the Academy Award as best supporting actress for her performance.

Why? Because we're wise enough to know that we must never forget. And we're smart enough to know that we might as well watch a good movie while we're remembering.

In real life, Anne Frank wrote her thoughts down in her diary, which is a good thing; otherwise, audiences might consider some of Anne's statements in *The Diary of Anne Frank* to be among the most implausible, far-fetched lines of dialogue ever uttered in a serious film. No one would ever believe that Anne, in the most hopeless hours of her family's horrible ordeal, would be so incredibly optimistic as to say, "I was going on a great adventure," after describing how her family must "disappear" into thin air as Jews in Amsterdam are being rounded up by the Nazis and sent to death camps. Or to say at the end, as the second bookend of her amazing diary, "In spite of everything, I still believe that people are really good at heart." Even her father admits that she puts him to shame.

The story and the dialogue are, of course, carefully constructed, or rather reconstructed, by Francis Goodrich and Albert Hackett, based on their play and the published autobiography, *Anne Frank: Diary of a Young Girl*. It's powerful stuff—almost powerful enough to overcome the unexpected casting of the then unknown Millie

higher than the box office receipts. Most people already know before seeing *The Diary of Anne Frank* that all but one of the major characters perish. Many are also aware that the vast majority of passengers aboard the *Voyage of the Damned* are sent to Nazi death camps. That's entertainment?

Yet we're compelled to see these movies when they first arrive at the theaters, we honor them with awards and profits shortly thereafter, and we watch them again when they're released on video or shown on television.

Perkins, who looks and acts far too mature for a thirteen-year-old girl. At times it seems that just what kind of adventure this Anne really would prefer could best be left to imagination rather than fact.

Nevertheless, Perkins has not only the touching and perceptive dialogue from Anne's real diary but also a stellar cast to surround and support her in director George Stevens's film. The cast includes Joseph Schildkraut and Gusti Huber as her parents; Lou Jacobi, Shelley Winters (who won an Academy Award as best supporting actress), and Richard Beymer as Mr. and Mrs. Van Daan and their son, Peter, with whom Anne develops a brief romance; Diane Baker as her sister Margot; and Ed Wynn as the finicky dentist, Mr. Dussel, who joins them all later on in the small attic above Mr. Frank's factory.

The opening scene in *The Diary of Anne Frank* fills the screen with clouds and birds, which is why our visit with them is especially harrowing. Instinctively, we know that there won't be clouds and birds for them much longer. Maybe never again. Director Stevens heightens the tension by keeping the actual set on which they shot the movie as claustrophobically small as it was in real life, and by keeping the set very hot on days when the real attic would have been hot, and cold when it would have been very cold. It is painfully obvious that the Franks, Van Daans, and Mr. Dussel don't have nearly as much as they need to get on with their lives in the style to which they are accustomed. But as Mr. Frank tells Anne when she's upset that they don't have candles to put on their Chanukah cake, "I'm sure that God understands shortages."

Despite and because of the insanity outside, the families have more than their share

Timing

You can only imagine what went through Otto Frank's mind when he saw Joseph Schildkraut and Millie Perkins reliving his and his daughter's lives in a crowded attic while visiting the set of *The Diary of Anne Frank* during its production.

Frank remained calm and astute. He went over to Shelley Winters and said, "I believe you will get the Oscar for this picture." He told her that she possessed the kind of courage, compassion, and sense of humor the real Mrs. Van Daan had possessed. Winters told him that if she *did* win the Oscar she would donate it to the Anne Frank Museum in Amsterdam.

In 1975, when Winters was in Europe making a picture called *Lucky Touch*, she stopped by the Anne Frank Museum, Oscar in hand. Although it hadn't been planned, Otto Frank walked in at that very moment. He told Winters that it was something of a miracle to see her there. "I only come to this museum twice a year, for about an hour," he said.

of jealousies and arguments inside. There is tension between Anne and her mother, between Anne and her sister, between Mrs. Van Daan and Peter, between Mr. Dussel and everyone. But instead of simply a bundled battle of wills from beginning to end, Stevens and the writers created an old-fashioned and quite effective cliffhanger, as well. At one point, Peter's cat walks gingerly on a shelf exploring some crumbs and almost knocks some cups onto the floor. Any noise in the attic during the day could arouse suspicions in the factory or the street below and put an end to their secret hiding. At another juncture, the families hear noises downstairs after hours, which could be an employee working late, a burglar, or even the Nazi-controlled Dutch police.

Desperation and resignation: Shelley Winters, Academy Award winner for best supporting actress, and Lou Jacobi bide their time in The Diary of Anne Frank.

"I don't know how we can go on living this way," Mrs. Frank cries.

But they do go on living—even adapting to it in some ways. There is a terrifying sequence when the city around them is being bombed, with flashes of light seen in the distance, dust raining from the ceiling, the attic shaking. But Mrs. Frank and Mrs. Van Daan just sit and sip their tea in the midst of it all, and when the noise and shaking in the attic end, the women are strangely calm, as if it were just a day like any other. Which, of course, for them it was.

One reason that *The Diary of Anne Frank* seems so real is that it was shot in sequence. Another is that George Stevens had already mined this emotional territory personally as one of the cameramen who filmed concentration camps as they were liberated at the end of World War II. He learned about horror. Horror is not a group of Jews bickering in a locked attic. Horror, true horror, is knowing that they will not be around to bicker for too much longer.

Truth is more frightening than fiction, as many Holocaust films attest. And like *The Diary of Anne Frank*, what happens to Corrie ten Boom and her father and sister in *The Hiding Place* happened in real life. The story might never have come to the screen at all if not for Ruth Graham, Christian evangelist Billy Graham's wife. Ruth, a friend of Corrie's since 1969, was fascinated by her book, which was "drawn from the writing and memories of Corrie ten Boom, her family, and those who—with them—endured the darkness," as the film version states.

The Hiding Place, written by Allan Sloane and Lawrence Holben and directed by James F. Collier in 1975, recounts the experiences of the ten Booms, teachers and evangelists, as they hid Jews in their home during the Holocaust, and as they themselves were captured and interred in a Nazi camp.

It opens in Haarlem, Holland, in 1940 with a message from the queen of the Netherlands being delivered on the radio. "The lights have gone out over free Holland," the queen says, offering a political perspective rarely heard in Holocaust films. "Where only two weeks ago there was a free nation, there is now the stillness of death. The unhappy people of Holland can only pray in silence."

Immediately we are taken inside the ten Booms' crowded clock shop. Papa ten Boom and his daughters Corrie and Betsie—played respectively by Arthur O'Connell, Jeannette Clift and Julie Harris—have all been rendered speechless by the queen's pronouncement. Then the Nazis come to collect all the radios. Their Jewish neighbors are harassed and expelled. Signs in restaurants along the street forbid Jews.

But the ten Booms, deeply religious Catholics, do not look the other way. Papa even stands in line along with his Jewish customers to receive a yellow star to wear.

Diary of Disappointment

The Diary of Anne Frank was one of at least two Jewish-oriented projects that Sam Goldwyn wanted to produce and later regretted not having made.

Goldwyn was the tough, opinionated head of MGM who was responsible for *Wuthering Heights*, *The Best Years of Our Lives*, *Stella Dallas*, and dozens of other top films. In the early 1940s he came upon a book called *Earth and High Heaven* by Gwethalyn Graham and clearly saw its possibilities as a motion picture. The story concerns a rich Protestant girl in Canada and the poor Jewish lawyer who wants her hand in marriage, despite her father's strong disapproval. Goldwyn believed that such a movie would not only give audiences a tender love story to enjoy but would also spotlight the effects of anti-Semitism on contemporary society. Several writers produced countless drafts of the screenplay, but Goldwyn was never satisfied. By 1947, when Darryl Zanuck produced the highly successful *Gentleman's Agreement*, Goldwyn had dropped the project in frustration.

Then in 1956 Goldwyn saw *The Diary of Anne Frank* on Broadway and instantly envisioned it as a film that would be as important as it would be enthralling. Otto Frank, Anne's father, owned the rights to the story and insisted on script approval. Goldwyn wouldn't hear of it and soon abandoned the idea. As things turned out, George Stevens produced and directed it three years later. Another credit was lost, and it is said that not making *The Diary of Anne Frank* and *Earth and High Heaven* were two of the biggest disappointments in Goldwyn's remarkable career.

Messages

From production to premiere, *The Hiding Place* was a place of assorted and sometimes sordid messages.

First there were the messages of love, as some very wealthy friends of Corrie ten Boom, on whom the story is based, continued to contribute large sums of money to keep the production afloat when it was in financial trouble.

Then there was the message of hate, when a member of American Nazi party tossed a tear gas bomb into the Beverly Hills theater where *The Hiding Place* was premiering in September 1975, apparently to protest the characters' love for Jews.

Corrie ten Boom was herself a message of hope and friendship. While visiting Israel, she presented the two-millionth copy of *The Hiding Place*, the book on which the movie is based, to Golda Meir, and then went with the prime minister into a private room at the Knesset to pray with her for peace.

"The God of Abraham and Isaac is my God, too," he says, adding that if everyone in Holland wore a yellow star, no one would know who was a Gentile and who was a Jew.

Soon the ten Booms take in a Jewish baby to live with them, which of course is now against the law. "We must obey the law of the state," Papa says, "if it does not go against a higher law of God. It is the Jews who gave us the Bible. And our savior." Then they take in other Jews. "My Lord Jesus tells me to open the door to whatever comes, and give his love to whoever I can. And I will listen to his voice."

While it is an evangelistic movie in several ways, it is also a powerful statement about human responsibility and a pretty good adventure drama as well. Scenes depicting how the ten Booms build a secret hiding place for their Jews—using bricks smuggled in grandfather clock cases and paint smuggled in milk bottles—are truly absorbing.

The Hiding Place was an independent production that used some top-notch talent. The cast is uniformly excellent and Collier's direction solid. Such confidence in the production even allowed gentle humor to be part of the tension; for example, when Corrie tries to squeeze into a narrow opening to test the hiding place, she grunts and says, "They better not send us anyone wider than me."

Like the Franks and Van Daans, who were hiding elsewhere in the same country at the same time, the ten Booms' Jews are not without their interpersonal problems. But still, as Jews, they are family, and it shows, particularly when they come together in prayer and harmony. "Are you crazy?" a neighbor whispers, rushing in to talk to Corrie with a worried look on her face, "the whole street can hear your Jews singing!"

But soon the Nazis uncover the secret, and the second half of *The Hiding Place* recreates the misery the family endures in a work camp. Through it all, they hold on to their Christian values. When Betsie is beaten, Corrie starts to go after her unsuspecting Nazi assailant with an ax. Betsie stops her and whispers, "No hate. No hate."

She too, would put some to shame.

Collier didn't make a fancy movie, but there is honesty and integrity in every frame; eighteen years before *Schindler's List*, *The Hiding Place* told an interesting and inspiring story of non-Jews helping Jews in this

Julie Harris and Jeannette Clift go from The Hiding Place *to a place from which they'd like to hide.*

traumatic period in history. It was also among the first of several Holocaust films in which a real person from the story appears; Corrie, in her eighties, is shown at the end of the film talking mostly about her love for Jesus. Perhaps that's one reason *The Hiding Place* is rarely mentioned in lists of "Jewish" movies. But what the list makers may not have considered is that the ten Booms were also victims of hate and prejudice, and that they survived with the kind of hopeful resilience that *did*, in fact, give them a certain kind of Jewish experience.

The experiences of the Jews aboard the *St. Louis*, a German passenger liner on its way to Cuba just as World War II was breaking out, may have been emotionally wrenching,

but as far as most film critics were concerned, *Voyage of the Damned* (1976) was just plain wrenching. The review in the *New Yorker* states that "not a single moment carries any conviction." Charles Champlin in the *Los Angeles Times* wrote that the movie "stays surprisingly distanced and impersonal."

But the weight of all the criticism does not lessen some basic appeal, similar to the appeal of other Holocaust movies, namely, that the events it portrays really happened. Also, *Voyage of the Damned* has just as much star power as *The Ten Commandments*: Luther Adler, Faye Dunaway, Denholm Elliott, Ben Gazzara, Lee Grant, Julie Harris, Wendy Hiller, James Mason, Malcolm McDowell, Nehemiah Persoff, Fernando Rey, Katharine Ross, Max von Sydow, Sam Wanamaker, Orson Welles, Oskar Werner, and others.

In May 1939, just over nine hundred German Jews were ostensibly granted the right to emigrate to Cuba. But it was all part of Hitler's scheme to show that even those countries protesting his anti-Semitic policies would refuse sanctuary for the Jews. It was never guaranteed that Cuba would accept them, and Cuba did not. Nor did the United States. Most of the Jews had to return to Europe, where many eventually perished in Nazi death camps.

What bothered most of the critics about the movie, written by Steve Shagan and David Butler and directed by Stuart Rosenberg, is that its all-star cast was given what amounted to a dull palette of clichés with which to emote, making the critics feel as trapped as the characters.

"Are we ever coming back?" the glamorous Denise Kreisler (Dunaway) says to her physician husband (Werner).

"It's only a temporary madness," he responds. "Of course we'll come back." For one of the smartest men on board, Dr. Kreisler should have known better. After all, he's the one who administers to an elderly passenger (Adler) who says, "I saw my books burned, my house defiled, we had to hide from people we thought were our friends."

Elsewhere, passengers have other stresses to deal with on board: They must see Hitler's photograph hanging on the dining room wall (until the sympathetic captain played by von Sydow has it removed); they have an anti-Semitic crew member on board; several feel the need to mutiny; there is lingering fear and growing depression from cabin to cabin.

A businessman named Estedes (Welles), the Cuban president (Rey), and assorted other nefarious players on land refuse to intercede on behalf of the *St. Louis* passengers, effectively dashing all hopes that the Jews will find a friendly port. The passengers don't quite know what's going on outside, but it would hardly matter. Any more depression would sink the ship right there in Havana's harbor.

There are several additional subplots (a suicide pact between a young passenger and a steward; the intervention of the prostitute daughter of one of the on-board couples with officials in Havana), but they have very little momentum and pale in comparison to the story of Morris Troper (Gazzara), the man who, more than any other, worked tirelessly to find a place for the *St. Louis* to disembark its refugees. *Voyage of the Damned* picks up its lost momentum during the much-too-short and far-too-few scenes in which Troper appears.

Troper was the European chairman of the Joint Distribution Committee who traveled to Paris, Brussels, and many other cities on the passengers' behalf, spending countless hours on the phone, writing telegrams, and pacing endlessly in empty waiting rooms. A true hero, Troper's story could have been a far more interesting aspect of the film than the episodes involving many of the other characters. Acting up a storm, Gazzara gives an award-winning performance in a movie that won no awards, although it garnered three Academy Award nominations: Lee Grant for best supporting actress, Shagan and Butler for their screenplay, and Lalo Schifrin for his score.

"Throughout the centuries we have survived because we have not lost hope," Troper says to the passengers when he demands to be let on board. But when the *St. Louis* is turned back toward an unwelcoming and unraveling Europe, it is hard not to wonder how many passengers, despite Morris Troper's conviction, finally did lose hope.

A fleeting, unintentional glance by director Louis Malle as a young student may have forever changed the lives of some of his Jewish friends at school. At a film festival screening of *Au Revoir, les Enfants* in 1987, film critic Roger Ebert said he saw Malle— who wrote, produced, and directed it—cry uncontrollably as his new movie was being presented. Presumably, Malle was reminded of that fleeting glance.

It is the recreation of that glance upon which hinges the dramatic and tragic turn of events in this intriguing French film that won Academy Awards for best foreign language film and best original screenplay for

Before the children say goodbye to one another, Gaspard Manesse and Raphael Fejto experience a special friendship in Au Revoir, les Enfants.

Malle. And it is just one of several haunting and realistic moments in a studiously paced film that is, in essence, another movie about non-Jews helping Jews and, from a different perspective, about being a child in Nazi-occupied France.

Julien Quentin (Gaspard Manesse) is a boy in a private school who is not unlike boys everywhere. He is impetuous and mischievous, he taunts and teases others, and he tries to make the new kids in school upset. "I'm Julien Quentin and don't mess with me," he says to Jean Bonnet, one of the new kids. But before he learns that Jean's last name is really Kippelstein, he discovers that he has a lot in common with this equally impetuous classmate, including a love of music and adventure.

Like many European films, *Au Revoir, les Enfants* is straightforward, unpretentious, and very visual storytelling. Malle lets the characters' actions rather than verbal exposition tell the story. When the boys are in the school's church sanctuary after classes, Jean is unable to say the prayers the others are saying. With nary a line of dialogue, it is instantly clear what kind of school it is, what kind of boys they are, and what very dangerous secret Jean and his schoolmaster must carry around with them.

It is also suggested that many young people at that time may not have known what made a Jew a Jew but did know what made a Nazi a Nazi. In a restaurant scene with Julien and his visiting mother and brother François (Stanislas Carre de Malberg), although François says the Jews are guilty of being smarter than they are and crucifying Jesus, he nevertheless wants to join the resistance because he knows the Nazis are doing something terribly wrong. He also delights in giving the "Krauts" wrong information whenever they ask for directions. Malle doesn't try to make any points about these characters and their thoughts; it's all just part of the story, part of the reality he remembers and retells on film.

Eventually, when a German officer stops by the school, Jean is found out.

"Your principal committed a serious crime by hiding him," the officer tells the other students. "The school is closed. You have two hours to pack your bags and line up in the yard."

Jean and the other Jewish students, we are told, died at Auschwitz. Julien, in a voice-over, says, "I will remember every second of that January morning until I die." He is crying when he says it. Just like the man who originally had that thought and scripted those words in the first place.

Perhaps the most famous Holocaust film to date is *Schindler's List*, Steven Spielberg's 1993 masterpiece, which won Academy Awards for best picture, best director, best adapted screenplay (Steven Zaillian), best cinematography (Janusz Kaminski), best original score (John Williams), best editing

(Michael Kahn), and best art direction (Ewa Tarnowska and Allan Starski).

Unlike some of its predecessors, which begin with clouds, birds, and other symbols of freedom, *Schindler's List* begins with the somber lighting of candles and the Hebrew blessing over wine. Spielberg and screenwriter Zaillian, basing their work on Thomas Keneally's book, did not really wish to concern themselves with lives before, but only lives during the Nazi horror. To have "opened it up" might have lessened its impact. Even a cloud would have been too glamorous.

"Who is that man?" People in the story ask this question about Oskar Schindler more than once, making him as enigmatic a character as Rick Blaine in Casablanca, although in quite a different milieu, and one of the most intriguing characters in all of Spielberg's filmography. A womanizer, gambler, opportunist, and member of the Nazi party, Schindler, skillfully played by Liam Neeson, hardly seems the type of man who would break down and cry, ever. But at the end, when he realizes that he could have saved even more lives than he did, that's just what he does, shamelessly and uncontrollably.

Schindler saved hundreds of Jews by hiring them to work in an enamel factory, an industry that was relatively safe from the Nazi authorities because its products were needed for the war effort. But he needs help to run the factory which the German authorities initially finance, and so he turns to a skilled Jewish accountant, Itzhak Stern, played with understated brilliance by Ben Kingsley.

"They put up the money and I do all the work," Stern says to his new boss. "What, if you don't mind my asking, would you do?"

"The panache," Schindler responds confidently, "the presentation."

Schindler's List was filmed on black-and-white stock to make it look as if it had been shot by actual observers. Ralph Fiennes is shown here as Nazi camp commandant Amon Goeth.

As Schindler begins to turn what was a bankrupt factory into a successful one, he reclines one evening on a comfortable bed and says to his mistress, "It could not be better." In the very next scene, a Jewish woman in a ghetto home says to her husband, "It could not be worse." At the same time as Schindler is enjoying his good fortune, he also acknowledges that it is not luck that's responsible for it, but war.

A Black and White Decision

Schindler's List in many ways had the look and feel of a fifty-year-old documentary. That was deliberate.

"We want people to see this film in fifteen years and not have a sense of when it was made," said cinematographer Janusz Kaminski, a Polish émigré. Director Steven Spielberg and Kaminski wanted to capture the feeling of actually being there, without benefit of lights, dollies, or tripods. They accomplished that by filming much of the movie with a handheld camera, working very fast, and shooting most of it in black and white.

The head of Universal Pictures, however, did ask Spielberg to shoot *Schindler's List* on color negative film, from which a black and white version could be made for theaters and a color version for home video. The executive thought that a color version would be a much more attractive consumer item. Spielberg flatly refused. In his words, he did not wish to "beautify events" in any way whatsoever. Pure black and white film stock, he said, was essential. Not surprisingly, Spielberg, arguably the most successful filmmaker in history, got his way.

Schindler's Journey

In 1980, novelist Thomas Keneally was in Beverly Hills to sign copies of *Confederates*, his latest novel. He stopped into a luggage store and talked with its owner, a Polish immigrant named Leopold Pfefferberg. When Pfefferberg discovered that Keneally wrote books, he said he had the greatest story in the world—and one that was absolutely true. The story he told was about Oskar Schindler. Pfefferberg was, in fact, one of the *Schindlerjuden*, the Schindler Jews.

After Keneally's *Schindler's List* hit the bookstores, Sid Sheinberg of Universal Pictures sent a review to Steven Spielberg to consider it as a possible project. Spielberg didn't feel emotionally prepared to make the movie at the time but was interested enough to convince Universal to buy the film rights for him. A year later, Spielberg began to meet with some of the Schindler Jews, slowly building the emotional and artistic foundation on which eventually to make the film. The first Schindler Jew he met with was Mr. Pfefferberg, the one responsible for the book in the first place.

It wasn't Pfefferberg's first involvement with movie people, however. After World War II, Schindler's business failed and several of the Jews he saved tried to help him out. In 1963, Pfefferberg met with executives at MGM to try to have a movie made about Oskar Schindler, partially as a way of making money for Schindler himself. The deal fell through, but Schindler earned nearly $40,000 during the project's short life at the studio.

Like *The Hiding Place*, *Schindler's List* is a movie comfortable enough with its cast, story, and intentions to use a little gentle humor. When Stern hires a man with one arm and Schindler angrily asks him about it, Stern calmly says about the man, "Very useful," much to Schindler's disgust. Moments later, when a suspicious Nazi officer asks Schindler why he hired a man with one arm, Schindler says, matter-of-factly, "Very useful."

More significant than the humor is the irony. When the Nazi camp commandant Amon Goeth, played with chilling evil by Ralph Fiennes, admires Schindler's silk collar shirt at a party, Schindler states with casual abandon, "I'd get one for you but the man who made it is probably dead. I don't know."

In a story like *Schindler's List*, humor and irony are very quickly and easily overshadowed by sheer horror: Jews with foolproof hiding places are suddenly caught because of noise they make when trying to sneak out; children don't give a second thought to hiding in latrines filled with human filth; Goeth relaxes in a chair on his balcony shooting Jews in the courtyard indiscriminately as if it were a carnival game. It is *Schindler's List* at its most uncomfortable.

"One day this will all be over," Schindler says to Stern in the middle of all the insanity. "We'll have a drink."

"I think I should have it now," Stern replies. It, too, is a chilling moment.

Schindler becomes quite skilled at saving his Jews. At one point he grabs a girl on her way to Auschwitz and shows her little fingers to a Nazi official to point out how it is only little fingers like hers that can polish the inside of small shell casings in his factory.

At the end of the movie, appropriately gray and damp, there is a light that shines on Schindler when he talks to the soldiers ordered to kill the Jews before the camp is disbanded. "Here they are," he says. "This is your opportunity. Or, you can return to your families as men, instead of murderers." The soldiers go, without firing a shot.

Upon first hearing the story of Oskar

Liam Neeson and Ben Kingsley bring panache and expertise to their respective roles in Schindler's List, *Academy Award winner for best picture of the year.*

Schindler, Spielberg knew that this was a motion picture he needed to make both as an artistic and as a personal statement. He became interested in the book upon its publication in 1982, though it was more than a decade before the film was completed. Although it does not concern itself with the previous lives of the *Schindlerjuden* (Schindler's Jews), the film does present them *after* this period of darkness. Several of them are shown at the end as we read in a postscript that the group Schindler saved has more than six thousand descendants.

"There will be generations because of what you did," Stern says to Schindler after presenting him with a ring the *Schindlerjuden* made for him. The ring has the inscription, "Whoever saves one life saves the world entire." And now there is a bigger world to appreciate the movie that was made about the one who saved lives.

Nazi of the House

Les Miserables, the famous Victor Hugo story, became an equally famous Broadway operatic musical. It has also been filmed at least six times, including three American versions with such stars as Frederick March, Charles Laughton, Debra Paget, Richard Jordan and Anthony Perkins. But it was a French version in 1995 that gave it somewhat of a Jewish identity.

That year, Claude Lelouch directed an adaptation of the sprawling story in which Jean-Paul Belmondo plays a man named Roger Fortin, who is very much like Jean Valjean, but this time he helps a Jewish family escape from Nazi capture in World War II France. Also worked into the story (which incorporates some scenes taken directly from the book) are episodes detailing the Nazi occupation of France and the persecution of its Jews. There was no choreography and no lyrical score, but this *Le Miz* was just as ambitious as its famous Broadway cousin.

7

A Funny Kind of Elation

Gentleman's Agreement

Crossfire

The Fixer

Chariots of Fire

School Ties

ONE GOOD THING CAN BE SAID about movies that cover anti-Semitism: They rarely discriminate. As far as major characters are concerned, such movies feature, among others, an Irish-American serviceman, a Russian-Jewish handyman, two British athletes—one an angry Jew, the other a Christian missionary—a prep school quarterback from the other side of the tracks, and a gentile writer pretending to be Jewish.

Movies like these are the very model of diversity.

Anti-Semitism has been part of the movie industry almost from the beginning, although not always as a narrative topic. In 1916 D. W. Griffith was forced to refilm the crucifixion scene in *Intolerance* when the B'nai B'rith protested the portrayal of Jews as Christ killers; in 1919 the producers of *The Volcano*, which concerned a Bolshevik spy ring on the Lower East Side of New York, were pressured by the Yiddish press and New York Governor Al Smith to dilute some of the anti-Semitic undertones of the movie with new dialogue; in 1927 Cecil B. De Mille acquiesced to Jewish groups that asked

Dorothy McGuire, Gregory Peck, and John Garfield discuss the ingenious plan and the sad realities in Gentleman's Agreement, *Academy Award winner for best picture of the year.*

him to delete anti-Semitic dialogue from *The King of Kings.*

But as far as movies *about* anti-Semitism are concerned, it has usually been the studios that have been intolerant. Although anti-Semitism has consistently been a problem in the United States, and despite the fact that the founding giants of the motion picture industry were disproportionately Jewish, it wasn't until 1947 that Hollywood moviemakers worked up the nerve or desire to devote movies to the subject, producing both *Gentleman's Agreement* and *Crossfire* that year. With World War II behind them, some filmmakers and producers had more of an impetus to approach the topic—yet even with that impetus these projects almost never made it to the screen. Louis B. Mayer, Sam Goldwyn, and Harry Cohn all advised Darryl Zanuck not to make *Gentleman's Agreement* because it would "rock the boat." It eventually won an Academy Award for best picture of the year. Similarly, the American Jewish Committee appealed to RKO to cancel its production of *Crossfire* because, they said, it might leave the wrong impression in the collective public mind.

It is important for filmmakers to rock the boat every once in a while. Unfortunately, a little bit of boat rocking and a little bit of Oscar winning will never stop anti-Semitism from being part of real life drama on the world stage.

It was Hollywood's only studio not run by a Jew that made *Gentleman's Agreement*. While other moguls did not want to stir up controversy, Darryl Zanuck of Twentieth Century Fox jumped right into it. Through the years he had witnessed, with various degrees of severity, elements of anti-Semitism around the circles in which he himself operated. He knew it was a problem and enthusiastically bought the film rights to a book on the subject by Laura Z. Hobson, which had already been read by twenty million Americans. Then he hired heavy hitters Moss Hart to write the screenplay, Elia Kazan to direct, and matinée idol Gregory Peck to star.

For all its great lines and good looks, *Gentleman's Agreement* surprisingly doesn't delve too deeply into the deepest roots of, and reactions to, anti-Semitism in America. That's because just about everything that happens in the movie happens to Phil Green, the gentile writer played by Peck.

But the lines *are* great and the characters are both good looking and interesting. Phil Green may be a tad mild-mannered to deal

Psycho

Anti-Semitism was such new territory for moviemakers in the late 1940s that many thought studies and surveys were necessary to gauge its effects. After the initial run of *Gentleman's Agreement* in 1947, psychologists at the University of Pittsburgh surveyed students who saw the movie and discovered that they had a "significantly more favorable attitude toward Jews" afterward than those students who did not see it.

Meanwhile, psychologists and educators directed controlled audience surveys around the country for *Crossfire*, the other 1947 film about anti-Semitism, and concluded that the movie changed attitudes about bigotry, but they issued no definitive statement on just how long the changed attitudes lasted.

It should be noted, however, that the professionals who conducted the *Crossfire* study had already concluded after viewing the movie themselves that anti-Semitic attitudes are too deeply ingrained in the minds of anti-Semites to be turned around by watching just one movie.

with it all, but that's Gregory Peck's style, and most moviegoers at the time wanted to see a movie with Gregory Peck a lot more than they wanted to see a movie about anti-Semitism. In fact, at the Academy Awards Zanuck stated: "I would like to emphasize that *Gentleman's Agreement* was primarily planned for entertainment rather than for any social message. I believe that is the chief reason for the success of the film."

It is Phil Green's publisher who first suggests he write a magazine series on anti-Semitism, and his charge to the young reporter is to find an entirely new angle with which to do it, something that will make people want to read it. "What could I possibly say that hasn't been said before," Phil complains to his mother (Anne Revere). But then he comes up with the idea of pretend-

Rank Rep

Although it was never part of anyone's acceptance speech, the creators of *Gentleman's Agreement* had U.S. Representative John Rankin to thank for their Academy Award-winning film.

Rankin, a Democrat from Mississippi in the late 1940s, had been an early chairman of the House Un-American Activities Committee (HUAC) and believed that Hollywood was rife with communist influences because of all the Jewish studio executives. In his presentations to the committee he used words like "Jew-boy" and called columnist Walter Winchell a "slime-mongering kike."

Laura Z. Hobson, a Jewish writer whose father was the editor of the *Jewish Daily Forward*, began to work on a story about anti-Semitism while following the progress of the HUAC hearings through media coverage, particularly Rankin's vicious oratory. Her story became the best-seller *Gentleman's Agreement*, which was then purchased by Twentieth Century Fox.

ing that he's a Jew—and when he does, the anti-Semitic floodgates open up wide. Phil is treated differently and spoken to differently by people who think he's a Jew.

Phil's childhood friend Dave, played by John Garfield (in a role originally offered to Marlon Brando), is the movie's real conscience. Dave helps Phil understand that what he has been experiencing for a few days is what many Jews experience their whole lives. Garfield was a huge star at the time, and it was uncommon for him to accept a role that, compared to the leads, was quite small. But Garfield felt it was a story that needed to be told—and he gladly played the character to help tell it.

It is not only Dave who sheds a light on the problem for Phil. When Phil's son Tommy (Dean Stockwell) comes home from the playground upset because some kids called him a dirty Jew and a stinking kike, Phil's girlfriend Cathy (Dorothy McGuire) comforts the boy, telling him it's not true,

that he's no more Jewish than she is. Phil yells at her and suddenly realizes the problem is not only hate, but fear, ignorance, and most of all inaction.

Even Cathy comes to realize the pervasiveness of anti-Semitism as she discusses it with Dave. She says she recently heard an anti-Semitic joke and just sat back after the punchline, silently.

"There's a funny kind of elation about socking back," Phil reproaches, gently.

Things work out well, though, as they can in the movies. Phil's articles flow out of him with the force of Noah's flood. Dave, who has been trying to find a home in the suburbs of Connecticut, finally finds one despite the town's anti-Semitic heritage. Cathy promises to stay nearby. "And if anybody dishes anything out," Dave tells Phil proudly, "Cathy will be right there to dish it back."

There's little room for humor in such a solid, serious film (except inadvertently, such as when Phil says that if going after anti-Semitism in print is going to work, "the only chance is to go whole hog at it"). Instead of intentional laughs, *Gentleman's Agreement* gives us good intentions, and a rare peak at Gregory Peck *almost* losing his temper.

As if anti-Semitism itself didn't create enough division between people, a divide of sorts developed between Twentieth Century Fox's Darryl Zanuck and RKO's Dore Schary because of *Gentleman's Agreement* and *Crossfire*.

Schary began actual production of *Crossfire* while Zanuck's *Gentleman's Agreement* was only being prepared, and Zanuck was convinced Schary was trying to outdo him and outmaneuver his studio at the box office.

Gentleman's Agreement was by far the more successful of the two films. Still, *Crossfire*, written by John Paxton and directed by Edward Dmytryk, had a high-caliber cast and an intelligently built murder mystery with which to make its point. But it was slower, darker, more somber, and entirely humorless.

Crossfire was filmed in twenty days for $500,000, and

Robert Young is a detective with an idea, and Robert Mitchum a soldier who is there to help out, in Crossfire.

it shows. Also, the anti-Semitism could have been anti-anything without too much of a dramatic stretch, and that shows, too. In fact, in the book on which the movie is based, *The Brick Foxhole* by Richard Brooks, the murder victim is a homosexual, not a Jew. But producer Adrian Scott and director Dmytryk both wanted to do a film on anti-Semitism, and *The Brick Foxhole* provided a way for them to do that.

The only Jew in *Crossfire* is the murder victim. The killer is an army sergeant on leave named Montgomery, played to smarmy perfection by Robert Ryan. Montgomery doesn't like Jews. No doubt about it. In one flashback before the murder, in the apartment of one Joseph Samuels (Sam Levene) whom he met in a bar, Montgomery is heard saying, "What's the matter, Jew boy, you're afraid we'll drink up all your stinkin' liquor?"

Robert Young is Detective Finlay. A tough, tired, though tireless cop, Finlay wants to get to the facts and uses his world-weary wisdom to do it. *Crossfire* could easily have been a movie about Detective Finlay alone, thanks to Young's cool and effective performance. Finlay realizes that neither Montgomery nor any of his army buddies knew Samuels well enough to have a motive. "The motive had to be inside the killer himself," the detective says. "Something he brought with him. The killer had to be someone who hated Samuels without knowing it, hated him enough to kill him." Hated him because he was Jewish.

As Finlay conducts his interviews (Robert Mitchum as another army buddy and

Crossfired

To read its list of honors, one would think that *Crossfire* is a true classic. But it is *Gentleman's Agreement*, the other 1947 film about anti-Semitism, that received an Academy Award for best picture, and is much more often discussed, revived, criticized, and studied.

Crossfire was nominated for several Academy Awards, including best picture, best director (Edward Dmytryk), best supporting actor (Robert Ryan), and best supporting actress (Gloria Graham). The film was also judged best picture of the year by the New York Film Critics Circle; selected as one of the top ten movies of the year by the National Board of Review, the *New York Times*, and *Time* magazine; named the best film of the year by Britain's *Film Daily* (which also named Dmytryk best director); and awarded the Grand Prix at the Cannes Film Festival as the best social film.

But producer Adrian Scott and director Dmytryk had both been called to testify before the House Un-American Activities Committee, had invoked the Fifth Amendment, and had been cited in contempt of Congress. As a result, their studio, RKO, fired them and subsequently denied them any studio assistance in campaigning for their Academy Award nominations.

characteristic conviction. "There's the you-can't-join-our-country-club kind, and the you-can't-live-around-here kind, and the you can't-work-here kind. And because we stand for all these we get Monty's kind. . . . Hating is always the same, always senseless. . . . It's hard to stop. It could end up killing men who wear striped neckties. Or men from Tennessee."

Crossfire is a small movie with a big message—and a lot of dark shadows, as if to say that anti-Semitism throws a shadow over the entire city. But in real life, as in movie theaters, when the lights go on, the shadows often disappear, and the problems linger on.

As a movie, *The Fixer* was as brutalized as the man it was about, not by anti-Semites, but by critics. Pauline Kael said it's a movie that "flogs you" with "dialogue as flat as unleavened bread." Arthur Schlesinger, Jr., said it is a "totally false film, devoid of a breath of human life or truth."

If not for the fact that the 1968 movie is based on a highly regarded novel by a brilliant writer, and that the story was based on a real historical event, *The Fixer* would be a cinch to ignore. If not for the fact that it had several performances of great nuance and appeal, it would be easy to dismiss. But *The Fixer* is the film version of Bernard Malamud's 1967 novel, winner of the National Book Award and Pulitzer Prize. Adapted for the screen by Dalton Trumbo and directed by John Frankenheimer, it uses the famous case of a man named Mendel Beiliss in prerevolutionary Russia as its core. That's why it can't be ignored. And Alan

Gloria Grahame as a tough city broad are among the guys and dolls involved), much is learned about soldiers on leave in New York in 1947—guys with striped neckties, guys from Tennessee—but not much is learned about anti-Semitism. Finlay, though, knows all about it, and he knows how to find the man who is the walking embodiment of it.

He sets a plan in motion that has Montgomery showing up at an apartment he would never visit if he were innocent. It's a trap, and it works.

"This business of hating Jews comes in a lot of different shades," Finlay says with

Bates and Dirk Bogarde, as the persecuted Jewish handyman and his sympathetic magistrate respectively, are enigmatic figures who leave a lasting impression, which is why it is hard to dismiss.

Bates, as Yakov Bok, has such unbelievable patience, resilience, and even a sense of humor in the face of utter hopelessness that his character lasts long after Kael's unleavened bread has crumbled away.

Bok, of course, has the misfortune to be a Jew, which means being poor and despised. But that doesn't stop him from trying to have a life worth living. One night he saves the life of a drunk who turns out to be an anti-Semitic aristocrat who then offers Yakov a job. Yakov, who had been planning to hide his Jewishness to get ahead, is inclined to tell the man that he is a Jew and that "if it makes any difference, you can go to hell and take your money with you." But when Yakov arrives at the man's house, he changes his mind—and his name—and accepts the job.

Neither is Yakov willing to give up love—or at least lovemaking (he and his wife separated after years of a childless marriage). When the aristocrat's homely daughter makes advances, Yakov says to himself, "The answer's no, absolutely no. On the other hand, it's been a long season without rain. Take off your clothes in the house of a goy in the most anti-Semitic town in Russia? Are you out of your mind? Yes."

He's not kidding. He *must* be out of his mind.

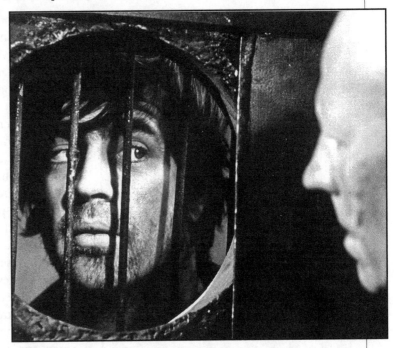

Alan Bates looks tentatively but optimistically into the future in The Fixer.

After some further adventures and misadventures, he is suddenly accused of murdering a boy he had previously chased off the brickyard where he has gotten a job. The boy was really killed by his mother's boyfriend, but it's convenient, easy, and almost foolproof to blame a Jew, and Yakov is the Jew conveniently blamed.

In prison, Yakov the Jew is the lowliest of lowly creatures, stepped on, crushed, swatted like a bug into a convulsing shell of a person on the hard floor. If not for Yakov's sardonic thoughts, arresting fantasies, and sheer willpower to live, such scenes of brutality would barely be watchable.

"All I ask is your confidence and patience," says Bibikov (Bogarde), the magistrate on his case, and the only man who has doubts about Yakov's guilt.

In a Fix

Although *The Fixer* was panned almost universally and performed terribly at the box office, Alan Bates, portraying the lead character Yacov Bok, was nominated for an Academy Award as best actor in 1968.

Bates, a serious and intense British actor who first gained prominence on screen in *The Entertainer* (1960), appeared in several notable films, including *Far from the Madding Crowd* (1967), *Women in Love* (1969), *An Unmarried Woman* (1978), and *The Rose* (1979). But despite his nomination for *The Fixer*, Bates has won no major awards.

In 1968 his fellow nominees included Alan Arkin for *The Heart Is a Lonely Hunter*, Ron Moody for *Oliver*, Peter O'Toole for *The Lion in Winter*, and Cliff Robertson for *Charley*. Robertson won. One commentator, apparently alluding to *The Fixer*'s disturbing nature and unsuccessful run and not the lead performance, said that Alan Bates must have been on the list only because the Academy needed a fifth nominee. In fact, many critics did cite Bates's fine performance, saying that it was the one bright spot in an otherwise dim motion picture.

"Confidence you'll get," Yakov grins. "Patience I've always had." Bibikov looks at him as if he's kidding—but he's not.

The New Testament is the only reading matter Yakov is given during his long internment. Where other Jews might forfeit the opportunity for a diversion, Yakov reads it willingly.

"I understand something," he says to his captors upon completing the book. "Who hates Jews, hates Jesus. To be anti-Semitic, you have to be anti-Christian." He may not have won any points in prison with his logic, but his mind is becoming even freer than it was before.

Then Yakov learns that the Tsar is celebrating the three hundredth anniversary of his dynasty with a general pardon of several classes of criminals—including Yakov. But Yakov committed no crime, needs no pardon, and wants to have his name cleared. He wants his day in court.

Malamud's original story had even more important points to make about justice and inner freedom, but some of it is lost in the movie because of the screenplay's exclusion of certain scenes, and because the excruciating episodes of degradation and despair seriously lessen its impact. It is sad to note that even those horrific images are pitifully close to the truth of what too many Jews over too many centuries have suffered. Malamud knew that well. "I know them," he once said about his Jewish literary subjects. "But more important, I write about them because the Jews are absolutely the very stuff of drama."

As Yakov might say, no kidding.

Despite its Academy Award for best picture of the year in 1981, it was neither the performances in *Chariots of Fire* nor the topic that left a lasting impression. Neither Ben Cross nor Ian Charleson became major stars (Charleson died in 1990), nor did the anti-Semitism that motivates Cross's character create much of a societal stir.

What left an impression and created a stir was its soundtrack. It, too, won an Academy Award (for composer Vangelis) and has

Ben Cross, an angry young Jew, is driven to succeed in the Academy Award-winning film Chariots of Fire.

been used a few million times since on countless television shows and films behind slow-motion running scenes—in addition to school events, dance recitals, and probably even a few weddings and bar mitzvahs.

But the music was new then, and the story it supported was intriguing and extremely well told. Its awards are all well deserved. *Chariots of Fire*, written by Colin Welland (who won an Academy Award for best original screenplay) and directed by Hugh Hudson, is presented almost as two separate mini-biographies, one about Harold Abrahams and the other about Eric Liddell. It explores the motives behind each young man's need and desire to run before the script puts them together at the Paris Olympics of 1924.

Eric runs for faith. "Commit yourself to the love of Christ, and that's how to win a race," he tells a group of admirers in his native Scotland.

But Harold runs for a different reason. "It's a compulsion, a weapon," he admits to a sweet young woman with whom he dines one evening.

"Against what?" she asks.

"Being Jewish, I suppose."

"You're not serious."

"You're not Jewish, or you wouldn't ask," he responds. "I'm what I call semideprived."

Chariots of Fear

After having won four Academy Awards in 1981—for best picture, adapted screenplay, score, and costume design—*Chariots of Fire* became a source of concern for many in the Hollywood community worried about a British invasion into American theaters.

"Look what you've done for the British film industry!" one writer said about the film and its creators. "You may have started something: The British are coming!" Producer David Puttnam didn't help matters when he was quoted as saying that Hugh Hudson, who lost the best director award to Warren Beatty (for the movie *Reds*), "is without a doubt a better director than Warren is or ever will be."

Emotions ran so high that the *New York Post* had a headline shortly thereafter that said, "Hollywood Fuming Over Win By *Chariots of Fire*." As it turned out, it *was* a trend, although a short-lived one: The following year, *Gandhi*, a British-Indian coproduction, won nine Academy Awards, including best picture, actor (Ben Kingsley), screenplay (John Briley), and director (Richard Attenborough).

"What does that mean?"

"It means they lead me to water but they won't let me drink."

The story never shares much detail about what Harold has been through as a young Jew prior to arriving at Cambridge's Caius College in 1919, but as a student in that elite British institution it is obvious not only that he is sensitive to anti-Semitism, but that anti-Semitism hovers as an almost palpable and ubiquitous presence throughout those hallowed British halls. "Arrogant, defensive," one college administrator says about Jews in general and Harold in particular, after Harold makes and wins an impromptu challenge to race another student to break an old school record.

Other students, too, cast aspersions on Harold and his heritage (his father was a financier). That he *is* arrogant and defensive is obvious in Cross's characterization—but it is the reaction of others to him that color it as a character flaw instead of just a character trait. It is not that all Jews are arrogant and defensive, it's that Harold Abrahams is.

The anti-Semitism Harold experiences seems almost harmless compared to what Samuels in *Crossfire* or Yakov in *The Fixer* go through. But where there's smoke there's fire, and Harold does indeed feel the heat of his personal goals breathing down his neck. So he hires a trainer (Ian Holm), a man he trusts and admires, to help him prepare for the big race.

Both Harold and Eric are winners in the end, victorious in different ways for different purposes. As a dual character study, the film is as good as it gets. Eric, for example, a staunch Scottish Presbyterian, refuses to race on Sunday and makes sure to shake each opponent's hand to wish him luck before each race. But as an indictment of anti-Semitism, *Chariots of Fire* simply runs out of steam.

Harold Abrahams used his legs against anti-Semitism. David Green uses his arms.

As a talented high school quarterback in *School Ties*, a 1992 movie written by Dick Wolf and Darryl Ponicsan and directed by Robert Mandel, David knows that his performance on the field could prove to his small circle of new, proud and privileged friends that being a Jew is no cause for lack of pride or privilege.

Well played by Brendan Fraser, David is a poor, working-class senior who wins a scholarship to an exclusive prep school in Massachusetts. The school is almost a guaranteed entrance to Harvard, where he wants to study after graduation. Then he meets, among others, fellow students Charlie Dillon (Matt Damon), Chesty Smith (Ben Affleck), and Chris Reece (Chris O'Donnell)—all before those actors were stars—and learns from some of them that even the proud and privileged can be ignorant. Within his first week at the new school, David hears several comments about cheap Jews, the physical traits of Hebes, and other anti-Semitic remarks. Even his football coach (Kevin Tighe), worried about David's successful assimilation, says, "Don't tell people more than they need to know."

School Ties is filled with interesting little moments that all add up to the general feeling of isolation David must deal with. When he takes off his shirt for the first time since arriving at the school

Brendan Fraser gets more than he bargained for after winning a football scholarship in School Ties.

he realizes he is wearing a Star of David and quickly hides it in a bandage box. Another moment finds David's roommate glancing at him suspiciously while he tucks a *yarmulke*—a skullcap worn for prayer—into a drawer.

"You people are very determined, aren't you?" says the headmaster (Peter Donat).

"Sometimes we have to be," David says.

Things get worse before they get better. He likes Charlie's girlfriend, Sally (Amy Locane), but when Charlie finds out that David is Jewish he knows he can make trouble for him—and he tries. Before long, a swastika and the words "Go Home Jew" are written on a dormitory wall.

After David is falsely accused of cheating on a test, school tradition allows a jury of his peers to decide his guilt or innocence. Some of the boys admit to believing that Jews are greedy and pushy. Hardly any of the jury members, however, feel good about what is going on, since most want to believe that the friendly and personable David is

Studio Ties

Major producers often produce major films. Occasionally, however, novice producers produce major films too. Of course, major producers can also produce modest films, and sometimes they do so deliberately as a personal statement or an attempt at artistic expression. Such was the case with *School Ties*, a rather unpretentious drama with a cast of unknowns. Its two producers, Stanley Jaffe and Sherry Lansing, are industry giants.

Jaffe, who produced his first movie, *Goodbye, Columbus*, at the age of twenty-eight, became head of Paramount Pictures in 1971, when he was only thirty. After he became an independent producer in 1979, his first project, *Kramer Vs. Kramer*, won an Academy Award as best picture of the year.

Lansing, who was a teacher and actress before she became a producer, was appointed president of Twentieth Century Fox in 1980 at the age of thirty-six. She was the first woman to hold that position in the industry. She and Jaffe had their own production company for a while and together produced *Fatal Attraction*, *The Accused*, *Black Rain*, and *School Ties*. In 1992 Lansing was named chairman of Paramount Pictures' Motion Picture Group.

innocent. It is Charlie who ultimately pays the steepest price for his own participation in the sordid affair, and David gets his funny kind of elation when Charlie is driven away from the school for good.

"In ten years," Charlie scowls, "no one will remember any of this. And you'll still be a goddamned Jew."

"And you'll still be a prick," David grins.

Ironically, that scene was reshot after the film was already completed, and Fraser said that the way he performed in the reshoot did not really "turn the screw" on Charlie as much as it needed to be turned. He is probably right. To make matters worse, when *School Ties* is shown on network or cable television, David's last line is often deleted entirely, which just proves that some people behind the scenes just have a funny kind of stupidity.

School Ties is an unassuming little movie in which the actions and words of the characters are more true to life than many Hollywood productions about high school tend to be. The script serves the competent cast well, which is partially why so many of them went on to fine careers in the 1990s, including Fraser.

The Old Jewish Neighbor Hoods

King of the Roaring Twenties: The Story of Arnold Rothstein

Lepke

Once Upon a Time in America

Bugsy

Homicide

THEY WERE GRAND VISIONARIES, ambitious dreamers, and debonair businessmen who could have been CEOs of Fortune 500 companies.

They were also ruthless criminals from the old neighborhood with names like Jacob "Greedy Thumb" Guzik, Louis "Shadows" Kravitz, "Tick Tock" Tannenbaum and Abner "Longie" Zwillman.

While there were more notorious Jewish gangsters in America in the first half of the twentieth century than many people realize—and more than most Jews like to admit—very

few movies have focused on them, and of those an even smaller number address their characters' heritage to any great degree. Maybe that's a good thing for those who feel that Jews have enough problems without the glamorization of their black sheep.

But even if there were twice as many such movies, it would hardly be an issue, because this wild Jewish bunch isn't glamorous at all. In fact, they're quite pathetic. David Janssen as Arnold Rothstein in a 1961 movie about the famous gambler may have had the dark good looks of a matinée idol (even though

David Janssen is a dapper numbers cruncher in King of the Roaring Twenties: The Story of Arnold Rothstein.

the real Rothstein was a tiny little tub of a man), but he's as tightly wound as a broken pocket watch and as square as a grandfather clock. Tony Curtis, as Louis "Lepke" Buchalter in the 1975 film about his life and times, may have had the raw, virile energy of a Sonny Corleone, but he was doomed from the start and seemed to know it all along. Even Warren Beatty, as Benjamin Siegel in *Bugsy* (1991), is as adorable as they come, to the point of reciting "Twenty dwarfs took turns doing handstands on the carpet" over and over to improve his diction, though on closer inspection he was certifiably nuts and frighteningly unreasonable.

There was nothing glamorous about any of these movie bad guys. Although the glossy filter of Hollywood *can* cast a rather innocuous shadow on the lives of Jewish no-goodniks, real and fabricated, nobody in his right mind would ever want to emulate them.

They're not even nice to their folks.

In real life, though not in the movie about him, Arnold Rothstein was called The Brain because he had an uncanny skill for numbers, odds, and investments, a talent he used for many illegal purposes while his pals from the old Jewish neighborhood used similar gifts to build legitimate corporate empires. But in *King of the Roaring Twenties: The Story of Arnold Rothstein* (1961), based on the book *The Big Bankroll* by Leo Kotcher, Rothstein's brain is missing the part responsible for personality. A black and white film with a jazzy score and a frenetic pace, *King of the Roaring Twenties*, written by Jo Swerling and directed by David Diamond, is more about an impeccably dressed smooth talker than a cool and calculating master criminal. In fact, in this movie Rothstein, played by Janssen, seems incapable of hurting a fly, even if it stains his tailored silk suit.

Nevertheless, Abe Rothstein, Arnold's father, doesn't like what he sees. "This boy has a *dybbuk* in him," bemoans the old man (Joseph Schildkraut). "How did you get into our family, who's always been taught to obey God, to respect the commandments and the law?"

He poses a very good question.

According to the movie, once Arnold is

grown, it is less a *dybbuk* and more a far-too-creative accountant that old Abe needs to fear has inhabited his good-for-nothing son. The real Arnold Rothstein was more nefarious than writer Swerling makes him out to be.

Like all good gangsters, Rothstein falls for a beautiful woman, Carolyn Green (Dianne Foster). But only Carolyn's roommate knows for sure that trouble lurks around the corner. A gambler for a husband is bad news, she tells Carolyn. "One day he won't come home."

And like all good gangsters, Rothstein's headaches build up one by one. His gambling club partners lose faith in him and he loses faith in his ne'er-do-well childhood friend, Johnny Burke (Mickey Rooney). He certainly doesn't need the added burden of a father who doesn't like his choice of women.

"You are not of our faith?" old Abe asks Carolyn.

"No, Mr. Rothstein," Carolyn says.

"Then, if you marry Arnold you are prepared to change your religion?"

Arnold interrupts, yelling that religion is not important to him, but Abe, ever the good-hearted Jewish father, looks out for the girl's welfare—even her financial future. Arnold, of course, knows this is a ridiculous thing to discuss, since he has plenty of money. But old Abe glares him down:

"I don't think we need to go into the sources of *your* income, Arnold, do you?"

Eventually, Arnold starts losing money and patience—just as his associates lose patience with him. But this is one of the least violent gangster movies in the history of gangster movies; even after Arnold is shot twice during a game of craps, there's not a drop of blood to be seen.

There is only one line in the film about the fixing of the 1919 World Series, with which Rothstein is generally credited, and there is nothing about shady bankrolling, bootlegging, or his work with a fellow named Waxey Gordon and their dealings in dope and robbery—the kind of stuff that, for better or worse, would have made him a slightly more interesting movie character. In *King of the Roaring Twenties*, Arnold Rothstein is so bland that he could easily have been a model for Sears menswear. And he could have owned the company.

While Arnold Rothstein was pretending to run legitimate social clubs, a kid named Louis Buchalter, Lepke to his Jewish family and friends, was pretending to be a teenage dapper don. In *Lepke* (1975), the young angry hood (Barry Miller in his film debut) robs a store in the very first scene; moments later, as an even angrier adult (played by Tony Curtis), he pushes a garment executive out of a tenth floor window in Manhattan.

"When are you gonna start using your brain instead of your *kishkas*?" an associate asks him as the executive hits the ground below. (A Jewish associate, no doubt, for only a Jew would use the word *kishkas*, meaning raw guts. It literally means intestines.)

But in the movie, written by Wesley Lau and Tamar Simon Hoffs and directed by Menahem Golan, it is Lepke's *kishkas* that drive the story from beginning to end; his brain is nowhere in sight. Never friendly, destructively short-tempered, always suspicious, Lepke's life mission is to be meaner

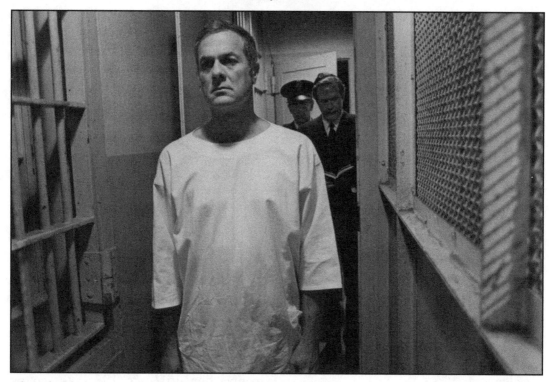

The end of the line—and a violent one it was—for Tony Curtis.

and more ruthless than all his underworld colleagues. "The top of the heap," he declares, "miles above them Italian *gonifs* [thieves]. I tell you, you don't know what good is yet."

Curtis made the choice to play him that way. "The original concept," he explained in his biography, "was that Lepke was just manipulative and shrewd, but I envisioned him differently, and that's the way I played him: aggressive and angry."

The story moves faster than a speeding getaway car, introducing several subplots along the way involving the likes of Albert Anastasia, Lucky Luciano, Dutch Schultz, Walter Winchell, Lepke's friend and onetime attorney Robert Cohen, and his girlfriend Bernice Meyer (Anjanette Comer). Cohen

(Michael Callan) becomes Lepke's lawyer but then asks to be released so that he can join the U.S. Justice Department in its narcotics investigations. Meanwhile, Lepke has an acrimonious split with fellow mobster Dutch Schultz (John Durren), who wants to knock off New York District Attorney Thomas Dewey, though Lepke doesn't think that's a wise move.

The only time Lepke isn't aggressive and angry is when he's with Bernice, the Jewish woman he loves and tries desperately to shield from his violent ways.

Bernice's father is played by Milton Berle in one of the many dramatic roles the comedian performed throughout the years. As Mr. Meyer, he wants things "to be kosher" when Lepke marries his daughter. Mr. Meyer

A Change of Plans, Part III

There was another *Lepke*. Almost.

In 1969 Peter Falk, Stuart Whitman, and an impressive list of supporting players began making a movie called *Lepke*, about the famous crime syndicate Murder, Inc. But somewhere along the line it was determined that the movie, more about the syndicate in general than any one individual, should be called *Murder, Inc.*, and that's how it was released.

Among the other Jewish movie name changes are *The Frisco Kid* and *Crimes and Misdemeanors*. In 1979, Robert Aldrich's western comedy starring Gene Wilder and Harrison Ford had a very unfunny title while it was being made—*No Knife*. It wasn't until production was well under way that the name *The Frisco Kid* was chosen. Woody Allen is one writer and director who often doesn't choose the titles of his movies until after they're shot and edited. While making *Crimes and Misdemeanors*, the titles he considered included *Windows of the Soul*, *Decisive Moments*, *Moments of Good and Evil*, *Make a Killing*, *Hope and Darkness*, and *Split Decision*. One of his working titles actually made it sound more like a Mafia story than a Woody Allen movie: *The Brothers*.

must not have been paying attention, because nothing is ever kosher in Lepke's life—except his execution, in a manner of speaking. In fact, a rabbi was on the movie set when Lepke's electric chair scene was filmed, acting as technical adviser and even reading the Kaddish prayer as the cameras rolled.

"You married me, rabbi, you bar mitzvahed my boy. Now you're gonna bury me," Lepke says. The line reading was among the most emotional in the film, yet still cold and bitter. Louis Buchalter was not repentant about the life he had led. He was just angry that he got caught.

Once upon a time there was an Italian film director named Sergio Leone who spent twelve years trying to bring an epic about a couple of American Jewish hoods to the screen. The movie, *Once Upon a Time in America*, was loosely based on a novel called *The Hoods* by Harry Grey, and it took seven screenwriters, including Leone, to help him find the structural vision with which to do it: Leo Benvenuti, Piero De Bernardi, Enrico Mediolo, Franco Arcalli, Franco Ferrini, and Stuart Kaminsky. *The Hoods* might have been a more accurate title (shorter on the marquee, too), because ultimately the $32 million movie, finally made in 1984, is nothing more and nothing less than that—the story of a couple of hoods, cunning, intriguing, and incredibly lucky hoods, but hoods nonetheless. Its title is a nod, though, to Leone's own *Once Upon a Time in the West*, made in 1969. Like that one, *Once Upon a Time in America* is a personal, arty, grand cinematic vision with little hold on reality, or even on America, for that matter—these hoods could have lived anywhere at any time—but it is a vision that demands attention because the atmosphere is so rich.

Leone's vision has many long, almost dreamy sequences without dialogue and a time line that does not sit still. That can be annoying at times. But it also has a large, skilled cast headed by Robert De Niro and James Woods as Noodles and Max, the two Jewish thugs who live, learn, lose, and lie their way through very isolated lives in New York's shadow world. Noodles wants to believe he lived and can still live a life he is totally incapable of living, and his thirty-five-year exile from society serves only to cloud his memories and fantasies. Max is

Robert De Niro and James Woods have a long and unbalanced story to tell in Once Upon a Time in America.

stand the chance of being somber long after they get home from the theater.

As soon as they meet, Noodles and Max (extremely well played as youngsters by Scott Tiler and Rusty Jacobs) begin to lead lives of crime with a few other friends who look up to them. Loyalty is their middle name. Beginning in 1921, jumping to 1933, and concluding in 1968, the story follows the gang into and out of Prohibition through plans and schemes, close calls and jail, a faked death, personal betrayal—and an opium den where Noodles tries to make sense of it all, or at least to forget it all.

It is De Niro who comes through as the central character and the one into whose head Leone tries to take the audience. The audience, in turn, feels everything Noodles feels, except for the opium, which actually might have helped.

The cast includes Elizabeth McGovern, Treat Williams, Tuesday Weld, Burt Young, Joe Pesci, Bill Forsythe and Danny Aiello (playing a character named Chief Aiello), but for all their skill, none of them is in it long enough to make a lasting impression.

even more unrealistic, in a deranged sort of way. Though best friends, they are not a very good match.

The movie may be a victim of the very vision that created it, for many viewers may have felt as isolated and unbalanced as Noodles and Max, far away from any light, laughter, hope, or happiness. Moviegoers

We know that Noodles, Max, and the gang are Jewish only because they seem entirely comfortable and natural with their occasional Jewish phrases and expressions. And the lack of other central characters keeps *Once Upon a Time in America* focused on the fact that they were Jewish juvenile delinquents who graduated into Jewish grownup hoods with quite a lot of style, but certainly not much substance.

If Ben Siegel were alive today, actor Warren Beatty, director Barry Levinson, and screenwriter James Toback might have to run for the hills. It is not that Beatty, Levinson, and Toback conceived a character that wasn't embraceable and exalted enough for the late Jewish gangster's taste. It's just that Siegel hated the name Bugsy with a passion and might even kill you if he heard you use it. And the name of the 1991 movie Beatty, Levinson, and Toback made, after all, is *Bugsy.*

All of Ben Siegel's friends knew this about him, particularly his Jewish mentor, Meyer Lansky (Ben Kingsley), but it took them all some time to realize that it was a character trait indicative of a man with major psychological problems, perhaps even a death wish.

Beatty's character is far less endearing than most of his other roles, although as written, Ben Siegel can be charming and even adorable. But just as Tony Curtis played Lepke as an aggressive malcontent, Beatty plays Bugsy as a certifiable loon. After all, he beats people up during formal dinner parties and kills one of his oldest friends, Harry Greenberg (Elliot Gould). In short, he's not a nice man to have over for coffee and cake.

Bugsy is as serious an attempt to turn a gangster's life into cinematic art as there ever has been, even more than *Once Upon a Time in America*, thanks to Beatty's carefully con-

A Movie Massacred

Leave it to the boys with the scissors.

Once Upon a Time in America was over three and a half hours in length when director Sergio Leone got through with it—but that's not how it opened in American theaters. Leone, known for his epic storytelling in such films as *Once Upon a Time in the West* and *The Good, the Bad, and the Ugly*, conceived and filmed a sprawling story with many flashbacks and long, contemplative sequences.

Warner Brothers decided it was *too* long and edited it down to just over two hours, throwing out scenes and attempting to put it into chronological order. But the result, according to most critical accounts, was disastrous. "I don't believe I've ever seen a worse case of mutilation," said critic Pauline Kael, who saw both versions. "I defy anyone to understand the plot of the short version," echoed Roger Ebert.

Even the original long version, now readily available on home video, almost never got made. First, Leone's concept of using hard-boiled movie veterans like Glenn Ford, George Raft and Henry Fonda, all of whom expressed interest, didn't work out. Then other production deals fell apart, and it was only after twelve years of international negotiations that *Once Upon a Time in America* finally began shooting.

structed performance; Toback's intelligent script, based on Dean Jennings' book, *We Only Kill Each Other: The Life and Bad Times of Bugsy Siegel*; a highly detailed 1940s production design; and the sharp, polished direction of Barry Levinson. *Bugsy* is fluid and smooth, with a jazzy score by composer Ennio Morricone (who also scored *Once Upon a Time in America*) and an inventive style.

Too bad all that skill and effort was on behalf of a cold-blooded killer.

The story turns both on his torrid relationship with Hollywood starlet Virginia Hill (Annette Bening, who later became Mrs. Beatty) and his plan to create an entertainment and gambling paradise in the

Conversation, cocktails, and a gun: Warren Beatty is Bugsy.

Mussolini to stop them from "trying to knock off every Jew on earth."

But the devotion, earnestness, sincerity, and piety add up to nothing much. He soon cheats on his wife Esta (Wendy Phillips), and ultimately leaves her and their kids. At heart he's just an egomaniacal, greedy, lying killer whose fatal mistake is misleading his Mafia compatriots.

Sitting in jail, Ben turns to his friend Mickey Cohen. "What kind of vile, despicable people write this?" he asks about newspaper accounts of his arrest for killing Harry Greenberg.

"I agree with you 100 percent," Mickey says. "They got no morals, those people."

The two Jewish hoods knew they were being funny. They weren't dumb. They were as capable of charm and humor as the next guy. But nobody has the last laugh in *Bugsy*. It ends in a horrific barrage of bullets, deception, broken families, and wasted lives. There's nothing left. Absolutely nothing.

Except Las Vegas, of course.

middle of the Mojave Desert—"five hundred miles from the nearest toilet bowl," as Lucky Luciano complains to the Mafia commission bankrolling the idea.

It's not hard to enjoy Mr. Siegel a little at first. He seems devoted. Shortly after meeting Virginia in Los Angeles he tells her that he can't see her on New Year's Eve because his wife back east would normally be his date—and he doesn't lie to his wife. He seems earnest when practicing his diction for a Hollywood screen test. He seems sincere when he demands that his Las Vegas plans be designed for the maximum enjoyment of his paying guests. He seems pious when his latest goal is to kill Hitler and

There are Jewish gangsters and there are Jewish cops—and the bad guys don't deserve *all* the movie deals.

Several films have featured Jewish detectives—George Segal as Morris Brummel in *No Way to Treat a Lady* and Richard Dreyfuss as Moses Wine in *The Big Fix* are two of the most interesting—but *Homicide* (1991) is about a Jewish cop on a relatively "Jewish" case, facing a Jewish identity crisis. All of which make it perhaps the most Jewish cop movie of all.

A Star Is Made, Part II

Bugsy Siegel, who usually got what he wanted, never became the actor he wanted to be. *Bugsy* director Barry Levinson, however, made it onto the screen with much greater ease, and he probably didn't even threaten anyone to do it. The director of *Diner*, *The Natural*, and *Good Morning, Vietnam* gave himself the part of a caring and cautious doctor in his own *Rain Main* (1988) and portrayed television host Dave Garroway in Robert Redford's *Quiz Show* (1994).

Jewish crime boss Marty Augustine, a character in Robert Altman's *The Long Goodbye* (1973), was portrayed by Mark Rydell, a director who made the popular 1981 film *On Golden Pond*, for which Katharine Hepburn and Henry Fonda both won Academy Awards. As a young Jewish actor, Rydell was featured in the television and movie versions of *Crime in the Streets* (1955 and 1956 respectively) and also appeared in *As the World Turns* in 1959. In addition to *On Golden Pond*, he went on to direct such acclaimed movies as *Cinderella Liberty* and *The Rose*.

Joe Montegna in Homicide.

It is also surely the most foulmouthed, with enough four-letter words to embarrass even the likes of Louis Lepke. David Mamet's dialogue is said to be an accurate reflection of the way policemen talk among themselves in real big-city precincts. It's gritty and raw. Mamet, who first achieved fame as a playwright (*Glengarry, Glen Ross*; *Sexual Perversity in Chicago*), also directed the movie, which is unfortunate, because he's a much keener writer than director. *Homicide* may be a few days in the life of a city cop, but that doesn't mean it has to be as bumpy as a taxi ride through the city. A more skilled director might have done a smoother job.

Homicide stars Joe Montegna as Bobby Gold, a chain-smoking, curse spewing, insomniac detective and hostage negotiator who is taken off a case he had been working on with his partner (William H. Macy) in order to investigate the murder of an elderly shopkeeper. When he gets to the crime scene, he notices a Star of David around the dead woman's neck. He might not have given something like that much thought before—he has already indicated to his pals that religion means nothing to him—but Gold has recently had a run-in with a spokesman from the mayor's office who called him a kike. Suddenly, the Star of David has a new meaning for him.

Then the clues pile up.

"It never stops," says the victim's grown son.

Green with Envy

Like it or not, Jewish gangsters in the movies are among the most colorful characters around, and many actors love to play them. Alex Rocco's Moe Green in *The Godfather* ("I made my bones when you were going out with cheerleaders") is loosely modeled on real-life bad guy Bugsy Siegel, and Rocco cut quite a memorable portrait in his one major scene. In the sequel, *The Godfather, Part II*, Lee Strasberg plays Hyman Roth ("Michael, we're bigger than U.S. Steel"), a thin yet sharp imitation of Siegel's mentor, Meyer Lansky.

In between both Godfather films was *The Long Goodbye*, a sardonic spoof of a Philip Marlowe tale, with Elliott Gould as the scrubby detective and Mark Rydell (primarily a director) as the vicious Jewish crime boss Marty Augustine. "Her I love; you I don't even like," he says after smashing a bottle into his girlfriend's face to show Marlowe he means business. If only Marlowe could have taken Augustine's Star of David necklace and wrapped it around his fat neck . . .

There are also prominent Jewish gangsters, fictional and fact-based, in *Casino*, *The Cotton Club*, *Miller's Crossing*, *Mobsters*, *Murder, Inc.*, and *Naked Tango*. In *Naked Tango*, Esai Morales plays a Polish-Jewish-Argentine criminal, proving that not all bad Jews are made in America.

"What never stops?" asks Detective Gold. "Against the Jews," is the somber reply.

They're clues, all right—but not necessarily clues only to the murder. Rather, they are clues to Gold's reassessment of his own heritage. Still, he tries desperately to remain a cop first and a Jew second, primarily by raising a fuss about being taken off the first case on which he knows his skills can be valuable.

Also, Gold remains cool and aloof, at least on the outside, about the Jews with whom he is dealing on the shopkeeper case. The dead woman's granddaughter overhears him on the telephone talking crudely of "those rich Jews." Gold sees her standing behind him, realizes he was overheard, and feels truly awful about it. It's a turning point. He swears to her, at that decisive moment, that he will find her grandmother's killer.

Ironically, now his boss wants him back on the first case because it requires a skilled hostage negotiator. That's another turning point. Gold starts to believe that he gets the jobs he does on the force *because* he's a Jew, an outsider, someone who knows how it feels to be oppressed, alone, and angry.

The movie then takes a turn toward an unconvincing conclusion. Gold's investigation first leads him to a group that prints virulent anti-Semitic literature and then to a second group that wants to blow up its headquarters—which Gold does for them. It becomes obvious at this point just how much of a story Mamet wanted to pack into his movie: police work, anti-Semitism, guilt, and faith, among many other topics. He needed far more than his hundred minutes in which to do it. He could have had it, too, for as much as it might be a raw and authentic slice of police life, fewer four-letter words in *Homicide* would have given him a hell of a lot more time to get it all in.

9

The Two-Thousand-Year-Old Patient

Sword in the Desert

Exodus

Cast a Giant Shadow

Operation Thunderbolt

Hanna's War

INDEPENDENCE IS BUILT on the shoulders of heroes and idols, so it makes perfect sense for movies about independence to be built on the shoulders of Paul Newman and Kirk Douglas.

But independence can also be built on the backs of uncommitted mercenaries and even passionate martyrs who may never live to see it, which is why movies about Israeli independence, though few, are broad in the characterizations they bring to life.

"Everybody tells me the patient is dying," says the Israeli Defense Minister at a crucial moment in *Cast a Giant Shadow*. "The patient has already lived two thousand years after the doctors gave up." It's because of the cast of characters involved—some fictional, most of them real—that the tiny nation has been so resilient.

Sword in the Desert (1949) was the first American film to cover the Israeli fight for independence, made barely a year after the establishment of the state. In almost every decade since, at least one filmmaker has been bitten by the Israeli independence bug, either because of a stirring book that was pub-

Cast a Giant Series

Dr. Bellows and Sergeant Pepper both appeared in birth-of-Israel films, and other minor characters also show up later in major television roles.

In *Sword in the Desert*, Captain Beaumont, one of the tough British officers who interrogates a captured Jewish freedom fighter, is played by Hayden Rorke, the always befuddled Dr. Bellows in *I Dream of Jeannie* from 1965 to 1970. In the same movie, Jack Webb, the irrepressible Sergeant Joe Friday on *Dragnet* from 1952 to 1955 and from 1967 to 1970, and Jerry Paris, who was Rob Petrie's dentist and neighbor in the hit sitcom *The Dick Van Dyke Show* from 1961 to 1966, both play young Haganah soldiers who appear on screen for just a few moments.

In *Exodus*, one of the many young Jewish characters fighting for independence is George Maharis, who crisscrossed the country from 1960 to 1963 in *Route 66* with Martin Milner and a Corvette.

In *Cast a Giant Shadow*, Angie Dickinson was left behind the scenes for most of the movie waiting for her husband Kirk Douglas to come home from Israel. However, in her role as the resourceful Sergeant Pepper Anderson in the 1974 to 1978 hit series *Police Woman*, nobody ever thought of leaving her behind.

"I grew up in Israel with the stories, songs, and diaries of Hanna, like any child in Israel," Golan said. "She became part of our education in primary school." The benefit of motion pictures is that inspiring stories like those of Hanna Senesh can be taken far beyond the classroom and shared with people all over the world—at least with those who are genuinely interested in the subject. The rest can go see other Paul Newman and Kirk Douglas movies.

The solemn freedom fighters in pre-1948 Palestine could have used a George M. Cohan to liven things up a bit. *Sword in the Desert*, the first feature film about the Israeli struggle for independence, was written and produced by Robert Buckner, who also wrote *Yankee Doodle Dandy*, a film about the life of the famed song-and-dance man. Although the *Sword* film was certainly far more serious than the *Dandy* film, it is perhaps a bit too austere and one-dimensional to work really well as a political adventure.

In their relentless pursuit to move the story forward at breakneck speed, Buckner and director George Sherman seem to have accepted some mediocre acting and some less than inventive cinematography—the movie is in black and white—along the way. Intentionally or not, they also ended up with a picture that made everyone but the new Israelis look bad, particularly the British,

lished or a reawakening of pride for the resuscitated patient. MGM chief Dore Schary, for instance, put the gears in motion for Leon Uris to research and write a story that eventually would become *Exodus*, having been interested in pursuing a project about Israel ever since he had been moderately successful with *Crossfire* in 1947. Writer and director Melville Shavelson was consumed by the topic of the Israeli war of independence once he read Ted Merkman's biography about Colonel Mickey Marcus, and he eventually made *Cast a Giant Shadow*. Israeli-born director Menahem Golan hurriedly bought the film rights to Israeli martyr Hanna Senesh's story from her mother, then lost them, later reacquired them, and eventually made the film *Hanna's War*.

which was a bit of an embarrassment for the studio after the movie opened.

Sword in the Desert actually has several heroes, among them many Jewish freedom fighters but also one doleful American skipper. The Jews are played by Steven McNally, Jeff Chandler, and Marta Toren, all with a sense of scripted determination. The American boat captain, Mike Dillon, is played by Dana Andrews with the world-weariness of a second-string Indiana Jones. Dillon doesn't want to get involved in the conflict, other than to collect $125 for each Pole, German, Romanian, and Hungarian who successfully disembarks his boat and slips ashore on the coast. But like Indiana Jones, Dillon succeeds one moment, is caught the next, escapes again, and then must hide once more.

Once, when hiding out with the refugees, Dillon makes an almost fatal mistake by sneaking off to a radio transmitter to call his ship at sea; the call is intercepted by the British, who are then able to locate the refugees and round them up as prisoners.

Sword in the Desert is a movie of ingenious plans, midnight raids, courageous breakouts, tense interrogations—and dead seriousness from beginning to end. The one and only lighthearted moment in the entire film is when a sailor on Dillon's boat questions whether or not they have really reached Palestine, and a fellow mate quips, "Maybe you'd like me to swim ashore and come back with a matzah ball." Of course, the lack of humor may have been intentional and also unavoidable; it was only 1949 when the film was made, and the situation in Israel was still tenuous.

It is also a movie of poignant messages, attempting to put years of division into a

Dana Andrews (foreground) is torn between the freedom fighters and the authorities in Sword in the Desert.

few lines of dialogue. A British officer says at one point, "This isn't an Arab or Jewish problem, it's the problem of mankind." Toren, as a captured freedom fighter named Sabra, says to her interrogators, "Whoever I am, I am still a Jew, and this is my country." When the boat refugees land ashore, a son says to his elderly father, "How long did it take you to get here?" The father replies, "Two thousand years."

Paul Newman is a rebel with a cause in Exodus

Near the end, the British officers in pursuit of the illegal Jewish refugees and their Zionist protectors capture Captain Dillon and find out all they can about him. They know they can make life very difficult for him unless he cooperates and points out the Haganah operative they want more than any other. Dillon is just about to do it, too, to salvage his career and his freedom, but then someone points out a tree in the distance and tells Dillon it is a Judas tree. Dillon thinks back over his days with the intrepid bunch—so few, so displaced, so passionate—and changes his mind. He keeps quiet and says nothing to the British.

Just as Indiana Jones would have done.

The *Exodus* was a bigger boat than Captain Dillon's. And *Exodus* was a bigger movie than *Sword in the Desert*. It told a similar story but had more passengers (four hundred), a far lusher score (for which Ernest Gold won an Academy Award) more than double the running time, Paul Newman—and color film stock. While not the acclaimed epic producer and director Otto Preminger had envisioned, *Exodus* has zeal and integrity in each of its two hundred and thirteen minutes.

Although the idea apparently started with MGM's Dore Schary, it ended up with Preminger, an independent filmmaker, with Dalton Trumbo providing the screenplay for the 1960 film. It was one of the first motion pictures Trumbo had penned under his own name since being blacklisted in the late 1940s and 1950s.

Paul Newman wanted to be involved almost from the beginning, partially as a tribute to his late Jewish father. He accepted a salary that was half what his agent had originally requested, and even took wife Joanne Woodward and baby Nell with him to Israel and Cyprus for all the months of shooting. His portrayal of Haganah leader Ari Ben Canaan, however, was steely, almost emotionless.

The story concerns Ari's plan to take a shipload of refugees to Palestine from their internment camp on Cyprus, despite the strict limits on immigration imposed by the British mandatory government. As a leader of the tough, ruthless, underground Jewish defense corps, Ari's goals are not only humanitarian but also militaristic. Things can get nasty, if they have to.

But first the handsome fighter must meet a beautiful girl, and sure enough Ari bumps into nurse Kitty Fremont, played with an uncertain interest by Eva Marie Saint. Kitty follows the travails of the ship not only because she's interested in its fate but also because she takes a liking to a young girl on board named Karen (Jill Haworth), whose parents were victims of the Holocaust. Needless to say, she also likes what she sees in the dark, determined Ari. Her relationship with him, like her performance, is cool, almost halfhearted. She finds it hard to commit so totally to his cause—and anyway, *his* first love is fighting for independence.

"Each person on board this ship is a soldier," Ari says to Kitty, "and the only weapon we have to fight with is our willingness to die."

"But for what purpose?" Kitty asks.

"Call it publicity, a stunt to attract attention."

The *Exodus* finally does make it to Palestine, but the refugees then encounter more than their share of renewed problems, struggles, capture, and human dramas all interwoven into a giant Middle Eastern soap opera. Refugee Dov Landau (an intense Sal Mineo, who was nominated for best supporting actor) joins an underground terrorist group, to which he is admitted only after being interrogated by his new comrades to determine just why he wants to join. What is revealed is quite harrowing. Young Karen, whom Dov also likes, is ambushed and killed by Arabs. Ari and his father, a local political and community leader named Barak (Lee J. Cobb),

The Genesis of *Exodus*

It was Preminger's film but Schary's idea.

Dore Schary, the head of MGM in the 1950s, was determined to make a motion picture about the birth of Israel and hired Leon Uris to create a fact-based epic similar to his book *Battle Cry*. MGM bankrolled Uris's two-year stay in Israel to gather material for the book that would become *Exodus*.

Book agent Ingo Preminger, brother of independent director and producer Otto Preminger, received an early copy of the manuscript and told Otto that MGM owned it and planned to film it. Otto read it anyway and couldn't put it down. *He* wanted to film it.

Preminger went to Joseph Vogel, president of MGM, and said he would save the studio a lot of money by taking *Exodus* off their hands, since it was likely they'd never really make it. Preminger told Vogel that sooner or later he would discover that all the Arab countries would close their MGM theaters and ban all the studio's films if they made *Exodus*, and MGM couldn't afford an Arab boycott. As an independent producer, Preminger said, an Arab boycott wouldn't affect him very much.

Vogel refused to sell the film rights at first, but after discussing the situation with other MGM executives, he changed his mind.

Ironically, Preminger had more than the Arabs to worry about. The British and Israelis gave him problems, too—the British because of the film's less than admirable portrayal of the British mandatory authorities, and the Israelis because the script could be interpreted as legitimizing terrorist underground forces such as the Irgun. The Israeli government thought that would be viewed as unflattering, and that too much credit would be given to them, and groups like them, for the birth of Israel.

does not speak to his brother Akiva, because Akiva is a leader of Dov's terrorist faction.

Loose ends aren't necessarily tied up—but neither are they in conventional soap operas. Ari meets with some success, particu-

The Power of Suggestion

Paul Newman did not particularly like his *Exodus* director, Otto Preminger, who by many accounts was a very difficult man to work with. During production of the 1960 film, the two did not get along well, and Newman exacerbated the situation by making innumerable suggestions about the production. At one point, Preminger was said to have blurted out to the young actor, "*I* am the director."

There are hundreds of Hollywood stories about friction on film sets, and one of the pettiest involves two top Jewish actors, Barbra Streisand and Walter Matthau. Streisand, like Paul Newman, was a professional who felt the need to make many suggestions to the director. The 1969 musical *Hello, Dolly!* was Streisand's second movie, but she shot it even before her first, *Funny Girl*, was released. Her constant suggestions to director Gene Kelly infuriated costar Matthau. "Who does she think she is?" he complained out loud on the set. "I've been in thirty movies, and this is only her second—and she thinks she's directing!" Streisand implied that Matthau was jealous because he wasn't as good as she was. "You might be the singer in this picture," he responded, "but I'm the actor! You haven't got the talent of a butterfly's fart."

work on many films, Preminger and Trumbo tried to tell *too* much, and the result, as most critics concur, is a lackluster blockbuster. In addition to its length, some critics blamed the heavy-handedness of Preminger's direction. Others pointed to a lack of chemistry between Newman and Saint.

Comedian Mort Sahl attended the film's premiere, and his oft-repeated jest in the middle of the show summed it up for many. "Otto," he cried, "let my people go!"

United Artists agreed to let Melville Shavelson make a movie about Israeli independence—and then decided to leave the words *Jews* and *Israel* out of all advertising because they were concerned with potential box office backlash due to its Jewish subject matter. Shavelson's *Cast a Giant Shadow* in 1966 was finally billed as "an adventure in the desert."

The hero of the story is the real-life character David Marcus, commonly known as Mickey. Almost everything that happens to Mickey in the movie happened in real life, while several other major characters are fictional composites of real people. The major departure from the facts is that the real Mickey was balding and wrinkled, and the movie Mickey is Kirk Douglas.

Colonel Marcus, a West Point graduate who saw action in World War II, was hired to help the Jews win their struggle for independence because he was a master strategist

larly in a climactic prison escape scene, but there's still a lot of work to be done. That, of course, is Israel's heritage.

The story is loosely based on fact. A real 4,000-ton steamer called the *President Warfield*, used in World War II, was sold for scrap in 1946, and a Haganah agent saw it in Baltimore and bought it for $40,000. A young merchant seaman from Cincinnati, Bernard Marks, took command and renamed it *Exodus 1947*. It eventually transported 4,500 refugees, but in the real story, the British intercepted the ship and removed the passengers to camps on Cyprus.

It is quite an interesting story, as is the story of the Haganah and its violent little sister, the Irgun, all of which is touched upon in *Exodus*. But like many filmmakers who

with the guts, skill, and flair to organize a rather disorganized army. He became, in effect, the first general of a Jewish army since Judah the Maccabee.

After the relentlessness of *Sword in the Desert* and the ponderousness of *Exodus*, *Cast a Giant Shadow* seems to have made a conscious decision to lighten up with a dash of humor, a cup of tension and romance, and a sprinkle of irony and irreverence. The result is a combination of *Patriot Games*, *Patton*, *Kelly's Heroes*, *Sorcerer*, and probably two or three dozen other movies. Unfortunately, it has no real identity of its own, other than being a troubled production that failed at the box office.

Mickey may have had an adventure in the desert waiting for him, but he also had Angie Dickinson as his wife, Emma, waiting for him at home. While holiday shopping at Macy's, he is intercepted in the store by an agent of the Haganah who says:

"We need an experienced military adviser. We came to you, frankly, because no one else wanted the job."

But thinking of Emma, Mickey says, "Would you give up everything you love to fight an insane war for a little country that will get its brains blown out in a couple of weeks?"

The answer, of course, is yes, absolutely, no question—and Emma grudgingly accepts it. "If they hadn't come looking for you," she says, "you would have started your own war."

As an American military man, Mickey was always a bit undisciplined, taking unauthorized trips in military vehicles, talking out of line, criticizing his superiors. With a little bit of that same old irreverence, he makes it clear to the Israelis that he is helping out as an adviser and nothing more.

Kirk Douglas, in Cast a Giant Shadow, *led a cast of giants in pursuit of Israeli independence.*

Mickey soon begins to experience the unpredictable—although for him, energizing—world of young Israeli society, which gives him (and the audience) a *Reader's Digest* version of much of what happened in the months just prior to the truce that solidified Israel's independence. In one of his first desert adventures, Mickey rides in a civilian bus, more a tank than a bus, which goes through an ambush and arrives at its destination covered in blood and riddled with bullet holes. In a far less violent but no less exciting episode, he witnesses a large group of Jews exchanging clothes on the beach so that the British soldiers won't be able to tell the legal citizens from the illegal immigrants. Mickey actually seems to be enjoying his stay, bullets and all.

He also meets Magda, a beautiful soldier

Dark Shadows

There was one day during the production of *Cast a Giant Shadow* in which fate cast the biggest shadow of all. It was during the filming of a battle scene in the Negev Desert, which used real Israeli soldiers, tanks, machine guns, and other artillery.

First, the temperature was 126 degrees. Then, a $40,000 camera lens was shattered to bits when a cannon fired. After that, half the jeeps in the scene broke down. They were towed by the other half, which soon broke down, too.

Then, as filming continued, some of the dummy ammunition fired from machine guns, which were sealed with wooden plugs designed to disintegrate on firing, didn't work as intended. Three soldiers were seriously wounded. Many who weren't wounded fainted from the heat. Finally, a column of jeeps that were being filmed plowing into action didn't stop when they were supposed to and continued rolling right toward the cameras. When the director shouted in panic, not least because only half the scene had been shot, he was told that the soldiers had officially been ordered to leave. Syrian commandos had raided the Galilee border, and the soldiers were needed there to man more modern tanks on that front.

The soldiers and tanks never returned to the set.

---

played by Senta Berger, whose looks and courage attract and tempt him to levels dangerous enough to start another war.

Meanwhile, Mickey has a job to do. "Surprise and bluff are your major weapons," he tells his fellow officers, including Yul Brynner as Israeli commander Asher Gonen, as the Arabs prepare to attack just after independence is declared. His plans and leadership ability are put to good use, and quite successfully. But then comes the biggest problem of all. The Arab Legion has blocked the major road to Jerusalem, which the Israelis need to transport essential supplies. Mickey needs to accomplish with common folk and human ingenuity what can normally be done only by mechanical engineers and heavy machinery: quickly carve a road out of the rocky, jagged hills that bypass the blocked road, while staying out of sight of the Arabs.

"We made it across the Red Sea, didn't we?" Marcus says to Asher.

"Mickey," Asher says proudly, "that's the first time I heard you say 'we.'"

Cast a Giant Shadow is as interesting for its supporting players as it is for the events it recreates. In addition to Brynner, who plays Asher with an admirable and likable authority, Frank Sinatra is on hand as Vince, a devil-may-care pilot, John Wayne is General Mike Randolph, who is man enough to be sickened by the horrors he sees (in a flashback) at a liberated Nazi death camp, and Topol provides the biggest laughs of all as Abou Ibn Kader, a friendly, spicy-tongued Arab grand mufti, who helps his old Israeli friends in the interest of peace.

Unfortunately, Shavelson's desire to make the film all things to all people doesn't really work. At least it immortalizes on screen one of the era's most fascinating real-life characters, Colonel David "Mickey" Marcus. That's why Marcus's fate at the end of the movie, based on the actual facts (with slight modifications) of his shooting death by a confused Israeli soldier, is such a terrible shock. It matters little that the real man was balding and wrinkled. Douglas brings the legend to life long enough for us to admire and remember him, even if we are forced to remember him, however inaccurately, with a cleft chin.

The can-do spirit of Colonel Mickey Marcus has never died in Israel since independence was achieved, and it has come in handy thousands, if not hundreds of thousands of times since. Israeli commandos took that very spirit and used it to rescue a planeload of Israelis and others held hostage in Uganda in July 1976.

Seven German and Arab terrorists had hijacked an Air France plane on a Tel Aviv to Athens to Paris flight. Of its 257 passengers, 70 were Israelis. The terrorists, members of the Popular Front for the Liberation of Palestine, demanded the release of 53 imprisoned Palestinians and pro-Palestinians held in Israel and four other nations in return for setting the hostages free.

Less than a year later, an Israeli-produced movie called *Operation Thunderbolt*, written by Clarke Reynolds and directed by Menahem Golan, dramatized the story of how a group of commandos killed the hijackers and took the hostages home. It was a feat of great skill and courage that would have made Mickey Marcus and Ari Ben Canaan very proud—just as it made millions of Jews, and non-Jews, proud to be on their side.

Operation Thunderbolt was particularly realistic because Golan (*Lepke, Over the Brooklyn Bridge*) had the cooperation of the Israeli government and military in making it. Prime Minister Yitzhak Rabin, Defense Minister Shimon Peres, and Foreign Minister Yigal Allon even played themselves (in documentary style, without actual dialogue).

The entire production is documentary in style, building the story piece by piece, piling one element on top of the other until everything comes crashing down on the hostages, the Israeli government, and eventually the terrorists themselves.

The Duke of Palestine

When writer and director Melville Shavelson anticipated problems getting *Cast a Giant Shadow* in front of the cameras, he decided to try to enlist a couple of tough guys to help get it the green light—including John Wayne.

Shavelson had worked with John Wayne in the 1953 sentimental drama, *Trouble Along the Way*. When he met Wayne at his office on the Paramount lot a decade or so later, he told him the entire story of Colonel Mickey Marcus—how he was a West Point man, how he became a true military giant, how he risked all to help a virtually defenseless little country, how he died while lighting a cigarette in the middle of the night while bunkered down in the midst of battle.

Wayne loved everything about it and said it was the kind of story about an American hero he would love to make—especially in the mid-1960s when so many people were speaking ill of the United States' military involvements.

He also thought Shavelson was asking him to play Marcus.

Before long, however, even Wayne himself acknowledged that he might be too old and didn't really have the right look to play the part. He was fifty nine at the time and had recently undergone major surgery.

Without hesitation, Wayne agreed to the cameo of two-star General Randolph, and Shavelson remained awed by the Duke's dedication to the project.

We learn that the terrorists (Klaus Kinski plays the leader, and he's very scary) were able to get their weapons onto the airplane by turning off the electricity for a few seconds at the Athens airport where they boarded; that they hid grenades in champagne bottles; that the Israeli commandos, led by Yonatan (Yoni) Netanyahu (Yehoram Gaon), are kept wondering until the last possible moment whether or not the mission will go forward; and that the Israeli Knesset came perilously close to breaking a long-held resolve never to negotiate with terrorists. At least that's the impression they

Klaus Kinski is all too menacing as one of the terrorists in Operation Thunderbolt.

gave to the world; in actuality, it was more likely a stalling tactic.

In short, *Operation Thunderbolt* is a blueprint of the operation and a history lesson rolled into one, and as such, it is rather dry and impersonal, although Golan and Reynolds do take us briefly into the homes of some of the commandos and, with Gaon's help, build Yoni into a very admirable and personable hero.

"If we don't save them, nobody will save them for us," he says—and that's the spirit that drives the soldiers, all of whom are young men on a very dangerous, potentially suicidal mission—men just at the beginning of their adulthood.

Ugandan President Idi Amin, all smiles and salutations, is a friend of the terrorists, and he soaks up the international spotlight like a Shakespearean king. "They can't be stubborn, they must be reasonable," he declares about his "friends" in the Israeli government.

With understandable anxiety, the loved ones of some hostages also implore Rabin, Peres, Allon, and others in the Knesset to be reasonable. "Don't play roulette with the lives of our children," one shouts.

On the flight over to Uganda in military planes, the Israeli commandos feel that God is on their side. "Let's hope that tonight he puts in some overtime," one of them says.

The story is almost legend now: The Israelis drove up to the terminal at Entebbe Airport in a black Mercedes that resembled Idi Amin's, surprised the terrorists, killed them, blew up the Ugandan planes, and took the hostages home. Three hostages were also killed, as was Yoni Netanyahu.

The hostages, too, were heroes, remaining relatively calm and optimistic throughout the ordeal while being held at the terminal. At one point a child asks her mother why the terrorists have separated them from the Jewish passengers.

"Because we're not Jewish, darling," her mother answers.

The child looks toward the group being led into a separate room and wonders aloud, "What's Jewish?"

Jewish is knowing all too well why there had to be an Operation Thunderbolt—and why it had to work.

Operation Victory Raid

Real-life dramas, heroes, villains, Long Island Lolitas, and other natural disasters have been responsible for giving more actors work than John Grisham has. In fact, just one headline-grabbing event can spawn several productions, as was the case with the 1976 Israeli commando raid at Entebbe Airport in Uganda to free over a hundred hijacked passengers. In addition to the Israeli film *Operation Thunderbolt*, *Victory at Entebbe* and *Raid on Entebbe* were made for American television.

All tell the same basic story, although in slightly different ways with different details. In *Victory at Entebbe*, when the commandos drive up to the airport in a duplicate of Idi Amin's car, there is a black man in the car where Amin would normally sit in order to fool the terrorists. In *Raid on Entebbe*, the commandos in the car pull black hoods over their faces. In *Operation Thunderbolt*, the head commando insists the raid will be so quick and surprising that it won't matter how they appear.

Victory at Entebbe, the first film shown, was written and shot so fast that its clichés are all but inevitable. Among those in the cast were Burt Lancaster, Richard Dreyfuss, Anthony Hopkins, Theodore Bikel, Helen Hayes, Kirk Douglas, Elizabeth Taylor, Linda Blair, and David Groh. Godfrey Cambridge, who was to have played Idi Amin, died during filming and was replaced by Julius Harris.

Raid on Entebbe, which was shown on television a week later, avoided many of the clichés, although like *Victory* it has the kind of all-star cast that simply makes it *seem* cliché, including Peter Finch (his last performance, for which he earned an Emmy), Charles Bronson, Martin Balsam, Jack Warden, James Woods, and Yaphet Kotto.

Menahem Golan, who directed *Operation Thunderbolt* (and many other Jewish motion pictures), never wanted to make a horror film, so he almost didn't make *Hanna's War*.

Like that of Yoni Netanyahu, the name of Hanna Senesh will live forever in the an-

Pretty Offensive

It was a movie about a woman who moves to Israel to find her husband that made Sophia Loren a criminal.

In the early 1960s, Paramount Pictures chief Jacob Karp was one of the most enthusiastic supporters of a motion picture project called *Judith*, which was to star the beautiful Loren. It was about a concentration camp victim who moves to the Promised Land because she suspects her Nazi husband has taken their child there.

Karp had always been interested in the continued success of the tiny nation of Israel and thought *Judith* would enhance its image. Screenwriter J. P. Miller was hired to prepare the script and spent several weeks in Israel on a kibbutz conducting research. Miller sympathized deeply with the Israelis and his script showed it in the anti-Arab sentiments of his story. But when Loren's husband Carlo Ponti read the script he hit the roof because Sophia was a big box office attraction in the Arab world. Miller promptly toned down those sentiments, but Ponti still didn't like it and Miller quit the project.

Judith finally did get made and opened in 1966. Almost immediately, the Arab League condemned Sophia Loren and forbid any of her movies from being shown in Arab countries, and Arabs in other countries also were urged to boycott her films in response to her crime of making pro-Israeli propaganda.

had addressed the Israeli struggle for independence. During those twenty years, many filmmakers still wanted not to incur Arab boycotts and therefore avoided the topic. Others feared being called racist. Also, in the 1970s more Americans had begun questioning the U.S. role in Israeli politics and wondered if the tiny country was actually hindering the Mideast peace process.

Golan avoided the politics by concentrating exclusively on a woman with a gigantic smile and an even bigger patriotic streak. Interestingly, it is not a patriotism she was born into, for Hanna Senesh was a Hungarian whose life in the late 1930s is made difficult because of the growingly anti-Semitic policies of her government. Despite the love she has for her city of Budapest, her friends, and her family (Ellen Burstyn plays her mother), Hanna runs off to Palestine, where she works on a kibbutz near Haifa and announces, with heartfelt intensity and a wide, emotional smile, "Now I am home."

Then follows a montage of scenes showing Hanna's acclimatization into the world of the kibbutznik in the Promised Land—scenes filmed on location in Israel that, although too short, look as real and honest as any film covering similar territory. And Hanna herself, in a very strong performance by Maruschka Detmers, is very likable, incredibly winning, and entirely believable. In a way, though, she's almost *un*real in the manner in which she can find a smile in virtually any situation, no matter how tense.

nals of the Jewish people, at least in Israel, where she is a national heroine. But the nature of Hanna's work with the Haganah and her subsequent torture by the communist Hungarian regime could have formed the elements of a grisly cinematic experience. However, once Golan determined that Hanna's story was a profile of patriotism during a horrific period in history instead of just a horror story, he knew he could make the picture.

Although much of it does not take place in the land of Israel, it is Hanna's love for her adopted country that drives the film.

Hanna's War, coscripted by Golan and Stanley Mann, was made in 1988, twenty years after the last major motion picture that

Recruited by the Haganah in 1943, Hanna is asked if she wants to take part in a mission to drop behind enemy lines in Eastern Europe, rescue prisoners and collect information, all for the Zionist cause. Told that it could possibly be a suicide mission, her only comment is, "When do we go?" She says it, of course, with a smile.

Once in Yugoslavia, she talks the resistance leader there into crossing over into Hungary, where her family still resides. These scenes in the movie were actually filmed in Hungary. But she is captured by the Germans and tortured. Still, Hanna's devotion, love, faith, and passion enable her to smile and radiate hope in the face of such dire circumstances—except when her trial for treason begins. Then the look of hope is replaced by the scowl of shame for her former government.

Marushka Detmers fights Hanna's War *with passion, dedication, and hope.*

"I remember when one quarter of this beautiful city of Budapest were Jews," she says to the court in a pre-trial hearing. "Artists, writers, here they wrote. Then I saw the leaders one by one stand up and vote for racial discrimination. I realized Hungary became a country without human dignity. Can anyone say they are proud of what they are doing? I am not a traitor. The traitors are the ones who brought the disaster down on the people of this country."

The panel of judges is scheduled to return to court the next day, but because of Hanna's impassioned speech, they stay away, shamed. But one of the new German leaders (David Warner, vicious as ever) insists that she's guilty and must face the consequences, namely, death.

Hanna Senesh was buried in the Budapest

The Impossible Dreamer

Twenty-seven years before the birth of Israel, an Austrian documentary called *The Wandering Jew* discussed, among other things, the birth of the father of modern Israel. The hourlong silent, made in 1921, is a biography of Theodor Herzl, the founder of modern Zionism. The film explores early influences on Herzl's life, his reaction upon learning of Jewish persecution through the ages, and the development of his theory of political Zionism as the one and only true solution to the problem of Jewish displacement and anti-Semitism.

The Wandering Jew also documents Herzl's efforts to convert European leaders and ordinary Jews to his passionate and seemingly impossible plan.

Jewish Cemetery. After 1948, a new grave was dedicated at the military cemetery on Jerusalem's Mount Herzl, alongside other Jewish martyrs, heroes, and heroines, a monument more of hope than horror.

10

Between Two Worlds

The Pawnbroker

Hester Street

Lies My Father Told Me

The Chosen

A Stranger Among Us

LEAVING SPOUSES, BREAKING hearts, abandoning generations of tradition, being cut off from society, even kissing Melanie Griffith . . . these are among the choices Jews have had to make in the movies over the years, usually because America is a land of choice.

Frequently, such choices are made by people who are, in one way or another, between two worlds: the world of the eastern European *shtetl* and the world of the Lower East Side; the world of the ultrareligious Hasidim and the world of modern Ortho-dox Jewry; or even the world of mysticism and the world of *shikse* policewomen.

Because of their potentially narrow appeal, such movies are never guaranteed successes—which is why almost invariably they have been projects about which the filmmakers were quite passionate. Sometimes it is only passion that can get them made. Joan Micklin Silver, writer and director of *Hester Street*, said it had been her goal to make a movie "that would count" for her family. Jeremy Paul Kagan, director of *The Chosen*, said he hoped the project would reawaken his interest in Judaism.

When the Memories Start

The Pawnbroker was edited by Ralph Rosenblum, whose filmography features a great number of motion pictures with major Jewish themes and characters, including *Bye, Bye Braverman*; *The Night They Raided Minsky's*, *The Producers*, *Goodbye, Columbus*, and *Annie Hall*.

Rosenblum's input as an editor was often credited with turning projects around and putting them on the track of critical acclaim. In *The Pawnbroker*, most of Sol Nazerman's bitter memories are presented almost subliminally—a few frames at a time, barely perceptible to the human eye yet chilling once their substance starts to take shape. This is a method Rosenblum and director Sidney Lumet came up with at the request of the screenwriters, who knew that the story deserved a special way of handling flashbacks.

Rosenblum also produced and directed some television shows, but as his 1979 autobiography *When the Shooting Stops* explains, it was the process of putting together motion pictures that gave him the most creative satisfaction.

Some Jews stay entirely in one world, others successfully cross over into another, if only for a short visit, while still others become mercilessly stuck between the two. Being stuck is rarely a laughing matter. For many Jews, America means the land of the free and the home of the *traif* (traif foods, that is, meaning not kosher)—and to make fun of such a dilemma just isn't kosher.

When Rod Steiger was in Israel promoting *The Pawnbroker*, an Orthodox Jew, noticing that Steiger seemed somewhat edgy, approached the actor and asked what was wrong. Steiger said he was there as part of the film's publicity tour but feared desecrating the memory of Holocaust victims by participating in the event, particularly since he wasn't Jewish. The Orthodox man asked if he was indeed the actor who played Sol Nazerman. When Steiger confirmed that he was, the man replied, "Don't worry, you're Jewish."

Sol Nazerman is a bitter and lonely man, a pawnbroker in Spanish Harlem—bitter because everything he loved was taken from him by the Nazis, and lonely because he has decided to cut himself off from everyone and everything but the cold, heartless cash register in his crowded store.

In and around Sol's shop much happens that reminds him of the past that was stolen from him twenty-five years before. Hooligans fighting nearby remind him of a Nazi attack dog. A girl pawning her ring reminds him of the occasion when the Nazis took away his family's jewelry. When his assistant's girlfriend bares her breasts to try to induce him to lend her money, he's reminded of the time a Nazi officer raped his wife.

Based on a book by Edward Lewis Wallant, *The Pawnbroker* (1965), written by David Friedkin and Mortin Fine and directed by Sidney Lumet, is a somewhat bitter and lonely movie, like the pawnbroker himself. Even at the very beginning, when Sol recalls his happy family back in the old country, it is painful to watch because the idyllic memories are shown in slow motion, making them as frightening as any horror film.

Sol's assistant, Jesus Ortiz (Jaime Sanchez), looks up to him as a man who knows how to run a successful business, but Sol has no use for adoration. He just wants to be left alone with his anger and pain, his resentment and sarcasm.

"You want to know the secret of our success?" he barks to Ortiz after days of being badgered by the enthusiastic young helper, who thinks Jews, more than others, know how to be successful. "First you start off with a period of several thousand years during which you have nothing to sustain you but a great bearded legend. All you have is a little brain, but the legend convinces you that you are special, even in poverty. But this little brain, that's the real key, for with this brain you go out and you buy a piece of cloth and you cut this cloth in two and you sell it for a penny more than you paid for it..." until, Sol says, you realize you're nothing but a usurer, a pawnbroker.

The subplots in *The Pawnbroker* are not really subplots but part of the greater fabric of a New York that is not pretty and certainly nothing like the lovely fields in which Sol's wife and children frolicked long ago. The city's people are not pretty; its places are not pretty; its humanity, or lack of it, is not pretty. A social worker (Geraldine Fitzgerald) tries to help, but Sol, though he tries, cannot get himself to open up. A pimp named Rodriguez (Brock Peters), who is the real owner of the pawn shop, shows Sol no mercy when Sol confronts him about a business matter. A group of thugs botches a holdup of the shop

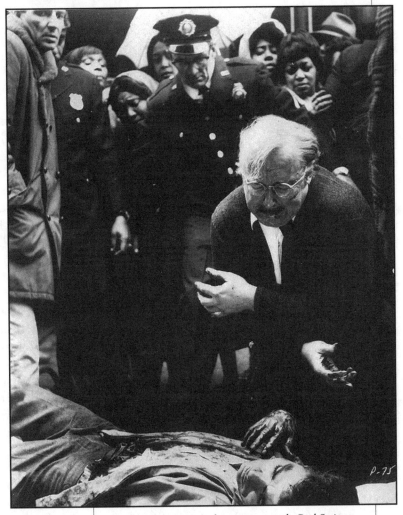

As if his past weren't shattering enough, Rod Steiger as The Pawnbroker *finds a new reason to be tortured in New York City.*

with tragic results for Jesus, who himself is a torn and confused New York immigrant. At the end, Sol still doesn't think he needs the great bearded legend—but no one knows for sure if one day he will turn to Him after all.

The Pawnbroker was the first major American film to portray a Nazi death camp, al-

Critical Mesh

At times it seemed as if *The Pawnbroker* had more troubles than the troubles of the pawnbroker himself.

Several Jewish groups complained that the movie had an anti-Semitic tone to it because the main character, Sol Nazerman, cared about nothing but making money. At the same time, African-American groups complained that it had an anti-black tone because of the insidious characterization of the man who actually owned the pawnshop. Furthermore, the Legion of Decency, a Catholic censorship board, condemned the film because of the scene in which the girlfriend of Sol's assistant bares her breasts in the shop. That prompted the Motion Picture Association of America to refuse to give it its seal of approval. Such a refusal in those days almost always had a negative effect on advertising and distribution. Fortunately, Ely Landau, the producer, vigorously protested the MPAA ruling and ultimately had it reversed.

Even years after its initial release, some writers and critics reevaluating *The Pawnbroker* decided that it did a disservice to Holocaust victims by meshing that issue with the social problems of urban blacks and Hispanics.

though *Judgment at Nuremberg* (1961) had used some documentary footage in its courtroom scenes. The question the movie really seems to raise is whether or not Sol Nazerman ever left the camp. Without a doubt he is one man who is not just stuck between two worlds, but virtually buried alive.

In the mid-1970s Hollywood was beginning to open a few more doors to women behind the camera and in the corporate boardroom. The studios, however, were not interested in Joan Micklin Silver's screenplay about Jewish immigrants in New York around 1900, which was based on a story by Abraham Cahan called "Yekl, a Tale of the New York Ghetto." So she and her husband privately financed, produced, and distributed *Hester Street* by themselves. In 1975, after a successful showing at the Cannes Film Festival, an equally successful European run, and an Academy Award nomination for Carol Kane as best actress, doors in Hollywood continued to open for more women.

A labor of love, *Hester Street* is the relatively simple story of a Jewish immigrant family in New York near the end of the nineteenth century. A sweatshop worker's wife suddenly arrives at Ellis Island with their son, but he is repelled by her old world ways. He insists that she no longer wear hats or kerchiefs, as she did in the old country. He even insists on Americanizing his son's name to Joey practically before the boy even sets foot on dry land.

As Jake, Steven Keats is not as strong a presence as Kane, who plays Gitl, the old-world wife, but he does an adequate job showing how he thinks of himself as a new-world man. He is almost silly, almost pathetic in the ways he thinks he is being a real American. "Here a Jew is a *mensch*," he says proudly. But a *mensch*—Yiddish for an honorable, decent man—is certainly not a word that can be used to describe Jake.

"I didn't know you at first," Gitl tells Jake shortly after arriving. "I thought you were a nobleman." But it is just the shock of seeing a Jake she hardly knows that blinds her, for Jake is neither a *mensch* nor a nobleman. He is a crude, loudmouthed braggart, perhaps because he thinks all Americans are. Gitl comes to know that before too long.

What Gitl *doesn't* know right away is that the money he had sent her when she was still in the old country came from a spirited, independent woman (Dorrie Kavanaugh) with whom Jake had been fooling around. Now, left to fend for himself, Jake needs to earn more money on his own, so he and Gitl take in a boarder, Mr. Bernstein (Mel Howard), who is also from the old country. But unlike Jake, Bernstein does not feel the need to change who he is and what he is. When Gitl sees him buried in his books, she admires his adherence to the tradition of study and tells him that to study Torah is to love God. "Not here," Bernstein says, with resigned wisdom. "When you get on a boat you should say, 'Goodbye Oh Lord, I'm going to America.'" Still, Gitl feels a kinship, or perhaps more.

As the story moves forward—at a leisurely pace and laced with gentle humor—Gitl begins to question her love for Jake. Not even their wise, concerned friend and neighbor Mrs. Kavarsky (Doris Roberts) can help any longer. "With one *tuchas* [backside] you can't dance at two weddings," she warns the young couple when it becomes obvious that they may break up.

Hester Street was Silver's first feature, but she recreates the Lower East Side of New York in 1898 with a thorough command of her art, despite a very small budget of $400,000. The screenplay and most of the performances leave you feeling that both Jake and Gitl, given time, will finally em-

Steven Keats and Carol Kane make Hester Street *their home—although not without a few major conflicts.*

brace the new world of America, under God, with liberty and justice for all. Having gotten to know Gitl through Kane's wonderful performance, we want true love for her, and she very well may get it. Having gotten to know Jake through the slightly less forceful Keats, we want a punch in the nose for him, and we don't really care who delivers it.

Forward Thinking

Writer Abraham Cahan, often described as flamboyant and ego-centric, was one of the most fascinating characters in the New York immigrant scene in the first half of the century. Born in 1860 in Vilna, Lithuania, Cahan arrived in the United States in 1882, became active in politics, helped organize the first garment workers' union, and cofounded the *Jewish Daily Forward*, which he edited from 1903 until his death at age ninety-one in 1951.

Cahan was a prolific writer. Among his short stories were "The Chasm," "In the Sweatshop," "The Daughter of Reb Avram Leib," "Circumstances," and "A Ghetto Wedding," in addition to dozens of magazine stories, short literary sketches in *McClure's* magazine, and editorials and criticisms in the *Daily Forward*.

But for movie makers his stories may have been too realistic, too unglamorous, and sometimes too painful echoes of the immigrant experience. Despite writing what was the first and one of the most highly acclaimed immigrant novels in English, *The Rise of David Levinsky* (1917), Cahan is represented only once on screen, with his story "Yekl, A Tale of the New York Ghetto," on which Joan Micklin Silver based her screenplay for *Hester Street*.

Little David Herman's problem is unique: He's not stuck between a world he once knew and a new one he must endure, but between the new world of his father and the old one of his grandfather.

Lies My Father Told Me, written by Ted Allan and directed by Jan Kadar, is a sweet 1975 Canadian film based on Allan's own childhood in Montreal's Jewish ghetto in the 1920s, and his own beloved *zaida*, the Yiddish term of endearment for grandfather. His screenplay was nominated for an Academy Award.

Zaida, played by Yossi Yadin, is the entire world to David, his guide to the universe, his teacher about life, his adviser in things spiritual, his partner in irreverent thoughts, his employer on their weekly Sunday rides through the city with their beloved horse selling rags, clothes, and bottles. It is clear that six-year-old David, played winningly by Jeffrey Lynas, loves living in Zaida's world and is trying desperately to keep his father's modern one far, far away.

But his father, Harry (Len Birman), will have none of it. "Zaida tells you a lot of superstitious idiocy," Harry tells his son, indelicately. "He thinks nothing's changed in five thousand years."

Harry, who is Zaida's son-in-law, fancies himself an inventor, an industrial visionary, an entrepreneur. He invents creaseless pants (or so he thinks) and announces, "This will do for pants what Edison did for lights!" He gambles. He connives. He yells at his wife, at his father-in-law, at David.

By contrast, Zaida is patient, warm, and loving. He answers all of David's questions, tucks him in at night, and enjoys his innocent ramblings.

David sees his world changing quickly as a result of two events. First, his father decides to move out of the ghetto—where Zaida's horse won't be able to follow—and then his mother gives birth to a baby, who instantly takes away all the attention he himself used to get. David is miserable. But suddenly, a miracle:

"We're not moving, we're not moving!" he shouts with joy, running through the streets of the ghetto. "My father's bankrupt! We're not moving! My father's bankrupt!"

Whether by design or budget, *Lies My Father Told Me*, though shot in color, has the feel of an old black and white one-reel comedy-drama which adds a very genuine dimension to the movie. Perhaps a brighter, smoother, slicker-looking film would not seem as real. And the acting is especially honest, with all of the performers, from the young Lyons to the elderly Yadin, inhabiting their roles to the core.

Though the heart of the story is the relationship between the boy and his father and grandfather, the movie also takes us along on a nickel tour of ghetto life and its people: the political Mr. Baumgarten—played by the film's author, Ted Allan—who badgers Zaida with socialist ideas; the local prostitute, who yells to her detractors, "Kiss my Royal Canadian ass!"; the neighbor who rats to the authorities about Zaida's improperly located barn—and onto whose steps David places a pile of horse dung, an idea he got from Zaida; and assorted other busybodies and whiners, or *yentas* and *kvetchers*, as Zaida would have called them in Yiddish.

"When God said 'Love thy neighbor,' he didn't know of this town," Zaida tells David.

The love between Zaida and David is strong and heartwarming. If Zaida were to go, one could only hope that David's memories of him would be enough to sustain him. But life changes, things happen, and sometimes real miracles are needed.

It becomes evident, in a movie like this, how cinematography, lights, music and almost every other element of filmmaking are perhaps half a step in importance behind the words of its writer. It is evident in conversations between David and Zaida, when what Zaida says in one exchange can explain thousands of years of Jewish sustenance.

"When people like us need a miracle," he tells David, "we'll have it. I have it from the highest authority."

Zero Tolerance

To little David Herman in *Lies My Father Told Me*, his grandfather was larger than life. Had Zero Mostel played the part, as originally planned, the performance itself would have been larger than life.

Mostel, a flamboyantly physical and vocal actor, brought brilliance to roles that required such a personality. But David's Zaida wasn't written with that kind of personality in mind. Nevertheless, Mostel was director Jan Kadar's first choice to play the part because Kadar had just directed him in *The Angel Levine* and was comfortable enough with his range and their working relationship to give him the role.

However, when Mostel met with Kadar and the film's writer, Ted Allan, he made so many suggestions for script changes that Allan had to say to him, "Zero, this picture is about my childhood, not yours."

That wasn't the only friction. Mostel wanted more money than the producers were willing to pay and stayed in New York during the first day of shooting in Canada as a bargaining tactic. When he finally went north, Yossi Yadin had already started playing the part.

"Do you believe in miracles, Zaida?" asks David.

"No," Zaida responds. "But I depend on them."

Zaida knows best.

To the uninitiated, the worlds of ultra-religious Hasidic and modern Orthodox Jews might seem close enough to be one. But to the Jews in *The Chosen*, based on the novel by Chaim Potok, they are indeed worlds apart.

The 1981 movie was adapted by Edwin

Robbie Benson gives one of his most moving performances as the Hasidic student Danny Saunders in The Chosen.

Gordon and directed by Jeremy Paul Kagan, who is the son of a rabbi. Set in the mid-1940s, it is the story of a growing friendship between Danny Saunders, the son of the grand rebbe of a large Hasidic sect in Brooklyn, and Reuven Malter, the son of a more secularized writer and scholar. It is also an exploration of Zionism, family traditions, soul searching, parental influence, and the pursuit of personal goals. That's quite a lot of serious and very Jewish content to load into one American mainstream movie, but *The Chosen* pulls it off. Part of the reason is its cast—Rod Steiger as Danny's father, Maximilian Schell as Reuven's father, Barry Miller as Reuven, and a surprisingly effective turn by Robby Benson as Danny. With characterizations and a production design so skilled and so complete, there is never

any question about who these people are, where they are, or even why they are motivated to do the things they do.

Danny is expected to inherit the mantle from his respected father and one day become the next grand rebbe. The problem is that he wants to study psychology. "I get tired just studying Talmud," he tells Reuven one day.

Ironically, Reuven, who is curious and slightly skeptical of the ways of the Hasidim, thinks he may want to become a rabbi. "I never realized how full the life of a rabbi could be," he tells Danny. "Babies to be blessed, boys to be bar mitzvah, disputes to be settled." He also happens to notice the fire of passion in just about everything Danny's father says and does, and it is a passion he himself would love to possess.

Reuven's father has passion, too, but his is for the founding of a Jewish state, a topic for which Rebbe Saunders has little patience. Only the Messiah, he says, can be responsible for a new Jewish state. This major difference of opinion almost destroys the friendship between Danny and Reuven—especially when Reuven's father makes a public speech about the need for increased Zionist activities.

The Chosen is also a story of good men, wise men, fathers who know that stubbornness is not an option when it comes to recognizing basic truths. For despite their differences in lifestyle and opinion, Reuven's father will not disparage the rebbe, the father of his son's best friend. "In a way it is that kind of fanaticism that has kept us alive," he says to Reuven about Rebbe Saunders. Nor is Danny's father one to force his son to lead a life he really and truly does not want to lead.

There is a lot of compassion in *The Chosen*. Perhaps Rabbi Kagan never intended his son Jeremy to become a filmmaker. But the young Kagan *did* become a filmmaker and he made a movie that was roundly praised. *The Chosen*, then, becomes a testament to following your dreams. That's where the compassion comes from.

Eric Thal and Mia Sara meet an outsider, Melanie Griffith, who needs to be on the inside to solve a murder in A Stranger Among Us.

The Chosen received many favorable reviews, which was a nice gift to Jeremy Paul Kagan, who had previously directed less than a handful of features. In startling contrast, *A Stranger Among Us* received almost unanimously negative reviews, despite the fact that Sidney Lumet had directed more than thirty-five features, including *The Pawnbroker*, *Twelve Angry Men*, *Serpico*, *Dog Day Afternoon*, *Murder on the Orient Express* and *The Verdict*.

In this 1992 mixed-world mystery-romance, written by Robert J. Avrech, Melanie Griffith is a sexy New York City detective who moves into a Hasidic enclave in Brooklyn to try to find a murderer and ends up falling for a handsome young rabbinical student, Ariel, played by newcomer Eric Thal.

One reviewer called Griffith, as Detective Emily Eden, "wildly miscast," while another critic called her "surprisingly credible." Whatever she is, the leggy blonde detective cannot be ignored by Ariel—not when she says things like, "You plan on jumping my bones?" or, "I guess you're not used to a woman like me, huh?" For the student Ariel, it is a test the likes of which he never had at *yeshiva*.

As Emily immerses herself in the mores and manners of the Hasidim in order to find clues to the murder, she necessarily spends much time with Ariel, the murder victim's best friend, and hears him quote many wonderful passages from the Torah and the Kabbalah—texts of ancient Jewish mysticism—leading her to develop an almost

The Antichosen

Every actor makes a bad choice every once in a while. As critics almost unanimously agreed, Kirk Douglas made a doozy in 1978 with a movie that had the same name as a far better picture made three years later—*The Chosen*.

An Italian-British coproduction, *The Chosen* concerned neither the Holocaust, as did Douglas's 1957 movie, *The Juggler*, nor the creation of Israel, as did his 1966 film, *Cast a Giant Shadow*. Nor did it have anything to do with the world of the Hasidic or Orthodox Jews, as did Jeremy Paul Kagan's film with Robby Benson and Barry Miller.

The Chosen with Kirk Douglas was about the antichrist who attempts to harness nuclear power to destroy the world. Douglas plays the antichrist's father. Originally, the movie was titled *Holocaust 2000*, which wouldn't have made it any better.

mystical infatuation with him. When at first she accuses him of not trusting her, he remarks, "Kabbalah says women are on a higher spiritual plane than men. Therefore it would be foolish of me not to trust you." She likes that.

Later, when discussing why some people have to split up, Ariel says, "Everything is predetermined. But we also have free choice. We don't always make the right choices." That's another notion she seems to appreciate.

These very exchanges are the only element to give this movie any spark at all, for there is none in the detective story itself. After Emily asserts that Ariel is probably not used to a woman like her, he says, "Is anybody?" And when Ariel explains the Kabbalah's decree that you never have to leave your home to find what you need, Emily says, "The Kabbalah never counted on me." Too bad relationships cannot survive solely on the power of their verbal exchanges.

Near the end, after Emily leaves the enclave and goes home, Ariel has to visit to tell her something; she answers the door scantily clad.

"Can you put something on?" he asks.

"If you don't like it," she responds testily, "leave."

He quickly concedes, "I like it. That's the problem."

Despite Lumet's track record, *A Stranger Among Us* just doesn't have the legs to stand on that Melanie Griffith has. It's a thin, sloppily told story. It's also much too squeaky clean, like Griffith's voice. The New York City in *A Stranger Among Us* just is not true to life. You can hardly see any grime at all. It is not so much a motion picture as it is a lithograph, a single frozen image.

The relationship between Detective Eden and Ariel is similarly thin, and ultimately wrapped up in a single antiseptic image: one passionate kiss. She wants him because he makes her feel safe, closer to a family than she has ever felt before, and open to all the wonderful possibilities of devotion. And he has grown to respect her as well. But she knows she'll never fit in because she is who she is, and besides, she's too late: Ariel is engaged to be married to a French student. Ariel knows, too, that he could not spend his life with Emily. He's already made all of his life's choices.

Eric Thal was an unknown when he auditioned for a small role in *A Stranger Among Us*. Lumet was so impressed with him that he offered him the lead instead. As a feature debut, this film offered little to the young actor—other than the dubious distinction of playing a love scene with Melanie Griffith that is among the shortest and cleanest on record.

11

In a Pickle

Goodbye, Columbus

Crossing Delancey

Driving Miss Daisy

Enemies: A Love Story

The Governess

JEWISH CHARACTERS IN THE MOVIES have been amazingly cunning, enormously spoiled, dangerously consuming, and annoyingly stubborn—and still, they have plenty of friends and lovers.

Good thing, too, because people do not grow intellectually or emotionally in a vacuum; it takes other people, often close friends, sometimes lovers, sometimes people who drive you crazy or put you in compromising positions, to help you grow. So the Jewish writers of these motion pictures have given their Jewish characters the chance to

do things, be things, and learn things that they might not embrace without the influence of their friends and lovers. Daisy Werthan, a rich southern Jewish widow, for instance, learns the value of befriending an uneducated black man. Rosina da Silva, a nineteenth-century British governess, discovers a special skill and the strength to develop it on her own. Neil Klugman, a librarian, finds the courage to stick to his own convictions.

Rosina, experimenting with the photographic process, learns with stunning artistry

Ali MacGraw and Richard Benjamin are intimate and obstinate lovers in Goodbye, Columbus.

to the universe. But first impressions aren't always accurate, and in the end, Neil, effectively played by Richard Benjamin, has far more substance than that. It's his lover Brenda who gives it to him, although she'll never know it. She's incapable of such self-awareness.

Brenda, equally well played by Ali MacGraw, is a classic Jewish American princess. "I was pretty," she says to Neal about her recent nose job, "and now I'm prettier."

Goodbye, Columbus, based on a novella by Philip Roth, was adapted for the screen by Arnold Schulman and directed by Larry Peerce ten years after the book was published. By that time all the hoopla about Roth's self-hating Jewishness in his early works had died down, and the movie was not nearly as controversial as it could have been and nowhere near as vile as the film of Roth's later book *Portnoy's Complaint*. In fact, *Goodbye, Columbus* is quite perceptive about morals and status and class and ambition, and it also happens to be extremely funny.

how to "fix the moment." That's an applicable metaphor for these movies as well, for they are fixed moments, captured images of interesting, lonely, troubled, intellectual, and passionate friends, lovers, husbands, and wives—and in one case (speaking of being in a pickle), *several* wives.

Brenda Patimkin is one cool kitten, with enough saucy come-ons and spicy bathing suits to keep Neil Klugman one hot guy. When we first meet Neil in *Goodbye, Columbus* (1969), he is a guest at an exclusive country club gawking moronically at breasts and buns as if, collectively, they hold the key

The Patimkins are a nouveau riche Jewish family with a very casual acknowledgment both of their good fortune and their own happiness. They seem detached from, perhaps even numbed by, their own lives. Phones ring in the house, but no one is ever sure whose line is ringing. The maid works hard, but no one ever bothers to thank her for all she does. The mother (Nan Martin) finds her greatest strength in criticizing ev-

Not So Private Ceremonies

As in real life, Jewish weddings in the movies are filled with laughter and tears, song and dance, crazy uncles and piggish cousins. Dozens of movies feature Jewish weddings of all types, as well as mixed ceremonies, among them *Goodbye, Columbus, The Heartbreak Kid, Fiddler on the Roof, The Duchess and the Dirtwater Fox, Sheila Levine Is Dead and Living in New York, The Chosen, The Frisco Kid, Private Benjamin, Yentl, Betsy's Wedding*, and *The Wedding Singer*.

When Paramount production chief Bob Evans saw an early cut of the movie *Goodbye, Columbus*, he complained that "all the ethnic stuff" was left out. So the director satisfied Evans' wish by reediting it to show many more wedding guests stuffing their faces with food. Ironically, this was the scene that many critics cited as being among the most offensive and unfunny scenes in the movie.

In *The Duchess and the Dirtwater Fox*, a comedy western in which con man George Segal teams up with saloon dancer Goldie Hawn, the pair stumble into a frontier Jewish wedding at which the cantor promises the married couple a life full of joy from their children, good crops from their fields, "and a pickle," and the rabbi implores them to "wear long underwear on the range so as not to catch a cold."

In *Private Benjamin*, where Goldie Hawn is a spoiled princess who learns self-respect the hard way, there are two weddings—one at the beginning (although the groom dies that night) and one at the end (although it never really gets under way because Goldie walks out defiantly).

Weddings in the movies indulge just about every catering stereotype. This one, from Goodbye, Columbus, *is attended by Michael Meyers, Lori Shelle, and Jack Klugman.*

eryone in the family. Brenda's brother, Ron (Michael Meyers), went to college for four years to learn how to say, "Come on, we don't have all day," over and over to the truckers who work for his father's company.

Jack Klugman, as Brenda's father, the patriarch of this dysfunctional clan, really does love his children, although money is too often the wrapping paper around his endless gifts of pride and affection. "You give me a lot of *nachas*," he tells Brenda, "a lot of joy. For a million dollars nobody could buy that joy. So, when you go back to school, and you're shivering, go to a store and buy yourself a leather coat with a fox fur collar."

Brenda loves Neil. He's reliable, a very good person, adoring. And Neil loves Brenda, even though she's spoiled. As far as

Brenda's parents are concerned, Neil may be a nice Jewish boy, but he's not ambitious enough for the Patimkins. After all, how much money can a librarian make?

When Ron gets married, the wedding scene gives Neil even more clues to the pity and pathos of the extended Patimkin clan. There's Uncle Leo, who can't figure out why he's at the bottom and Brenda's dad at the top, even though, as he tells Neil, "I got more brains in my pinkie than my brother Ben has in his whole head." There are two other uncles, both in the carpet business, who love to walk from one end of the reception hall to the other to measure the square footage. There are chubby little girls who gorge themselves on obscene amounts of food. It's the wedding from hell, although to Brenda's family it's just another fancy affair.

Neil must be wondering at this point about his own potential wedding. About life with Brenda. Like her family, Brenda seems not to think too much of Neil's job. And she'd probably die if she couldn't have a maid. She's rebellious yet still loves to play the dutiful daughter because she gets what she wants that way. What would she be like as a wife?

Then one day, at a motel with Neil, she realizes that she left her diaphragm in a drawer at home where her mother can find it. Was it by accident or on purpose, another one of her impetuous child-woman games?

Neil finally sees what he should have known all along—that Brenda is a victim of her own upbringing, spoiled, despondent, feeling some sort of pleasure in being a victim, as if she's earned her chic despondency. When she remembers where she put the diaphragm, Brenda cries and says she doesn't think she can ever go home again.

"Are you kidding?" Neil yells at her in a way he has never yelled at her before. "Your father will be waiting there with two coats and a half dozen dresses."

Brenda may be one cool kitten—but at least she'll never be cold.

A librarian is one thing. But a pickle man?

Crossing Delancey is a modest 1988 film from a modest play by Susan Sandler, who also wrote the screenplay. Joan Micklin Silver, of *Hester Street* fame, directed.

The movie is about two people thrown together to see if love takes hold, despite the way they are thrown together and the type of people they are. Amy Irving plays Isabelle, known as Izzy, an employee in an upscale bookstore, and Peter Riegert plays Sam, the pickle man. They're good-looking, they're Jewish, they're New Yorkers, and they're worlds apart.

Izzy's *bubbe* (grandmother) asks a matchmaker to find a prospect for her. She works hard at the bookstore, but for what? She has no one. "A college professor once said, No matter how much money you got, if you're alone, you're sick," Bubbe lectures her granddaughter.

Reizl Bozyk as the grandmother and Sylvia Miles as the matchmaker are like a couple of old Jewish con artists, only they know they're doing nothing wrong and not hurting a soul. Conniving and confident, they are able to set the events in motion only because Izzy *is* starved for love. She won't admit that, of course, but Bubbe knows everything. Bubbes always do.

"Maybe I don't want a husband," Izzy responds. "If I did, he wouldn't be a pickle

Amy Irving and Peter Riegert try to enjoy a date set up by matchmaker Sylvia Miles and Bubbe Reizl Bozyk in Crossing Delancey.

man." Especially one who sticks his hands in huge pickle vats all day long and has a sign on his awning that says, "A joke and a pickle for only a nickel." That's not Izzy's style. She's much more refined, more cultured than that. Sam the pickle man may be nice, decent, and honest, but he is after all just a pickle man.

Both Irving and Riegert walk through their roles leisurely, as if they have been playing Izzy and Sam all their lives. And neither do they just read lines; they are specific characters who handle emotions in specific ways. When Sam is frustrated with Izzy for being

so stubborn about not wanting to date him, he lashes out in one of the calmest, gentlest ways in movie history.

"You think it's so small, my work, so provincial," he says, stinging her without a trace of venom, "you think it defines me?"

Thank God for the arrogant, self-centered, two-faced author Anton Maes (Jeroen Krabbe) Izzy has to work with on behalf of her bookstore—he makes a move on her, very crudely, making her realize, at last, that a nice, decent, honest man like Sam is a rare breed indeed. But is it too late?

No, it's not. One late night Izzy comes

home and finds Sam waiting for her. As resilient as he is calm, Sam nevertheless has a few tricks up his sleeve to show Izzy he means business—and not just the pickle business.

"Go ahead, say it: 'Schmuck, what are you still doing here?'" Sam grins.

Izzy and Sam are from the same extended family tree, it's just that their branches grew in opposite directions. It might be possible, after all, to tie a swing between them and meet halfway. That's what *Crossing Delancey* is all about.

What the movie has going for it, in addition to believable central characters, is a much more authentic New York than certain other films. Fat people, skinny people, bookstore owners, *yentas*, pickle men. Here the city doesn't even seem to need an art director's, cinematographer's, or even screenwriter's creativity to present it in any light other than what it is, with all its ethnic and cultural diversity thrown into the mix.

Crossing Delancey never gets too deep or ponderous. It is a sweet Jewish love story. It doesn't necessarily make you fall off the emotional scale, but it doesn't put you to sleep, either. The author and director took a chance in even doing it—no sex, no violence, no foul language, no special effects. But the results are confident and were very well received by most critics. Sandler and Silver must have been as calm as a pickle man when they made it. With a few tricks up their own probably much better-smelling sleeves.

Driving in Prime Time

Not many Jewish movies are made into television shows. In fact, of those listed in this book, only *Private Benjamin* and *Down and Out in Beverly Hills* were turned into series, both of them short-lived. *Private Benjamin* ran from 1981 to 1983, and *Down and Out in Beverly Hills* ran for just the 1987 season. Also, *The Last Angry Man* was made into a television movie in 1974 with Pat Hingle in the lead.

There was one other attempt to turn a Jewish movie into a television show, but it never came to be. Joan Plowright (*Avalon*) was chosen to play Daisy in a pilot for a series based on *Driving Miss Daisy*. But African-American activist groups protested the show allegedly for perpetuating semicomical views of black servitude.

There are no lovers in *Driving Miss Daisy*. That's part of its appeal. The joy of the film is how two very different people become such close friends through necessity, selflessness, and time. What is also affecting is that Miss Daisy never even wanted a new friend in the first place. But when her son hires a black chauffeur to help her around town, fate more or less takes a hand.

Driving Miss Daisy was based on a Pulitzer Prize-winning play, by Alfred Uhry, and as well as it worked on stage, everything worked just as perfectly when it was brought to the screen in 1989 by Australian director Bruce Beresford—so much so that it won an Academy Award for best picture of the year, best screenplay (by Uhry), and best actress (Jessica Tandy as Miss Daisy).

Daisy is a rich Jewish widow living in Atlanta in 1948 who is getting on in years and inadvertently drives her Packard into a ditch.

Morgan Freeman is Hoke, the proud and simple man her son Boolie (Dan Aykroyd) hires as chauffeur. Like *Crossing Delancey*, the film is all character and story; no special effects, no sex and violence. Just the performances and the tale of friendship—and it's more than enough.

Uhry wrote his play based on people he knew growing up, and his genius is in telling a story that spans twenty-five years, covering everything from Hoke's illiteracy to Daisy's hidden prejudices—and leaving the audience hungering for more.

Boolie, who owns a factory where Hoke sometimes works, hires Hoke as chauffeur against his mama's wishes. Mama doesn't want to admit she's no longer as self-sufficient as she used to be. She doesn't even want to admit she's wealthy! Besides, what business does a liberal southern Jewish woman have keeping a chauffeur?

In fact, on their very first outing to the Piggly Wiggly supermarket, she even refuses to get in the car.

"I used to wrastle hogs during killing time," Hoke says after Boolie warns him that his mother is irascible and highly strung. "Ain't no hog got away from me yet." Later he tells Boolie that it took six days to get Miss Daisy into the car to drive her to the market. "Same time it took the Lord to make the world."

Driving Miss Daisy is also a comedy about extended families. Boolie's Jewish wife

Jessica Tandy and Morgan Freeman build a friendship—but not before driving each other crazy in Driving Miss Daisy.

Florine (Patti LuPone) loves to deck out her house in the grandest Christmas lights, wreaths, and decorations.

"I do enjoy Christmas at their house," Hoke tells Miss Daisy after attending another holiday party there.

"It's no wonder," Daisy replies drily. "You're the only Christian there."

It is also a history lesson about the times. When Hoke drives Daisy to hear Martin

King of the Rabbis

Alan King, who on screen has played more Italian *mafiosos* than most Italian actors, also has several business tycoons and a couple of rabbis on his resume (in addition to one Jewish *mafioso*, in *Night and the City*).

His rabbis have often been as acerbic as the comedian himself during his stand-up routines, which may, of course, be one reason he is asked to play them. In *Bye, Bye Braverman* he plays a rabbi at a funeral that George Segal and his friends go to by mistake. In one of Segal's daydreams, in which he envisions his own death, Rabbi King looks at the casket and says with all earnestness, "What do I know about him? Better I should say I'm glad I'm not in his place."

In *Enemies: A Love Story*, he's a rabbi who discovers that his ghostwriter (Ron Silver) is a man with a very interesting and embarrassing problem. "Don't worry," he deadpans at a party where too many guests show up, "I won't steal your wife—no matter how many you have."

In the 1994 cable movie, *The Infiltrator*, based on a book about a Jewish man who documents the growing neo-Nazi movement in modern Germany, King plays a real person, Rabbi Marvin Hier, dean of the Simon Wiesenthal Center for Holocaust Studies. It wasn't a funny role, but King enjoyed it immensely, particularly his tough, accusatory speech to the German government. About the leader of the new Nazi movement, King as Rabbi Hier says what King as King would have liked to say: "Get one of them, and the others don't sleep so well."

teaches him how to read. Why shouldn't a kind, gentle soul be able to read?

Jessica Tandy, who died in 1994, was not Jewish, nor is Dan Aykroyd. It doesn't matter. The acting and the script give us a real family we learn to love, and twenty-five years go by quickly, effortlessly, and quite emotionally. Without speechmaking, *Driving Miss Daisy* makes the point that true friendship is a gift, but one you have to work toward, even when your friend is a hell of a lot better behind the wheel than you'll ever be.

"The subject of my next speech: mixed marriages, the plague of the Jews," says Rabbi Lembeck (Alan King) in *Enemies: A Love Story*. Oddly enough, the problem that the film deals with is not simply one of a single mixed marriage, but several marriages, one mixed, the others just mixed up.

Such is the predicament created by Isaac Bashevis Singer, and the 1989 movie, adapted from his novel by Paul Mazursky and Roger L. Simon and directed by Mazursky, is one of the best translations of his work onto film.

Herman Broder, played with weary befuddlement by Ron Silver, is the main character in the story, which was Singer's first novel to take place in America. The setting is Coney Island in 1949, the epicenter of Herman's post-Holocaust world, a some-

Luther King speak at her temple, Daisy is pleased to tell him that things have changed in regard to race relations in the country. Hoke responds cautiously that they haven't changed all that much. And later, when both are traveling some distance to a relative's birthday party, they are approached by two policemen who smirk and mutter, "An old nigger and an old Jew . . ."

Time works its magic. Where once she accused Hoke of stealing a can of salmon (he had borrowed and returned it), she now

what crazy world where the present doesn't always count on the past and the past doesn't always accept the present. In Herman's case, the present is both his Polish gentile wife Yadwiga (Margaret Sophie Stein), who saved him from certain death in the old country, and his feisty lover Masha (Lena Olin), also a survivor, who wants him all to herself. The past, however, is his wife Tamara (Anjelica Huston), presumed dead during the Holocaust, but who "crawled over some corpses and escaped" to New York to confront them all. Talk about being in a pickle.

Tamara and Masha are strong women, yelling at and berating Herman at every turn. By contrast, Herman, a quiet little ghostwriter by trade, seems to be a bit of a *nebbish*, that is, a weak and helpless guy who doesn't have a clue. But working (writing for Rabbi Lembeck), making love, running around to prevent one woman from seeing the others—this is how a weak *nebbish* behaves? Herman certainly has the energy to do it; what he doesn't have are the answers. "The Talmud is such a good book," he laments, "why doesn't it say what to do with two wives?"

Enemies: A Love Story, one of many Paul Mazursky films with significant Jewish themes and characters, is evocative of the era, the places, even the people—although one wonders just how many refugees could

Girls Will Be Girls

"I didn't like vat Barbra Streisand did mit *Yentl*," Isaac Bashevis Singer said to director Paul Mazursky when he was discussing turning Singer's *Enemies: A Love Story* into a movie.

"Mr. Singer," Mazursky replied, "I can promise you that there will be no songs in *Enemies*."

He then proceeded to show Singer photographs of the actors he had chosen to play the characters in *Enemies: A Love Story*. Singer thought that Ron Silver, Anjelica Huston, and Margaret Sophie Stein all looked enough like the characters he envisioned and was pleased with the choices. Mazursky saved the photo of Lena Olin for last. Olin was to play the sexy Masha, and Singer, Mazursky recalls, was quite taken with her beauty.

"You will make a good picture," Singer smiled. "A nice picture."

Typecasting: Author Isaac Bashevis Singer was quite pleased with the choice of Lena Olin as Masha in Enemies: A Love Story.

possibly have been in the same boat as Herman, figuratively speaking. This is due to a cast and crew that obviously loved the project, as well as a good production design and a directorial style that is serious without taking itself too seriously. "The wallpaper was right, the actors were right," Alan King wrote about the experience of working on the film. "When I saw the completed picture, I could smell the potato latkes."

Herman is a lost soul, a wandering Jew, ultimately moving on to another place (a

Friends, lovers, and heartburn: Anjelica Huston and Ron Silver in Enemies: A Love Story.

place we don't see or learn much about), leaving two of his three women to assimilate without him in a most unusual though certainly not solitary way. But just before Herman goes for good, someone asks him if he's afraid.

"Yes, I'm afraid. Afraid of God," he says. A pretty forgiving God at that, to have let him go as far as he went without making him go absolutely crazy. After all, as one old man says to him at a party given by Rabbi Lembeck, "You refugees certainly know how to live. Us Americans are allowed to have only one wife at a time."

Rosina da Silva might never forgive God for taking away her father. She loses one of her best friends when she loses him. In *The Governess*, a beautifully rendered period film set in mid-nineteenth-century England and Scotland, written and directed in 1998 by newcomer Sandra Goldbacher, Rosina's father is the one who taught her about living, about laughter. He was the one who told her stories as a child to fall asleep, about the importance of family.

When her father is suddenly murdered and Rosina's Sephardic Jewish family is revealed to be deeply in debt, it is decided that Rosina must marry a merchant in order for them to have enough money to live on. But the beautiful and ambitious young Rosina, played by Minnie Driver, will not hear of it,

saying she'd rather be a prostitute "than be that fish man's
wife." She leaves on a train to
take up a post as governess to
a young girl on a remote Scottish island, studying math and
the New Testament along the
way in order to hide her
Jewishness.

The Governess takes place
mostly at the estate of the
Cavendish family, where Rosina
begins tutoring young Lily
Cavendish. But no sooner does
she meet the Cavendish family than she feels "the word
Jewess emblazoned on my fore-
head. I am not like them," she
narrates.

Mrs. Cavendish (Harriet
Walter) is pompous and opinionated, and Lilly (Arlene
Cockburn) is, in Rosina's words,
a rodent. There's even an annoying older brother, Henry (Jonathan Rhys-Meyers), who soon
professes his love for Rosina
with the gentility only a sex-
starved, angry post-adolescent
can display.

At least Charles Cavendish,

Minnie Driver takes charge of her own destiny as
The Governess.

the father (Tom Wilkinson), has a life that is
more than empty words and childish postur-
ing. He's a scientist working on perfecting
the photographic process, and Rosina feels a
kinship with him. They're both passionate
people, loners, perfectionists, dreamers—and
they end up using their *camera obscura* to
document the eroticism they feel but would
not be able to express without it.

Meanwhile, Rosina, who now calls herself Mary Blackchurch, keeps her heritage

hidden, for she doesn't want that discovery
to end the passionate lover's dream in which
she's living. She knows it *would* end, too,
because anti-Semitism hovers around the
estate like the sea mist. When she tells
Charles that someone once said she looked
like a Jewess, Charles says, "No. You're beautiful."

Rosina, celebrating a clandestine Passover

Seder in her room, inadvertently discovers a way to improve the photographic process because of the salt water she uses for dipping the egg during the Seder. When she shares her discovery with Charles, and together they see the fantastic results, he can no longer contain his lust. The passion explodes. But then he realizes that she is consuming him, making him think about things other than his work, "and I cannot be consumed!" he yells. When Charles meets with a member of the Royal Society to discuss his new photographic process, he gives no credit to poor Rosina.

The Governess sometimes strains credulity (imagine if photography *had* been invented by a Jew during a Seder), but it is also a beautiful, mesmerizing film, full of golden amber and sepia tones; haunting violin, harpsichord, and choral music; and a leisurely pace that lets the characters develop and the ambiance sink in.

Goldbacher directed documentaries, commercials, and short films for British television before writing and directing *The Governess*. She clearly had a vision for the project and quite a way with words and visual ideas to express its feelings and emotions. At the end of the movie, Rosina herself becomes a successful portrait photographer on her own back home in England. "They say I can capture the beauty of my father's people," she says.

So did the director.

12

Wandering Jews

The Golem

The Dybbuk

The Magician of Lublin

Crimes and Misdemeanors

Genghis Cohn

IF JEWISH MOVIES HAD BEEN around a few hundred years ago, there would be a few that only married men over forty would be allowed to watch.

According to Rabbi Joseph Telushkin, author of *Jewish Literacy*, some people hundreds of years ago were known to become mentally unbalanced while engaged in studying Jewish mystical texts (collectively known as Kabbalah). Seventeenth-century rabbis legislated that Kabbalah should be studied "only by married men over forty who are also scholars of Torah and Talmud."

Movies, while not real life, are sometimes made well enough to grab and hold audience attention from first frame to last as if they *were* real; that is why watching movies about golems, dybbuks, ghosts, magicians, and spirits might best be approached with some caution.

Of course, most moviegoers do know that motion pictures are no more than thousands of celluloid images merely giving the impression of movement as they pass through a beam of light (itself a mystical conception), so it is doubtful that anybody would be ad-

Light Work

Some cinematographers are noted for developing and perfecting a specific style of lighting and camera work for a specific effect, and it is often a style that follows them throughout their entire career.

Karl Freund wasn't one of them.

Freund, cinematographer for *The Golem*, began his motion picture career photographing German silents, including *The Last Laugh* and *Metropolis*. He then moved to England, where he became a Pathe newsreel cameraman, and subsequently made his way to the United States. There he first worked on several horror films for Universal, winning an Academy Award for *The Good Earth*. Then he moved to Desilu, the television production company, where he developed the three-camera shooting technique that became the standard for situation comedies from that time on.

Golem legends (*golem* is a Hebrew word for a shapeless mass) have been around since at least the times of the Crusades in the eleventh and twelfth centuries, and each new tale is a variation on the ones that came before. When Jews found it difficult to face the circumstances of difficult lives, believing in many cases that God had abandoned them, they created mythical golems, or redeemers, to protect them.

In *The Golem*, the first of three golem films Wegener was to make, the redeemer was a solidly packed hunk of clay—played by Wegener—who moved his massive frame through town inch by inch, disallowing anyone or anything from getting in his way, his square, stone-faced visage glaring at the Jewish populace he was created to avenge.

Wegener, of East Prussian descent, was a top German stage actor at the turn of the century and branched out into film as an actor, screenwriter, and director in 1913. Like the clay golem itself, Wegener was an extremely large man, giving this early Frankenstein a prophetic appearance for many dozens of movie monsters to follow. Peculiar though the movie may be at times because of its exaggerated silent-movie expressions and unsure pacing (you can read the dialogue cards ten times before the movie returns to live action), *The Golem* is a fascinating historical record of the world of the silent movie and the world of Jewish mysticism.

"The learned Rabbi Lowe reads in the stars that misfortune threatens the Jews." Although not the most surprising of revelations—they are Jews, after all—these words,

versely affected. On the other hand, the writers who create such myths, tales, and legends base them on such human perceptions and apprehensions as fear of persecution and punishment, along with an insatiable hunger to understand life, death, and guilt. Those are the perceptions and apprehensions that *can* affect movie audiences, if not adversely, then with mystical enjoyment. In short, they are movies that are fun to see.

With parental guidance, of course.

Was Frankenstein Jewish?

Unlikely. But if not for Paul Wegener's 1914 silent film *The Golem*, movie Frankensteins through the years might not have looked as menacing as they did. Almost all of them owe a debt of gratitude to Wegener's monster creation.

seen on the opening dialogue card in *The Golem*, drive Rabbi Lowe to create the dreaded but necessary redeemer.

Sure enough, an announcement comes from city authorities: "Decreed against the Jews, we can no longer neglect the popular complaints against the Jews. They despise the holy Christian ceremonies. They practice black magic. We decree they must leave the city before the month is ended."

The stars were correct.

With the clay golem created—and unwrapped, like Frankenstein—a magic word meaning "truth" is placed inside the amulet on its breast so that "he will live and breathe as long as he wears it."

As the golem prepares to defend the city's Jews and destroy their oppressors, it brings massive fear and destruction in its wake as if "Be careful what you wish for" were the subtitle of the film. And then, as if Jews didn't have enough problems:

"If you have brought the dead to life through magic, beware of that life," the rabbi is warned. In time "the lifeless clay will scorn its master and turn to destroy him and all it meets."

It may be too late for Rabbi Lowe to be careful what he wished for.

The Golem offers a few surprises beyond the cinematic birth of a Frankenstein-type monster. There are moments of great visual impact, such as an overhead shot of Jewish men praying, during which their fervor is quite clear, and special effects showing an exodus of people in a way that convincingly portrays their panic. An interesting plot twist at the end provides an intriguing surprise

Indirect Descendant

Although Sholom Ansky originally wrote his play *The Dybbuk* in Russian, the screen version, produced just after his death in 1920, was in Yiddish, but it was anything but a direct translation.

When Tsarist censors banned the play in Russia, Ansky translated it into Yiddish in hopes of getting a theatrical group in Lithuania, the Vilna Troupe, interested in producing it. They didn't. Meanwhile, the poet Chaim Nachman Bialik translated it into Hebrew for another theater company, but that troupe didn't produce it either.

In 1920 the Vilna Troupe finally decided to put it on, but the version they had by this time was Bialik's Hebrew version, which they retranslated into Yiddish. Simultaneously, the man who produced the Vilna play, Ludwig Prywes, approached writer Alter Kacyzna and asked him to write a *new* Yiddish version for the screen.

and is very effectively filmed: A curious five-year-old girl, playing with her friends, innocently pulls off the golem's amulet, rendering him lifeless once and for all—and just in the nick of time. If Wegener intended to make a point with his film, rather than just animate an old Jewish legend, it could be "Thank heaven for little girls."

For several years at the turn of the century, Yiddish theater populated its stages with cheap Jewish stereotypes (not unlike some seen in television sitcoms today). All that changed in 1920 with the first production of Sholom Ansky's play, *The Dybbuk* (meaning evil spirit), a mystical tale of a man's vengeful spirit lost in the soul of the young woman he was to marry. One of the most important and widely produced plays in Yiddish theater, *The Dybbuk* opened up new

Despite its limited resources, the young Polish film industry produced some very haunting pictures, like The Dybbuk *in 1937 with Lili Liliana.*

and much more serious horizons for Jewish writers, directors, and actors than any play before it had done.

The film was made in Poland in 1937, adapted by Alter Kacyzna and Marek Arenstein and directed by Michael Waszynsky. The cast and crew were Polish Jews who in the following turbulent years were either exterminated or scattered, like millions of other refugees. That adds a chilling postscript to the story. If only their own dispirited souls could have sought justice . . .

Ansky was moved to write *The Dybbuk* while leading a Jewish folklore expedition through eastern Europe in the early 1900s. He died in 1920 and never lived to see it produced. Had he done so, its success and theatrical power would surely have moved him immensely, as would the movie version. *The Dybbuk* is moving in its depiction of human needs and frailties, despite the fact that it is also long, dark, choppy, and technically crude; indeed, it often resembles a silent film, although it has Yiddish dialogue with subtitles.

The screenwriters wisely set the movie up as a tale told—not a slice of reality we are asked to believe at face value; a book blows open by the wind in the introductory scene, and thus the audience watches its story unfold. We learn right away that "when a man dies before his time, his soul returns to the earth so that it may accomplish the deeds it had left undone, and experience the joys and grief it had not lived through."

Two friends, Sender (Moishe Libman) and Nison (Gerszon Lamberger), vow that if one's wife delivers a boy and the other's wife delivers a girl, the boy and girl will marry. An ominous messenger (Isaac Samberg), who weaves in and out of the story in a ghostlike manner to warn and guide the human souls in his charge, appears and says to them, "Jews! Such things are not done without deliberation. You cannot pledge something as yet unborn."

But the pledge has already been made. As fate has it, Sender's wife dies in childbirth, and Nison drowns in a storm. Nison's son, Channon (Leon Liebgold), and Sender's daughter, Leah (Lili Liliana), seem destined never to meet to fulfill the promise between the two best friends.

When Leah is grown, her father promises her to someone whose father has a lot of money. Channon reappears and discovers that the numeric values of the names of the intended bride and groom indicate that it is a marriage arranged by Satan, not God. Then Channon dies.

Therein lies the opportunity for Channon's tortured spirit to enter Leah's body, bringing

with it misery for all, dementia for some, a joyous wedding for no one. Promises that should not have been made were made, but then promises that should have been kept were not kept. It's not that it's a cruel world—but people make it cruel. And the dead often suffer more than the living.

"There are no demons, but souls of people whose light went out too early," the messenger reports solemnly. "The souls of the dead return to the world and wander about. Sinful souls are transformed into beasts, fish, and plants. And there are souls that enter the living body of one they knew when they once lived. This is the dybbuk."

The characterizations in *The Dybbuk* are distinct, the now unknown actors being quite serious professionals in the young and ill-fated Polish film industry. Despite the need for English subtitles, there is never any question that Jewish crimes and misdemeanors, even for the mystically inclined, were nothing to joke about. It may just be a story, but for some these things were deadly serious.

"He's a street performer, he's penniless, he's married—and he's a Jew," says the genteel Emilia.

"And you love him," Emilia's daughter replies, with a don't-fool-me look on her face.

That about sums up this curious little tale from the imagination of Isaac Bashevis Singer—at least as much as a Singer tale can be summed up in a line or two. Like most of his stories, there are innumerable twists and turns and supporting characters in *The Magician of Lublin* (1979) who add light or

Alan Arkin is The Magician of Lublin, *and Valerie Perrine is more than just one of his illusions.*

shadows to the strange goings-on.

Yasha is a magician and illusionist in Lublin, Poland, who, whether by accident or design, is well on his way to breaking all of the Ten Commandments. Trusted neither by his Jewish neighbors—because he has no use for his Jewish heritage—nor the rest of Lublin's citizenry—because of his disconcerting talent ("With fingers like that," someone says, "he could clean out the pockets of the world")—Yasha is very much alone with his skills, his lovers, and his manager. Even audiences for his shows are hard to come by, Jewish magicians not being in such great demand at the time.

Alan Arkin gives Yasha the sly and ingenuous charms he expresses so well. The role of his manager, Wolsky, offers Lou Jacobi the chance to play another of the befuddled and stubborn old characters on which he built his career.

Together they attempt to book Yasha into bigger theaters in better cities. Along the way,

from the saloons of Lublin to small villages along the road, Yasha visits his various paramours, loving them and angering them at the same time. These include, oddly enough, his own wife, Esther (Linda Bernstein), who is mad that he's late for Passover.

When Esther tells him that she has found a holy man who could help them have a baby, he says he can't stay around to meet the man because magic shows on the road beckon. "I see less and less of you," Esther complains bitterly. "Well, that has its good aspects," Yasha grins. "We still hunger for each other." It is appropriate for a sleight-of-hand artist to be equally quick of tongue.

Yasha infuriates his women as he charms them—even to the point of attempted murder: His pretty assistant Magda (Maia Danziger), with whom he's been having an affair, changes the locks on his Houdini-type water torture trick during a performance, and the magician almost drowns.

Like Yasha, *The Magician of Lublin*, directed by Menahem Golan (*Lepke*, *Hanna's War*), is charming and infuriating almost simultaneously. It has scenes of incredible ambiance and tension, followed by scenes that stretch plausibility to the breaking point. The opening tightrope-walking scene in a crowded Lublin alleyway is particularly notable. But at times, Yasha's magic is so sloppy that you can actually see the camera tricks used to make objects disappear from his hands. And who takes care of the monkey he uses in his act?

The movie also has characters of great depth, passion, and humor, like Shelley Winters, who plays Magda's mother, a woman with enormous faith in Yasha. "Get yourself pregnant," she urges her daughter, "and you stay on top. It will be a son, and it will be ours forever."

Its flaws, though, soon dissipate, thanks to Singer's storytelling magic, which spirals to a most extraordinary finale. On the one hand, the final sequences feel as if they are from a different movie; on the other, they are mesmerizing. First Yasha doesn't show up for his biggest show to date, a performance in which he promised he would fly (although neither Wolsky nor the theater owner believes him). He follows that by trying to break into the safe of a wealthy man as an act of desperation. Finally, he finds that his assistant has committed suicide.

Then Yasha finds himself in a synagogue where he sees the Ten Commandments on a wall and realizes he has no choice left but to turn to God. He goes back to Lublin as a Jew, a very holy Jew, secludes himself in a hut, and prays all day and night for God to forgive his sins and give him eternal wisdom.

But Shelley Winters comes after him, angry to the core, determined to avenge the death of her daughter. With her hulking moose of a son she begins to destroy the hut, willing and able to tear Yasha limb from limb when the walls come tumbling down. Inside, Yasha prays fiercely.

When the hut is destroyed, Yasha is nowhere to be seen. He's gone. He *has* flown. It's his best show to date—even if *he* wasn't necessarily the magician responsible for the performance.

Oy Voila!

Yasha, in *The Magician of Lublin*, borrowed a few of Houdini's tricks, but not his marketing skill. Houdini's real name was Erich Weiss, but he changed it as a tribute to an earlier illusionist who had inspired him and also because the name had more mystique than Erich Weiss. It worked.

Yasha, however, was always Yasha.

Houdini, perhaps the greatest magician ever to have lived in terms of showmanship and the longevity of his legend, has been the subject of only one major motion picture, although several television productions have covered the same ground. Tony Curtis portrayed the great illusionist in the 1953 film *Houdini*.

In the film, directed by George Marshall, every possible reference to Houdini's life as a Jew disappears before our very eyes. Although the movie was noted for its sense of fun and the accuracy of the effects of some of Houdini's greatest illusions and escapes, one film writer calls it "more fiction than fact," and anyone who reads one of several Houdini biographies will certainly concur. For example, in the movie Houdini's mother, played by Angela Clark, always calls him Harry. In truth, Mrs. Weiss always called her boy Erich.

Curtis is more like Houdini than Yasha was in more ways than one. Both Curtis and Houdini had non-Jewish wives—Janet Leigh, who appears as Mrs. Houdini in the film, was married to Curtis in real life—and both changed their names. Curtis entered the world as Bernard Schwartz.

Take ragtime jazz, put it at the beginning of a Woody Allen movie, and you've got another *Sleeper*. Right?

Not even close. *Crimes and Misdemeanors*, written and directed by Allen in 1989, surprised critics and moviegoers alike. There's nothing mystical about that—Allen had long been creating emotional interper-

King Ant

Everyone thinks of Woody Allen as an auteur, a triple-threat moviemaker who writes, directs, and acts in his own pictures, as he did with *Crimes and Misdemeanors* and dozens of others. But there are exceptions. Several Woody Allen movies were written and directed by others—although none of them packed quite the same punch as those for which he wore all three hats.

In his third movie outing, *Casino Royale*, made in 1967, Allen plays the befuddled nephew of an aging Agent 007 (David Niven) in a mediocre James Bond spoof that had five directors behind it, including John Huston. Nine years later he fared much better in *The Front*, as the patsy asked by blacklisted screenwriters to pass their scripts off as his own. Directed by Martin Ritt, who along with cast members Zero Mostel and Herschel Bernardi actually had been blacklisted, *The Front* gave Allen some of his grandest reviews as an actor.

In took more than a decade for him to return to the set without an eyepiece, pen, or megaphone, in *King Lear* (1987), a strange, experimental, avant-garde updating of the Shakespearean tragedy, directed by Jean-Luc Godard. Allen played the jester and worked alongside Peter Sellers, Burgess Meredith, Norman Mailer, and Molly Ringwald. In 1991 he was paired with Bette Midler in *Scenes from a Mall*, a Paul Mazursky comedy about a married couple whose anniversary finds them revealing some very unusual things about themselves to each other. And in *Antz* (1998), Allen provided the voice of Zee, the worker ant with a severe case of depression, love starvation, angst, and fear. It was typecasting.

Judah's situation almost compels religious contemplation, and Judaism is "the only religion," Allen has said, "that I feel I can write about with any kind of accuracy... I have no feel for the details of Christianity." That's why *Crimes and Misdemeanors* is a Jewish movie.

Judah is played by Martin Landau, and his performance was nominated for an Academy Award as best supporting actor.

"The eyes of God are on us always," Judah remembers his father saying to him when he was a boy. But did Judah think of that when he embarked on an extramarital affair with Dolores Paley (Anjelica Huston)? He's an ophthalmologist; he should be thinking of eyes all the time. Of course, there would be no way to see that Dolores would become emotionally unstable and threaten to ruin his life if he doesn't divorce his wife and marry her.

But is there really a God (a question Allen asks often in his movies)? After all, Judah's friends and associates prove at the very least that life's twists and turns twist and turn for many people in many ways, sometimes making it seem as if there *is* no God to help them out. His friend, patient, and spiritual adviser, Rabbi Ben (Sam Waterston), is going blind and can only accept it with humility. His brother Jack (Jerry Orbach) is involved in crime and doesn't seem to have a guilty bone in his body.

"You don't think God sees?" Rabbi Ben asks, after Judah confides in him of his affair.

sonal dramas such as *Husbands and Wives* and *Hannah and Her Sisters*. What *is* mystical is just how earnestly instead of comically Jewish a story it is, and the eerie and affecting ways in which the central character, Dr. Judah Rosenthal, visits the family and religious influences from his past, which are often one and the same. He visits them in order to help himself be guided into a more agreeable future because of a misguided deed in his tormented present.

"God is a luxury I can't afford," Judah says, despondently.

Ultimately, and not without a lot of soul searching, Judah asks his brother to "take care" of his problem with Dolores.

"Sometimes to have a little good luck is the most brilliant plan," Rabbi Ben says—but now, the deed done, Judah must hope for a very different kind of luck: not being suspected of the crime.

Judah takes a journey to his religious childhood. "The eyes of God see all," he hears once again from the lips of a long-ago family rabbi. "There is nothing that escapes his sight. He sees the righteous and he sees the wicked. And the righteous will be rewarded. The wicked will be punished for eternity."

At a Seder in his boyhood home, Judah hears the guests talking of murder and faith in God, and his inquiring mind realizes that God is a luxury he *must* afford in order to return to the world of the righteous, where once upon a time he held an esteemed position.

While Judah's dilemma provides the ethical and spiritual heart of *Crimes and Misdemeanors*, in classic Woody Allen style there is an ensemble cast providing pointed and counterpointed story elements, with plenty of humor thrown in. Allen himself plays a down-on-his-luck documentary filmmaker named Cliff, whose big break comes when he's asked to make a film about his ex-brother-in-law, a pompous ass of a television producer named Lester (Alan Alda). Cliff falls in love with one of Lester's assistants, Halley (Mia Farrow), but then she begins an affair with the pompous ass, much to Cliff's chagrin. Talk about crimes and misdemeanors!

There is nothing derivative about the movie; it is entirely original for Allen, absorbing and entertaining for audiences. It takes a highly skilled writer and director to juggle all the pieces of a multicharacter, multistory drama-comedy and turn it into a cohesive spiritual opus. The only question left unanswered is just what it was that made Woody Allen focus on such a deeply spiritual project at this time in his life. Inquiring minds want to know.

Nobody, with the possible exceptions of Lenny Bruce and Andrew Dice Clay, becomes a comedian to make people angry on purpose. But Jewish comic Genghis Cohn, cutting Nazis down to size in 1933 Berlin, 1936 Vienna, and 1939 Warsaw, gets beaten up at every performance. He even goes so far as to have a ventriloquist's dummy in the guise of Adolf Hitler that acts, well, like a dummy.

His last performance before being sent to a concentration camp is indeed his last performance. He's shot dead.

That's when the fun begins.

In 1958 Genghis comes back to Bavaria as a ghost and haunts the Nazi officer who executed him, now a city police commissioner. Cohn himself executes an ingenious plan to exact revenge.

Genghis Cohn is a quirky 1993 film produced in England, written by Stanley Price and Romain Gary (based on Gary's novel *Dance of Genghis Cohn*) and directed by Elijah Moshinsky. Antony Sher's Genghis, with a little bit of Pee Wee Herman and Michael Keaton's Beetlejuice thrown into the personality, is a ghost with a mission and the driest and blackest sense of humor to

Antony Sher as comic Genghis Cohn *has a deliciously dangerous sense of humor.*

accomplish it. Sher, a South African-born Shakespearean actor and novelist, brings a joyous unearthliness to the role. Robert Lindsay, who starred in West End and Broadway musicals and on screen in *Bert Rigby, You're a Fool*, plays Otto Schatz, the ex-Nazi, and his performance is nearly a revelation of understated humiliation.

Genghis Cohn is wildly funny and at its best when Genghis appears to Otto and no one else (which is for most of the movie). When a series of murders occurs around town, Otto investigates and Genghis tags along, making a sarcastic nuisance of himself each step of the way.

"I'm glad you find murder so funny," Otto says to him, eliciting a sly and quizzical look from the slain comic. And when Genghis is particularly annoying, Otto says, "I should have gotten rid of all of you. You especially."

"You did!" Genghis responds. "Remember?"

Otto thinks it may be Genghis who is responsible for the murders, and so he feels he must study up on things Jewish to get closer to his suspect. But when he starts acting strange (thanks to Genghis's prodding), other officials begin to investigate Otto instead and find, among other things, that he checked out *The Diary of Anne Frank* from the library and looked up the meaning of the words *tuchas* (backside) and *meshugenah* (crazy person) and wrote them in his notebook. Then, Otto is also spotted when Genghis drags him to a synagogue to say Kaddish on the anniversary of his death.

Fast-paced and enormously clever, *Genghis Cohn* never surrenders its humor even as it promotes its deadly serious undertones. When Otto is in a mental hospital, having inadvertently convinced the authorities that he has gone crazy, there are no more murders in town. That convinces the authorities that he, Otto, is indeed the murderer.

"They need a scapegoat," Genghis explains to the broken Otto. "Believe me, I know."

Years later, released from the hospital, Otto, cured in more ways than one, has chosen a much different line of work. Genghis is free to wander off to start on another unwilling victim. Meanwhile, when Otto leaves work one day, he starts home and promptly gets beaten up. And we actually feel a bit sorry for the ex-Nazi. After all, he has become a Jew.

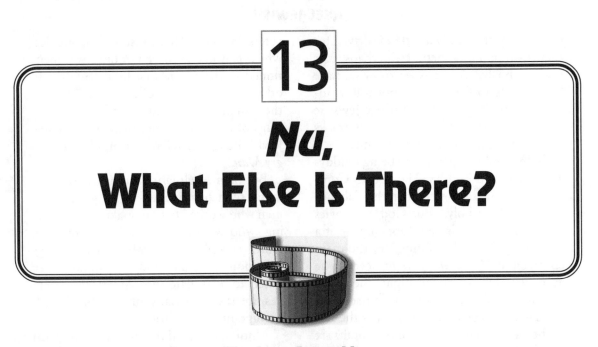

13

Nu, What Else Is There?

The Last Angry Man

The Apprenticeship of Duddy Kravitz

Next Stop, Greenwich Village

Joshua Then and Now

Mr. Saturday Night

THERE WILL ALWAYS BE DUDDY KRAVITZES, Larry Lapinskys, and Buddy Youngs—ambitious Jews who yearn to follow their dreams no matter how many commandments they have to break, even inadvertently, to get there. Sometimes they come across as "little Jewboys in the making," as Uncle Benjy says to his nephew in *The Apprenticeship of Duddy Kravitz*. "And boys like that," he adds, "make me sick and ashamed."

While greed, lust, guilt, Jewish mothers, even the fear of being left behind in the ghetto can contribute to "little Jewboys in the making," sometimes it's just a single broken commandment that is to blame: lack of rest.

"Food, money, sex," reflects Arthur Waskow in *Down-to-Earth Judaism*. "—Nu, what else is there? There is resting, which is always the 'rest' of life. That 'nothing' that gives meaning to everything."

In movies about driven, ambitious Jews, the characters almost never rest, never accept the 'nothing' that gives meaning to everything. They are almost maniacally driven to do, to be, to win, to prove, to accomplish. They are simply a little *too* driven for their own good. Sometimes, perhaps, it is understandable: As far as we know we have but one life to live, so why not follow instincts, especially in a world where Jews are occasionally stopped dead in their tracks from chasing the simplest of dreams?

So they overcompensate by being Duddys and Larrys and Buddys. The Fourth Commandment says, "Remember the Sabbath day to make it holy." But God, as movies consistently show, is very forgiving, so if a comedian like Buddy Young, Jr., the main character in *Mr. Saturday Night*, needs to be at a nightclub on Friday night, there's no reason he can't take it easy on Thursday instead—as long as whatever he does the rest of the week abides by most of the Torah's six hundred and twelve other commandments.

It is, after all, too much to ask Duddy, Larry, and Buddy to abide by *all* six hundred and thirteen; if they did, there would be almost nothing to make movies about.

The one exchange that doesn't ring true in *The Last Angry Man* (1959) is in the scene where Dr. Sam Abelman collapses on his front steps.

"How does it feel, Sam?" his friend Max asks, attending to the stricken doctor.

"It's no picnic," Abelman replies.

It doesn't ring true because Dr. Abelman doesn't seem the type *ever* to have gone on a picnic. He's been too busy being a doctor all these years, so how would he know what a picnic is like?

In his last role, Paul Muni as Dr. Sam Abelman creates one of his most Jewish char-

acters in one of his most Jewish movies, which is ironic because not once is it mentioned in the movie that he is Jewish, and other than a portrait of a Hasidic man on the wall of his living room and a passage he sings of a Yiddish song, there are very few Jewish images or references in *The Last Angry Man*.

But Sam Abelman's story is the story of many such Jewish men of his generation, men who worked hard to make a decent living, who were fiercely dedicated to doing right by people no matter how many wrongs were done to them, and who wanted very much to assimilate into American society despite their virtually unalterable Jewish immigrant personalities.

Muni once stated that he didn't ever wish to be typecast as a Jew, yet his Dr. Abelman is the quintessential old neighborhood Jewish doctor: he's slow when he walks but remarkably quick when it comes to telling a patient off; he's cranky and crabby every day of his life yet would give you the shirt off his back in a blizzard if it meant easing your pain.

The Last Angry Man is based on a book by Gerald Green, who also wrote the screenplay and as the son of a doctor knows this territory well from personal experience. The movie, directed by Daniel Mann, wastes no time introducing Brooklyn's Dr. Abelman and setting up the dramatic situation that can change his life forever. That situation involves an ambitious television producer named Thrasher (David Wayne), who wants to feature Dr. Abelman in a live, one-hour show on his network about real American heroes. "Drama, truth, real people," Thrasher says to his boss and the potential sponsor, trying to sell the idea.

Oy, has he got something coming to him.

In his last film, Paul Muni brought compassion and conviction to his role as The Last Angry Man.

As Thrasher soon finds out, there is more drama than he bargains for. Dr. Abelman may be *too* dedicated for his television idea. In fact, one of the first things Thrasher witnesses is a young kid running away from the doctor, who has just treated him, without so much as a smile or a thank you.

"Why do you break your back for an ingrate like that?" Thrasher asks.

"Because he's my patient," Abelman replies.

Thrasher should have been forewarned: patients first, television second. But Thrasher is as stubborn as the good doctor; as he tells

Dr. Abelman's friend Max (also a doctor), "Thirty million people will be watching Dr. Abelman. This will be good for him."

Good? Why would it be good for him? Does he need the publicity? No—Abelman already has too many patients, many of whom never even pay. Do Jewish immigrants like him need national exposure to complete the assimilation process? No—as much as Dr. Abelman reads Thoreau and other American writers, he'll forever be an angry old immigrant who knows that life is an uphill battle. Like Thoreau, he hears a different drummer, but heaven forbid he

Finish Line

When Columbia Pictures decided to turn Gerald Green's novel *The Last Angry Man* into a movie, Paul Muni was the favored choice to play Dr. Sam Abelman. The only one who wasn't so sure was Paul Muni. At sixty four, Muni had heart problems and wasn't certain he'd have enough energy to carry a major motion picture. He commented that if he read the script and loved it but ultimately couldn't do it, his heart would be even more broken, so he decided not even to read it.

But then director Daniel Mann heard that Muni was dropping out of a musical in San Francisco and had no other projects pending, so he sent him a copy of the book and the screenplay. Muni read the script and loved the character of Dr. Sam Abelman. He thought that the story was important and that it was a good idea to show what medicine and good doctors should be all about.

"So it'll kill me," Muni said to his concerned wife. "Abelman dies at the end of the picture. Make sure they schedule that scene last. He'll die and I'll die. It'll be a dramatic finish for both of us."

Muni was wrong. He lived another eight years, until 1967, although he did not make any more movies.

doctor? His patients would say yes. Max would say yes. Even Thrasher would say yes—although the television show never airs. But who knows what Dr. Abelman himself would say? First he would probably call you a big galoot, which is one of his favorite expressions. Next, he would tell you to take your damn hat off in his house. And finally, he'd make you completely healthy before kicking your *kishkas* back out into the street.

Who is to be blamed for Duddy? The tough Montreal ghetto in which he grew up? His brash, taxi driving father? The rich uncle who had no use for him? Or his beloved grandfather, Zaida, who told him that "a man without land is nobody"?

The Apprenticeship of Duddy Kravitz, based on a novel by Canadian Jewish writer Mordecai Richler and produced in Montreal in 1974, is an energetic little comedy as nervous and pushy as its hero. It is fast moving in its pacing, wide ranging in its narrative, and it grows on you with the earnestness of its highly strung young star, Richard Dreyfuss. Richler wrote the screenplay, and it was directed by Ted Kotcheff.

Dreyfuss was still basically an unknown at the time (he made the movie after *American Graffiti* and before *Jaws*), and it was this film that brought him to the attention of critics and studio executives because of his frenetically funny performance.

Zaida (Zvee Scooler) is really the only one who has had time for Duddy while he was growing up. His almost biblical pronouncement about man's need for land, born of years of *shtetl* life in the old country, is what drives the young Duddy through scheme

should ever march out of Brooklyn, where he knows he's needed.

Luther Adler, as Dr. Max Vogel, is nearly as prominent a figure in *The Last Angry Man* as Muni. He knows Sam well, knows what's in his heart and mind, and accepts him as a friend unconditionally. Trading barbs with him (the two together are often like an old Jewish version of Butch and Sundance), Max is the one who knows more than anyone else that when Dr. Abelman dies, it will only be because he was too stubborn to live for himself. Was it worth it for Abelman to be a

after scheme in order to reach that almost impossible dream.

"Zaida," Duddy asks in one of his calmer, quieter moments when he's not scratching himself to death, "if I get some land, lots of land, will I be somebody then?"

Though Zaida doesn't say it, Duddy quickly learns that all it takes is money—and *chutzpah*.

So first he becomes a waiter at a mountain resort, but he doesn't just follow the rules, he makes a few of his own. "He's got three more tables than anyone and still never stops," a jealous bunkmate comments. "It's little money-grubbers like Kravitz that cause anti-Semitism."

Next he tries operating a for-profit roulette wheel at the resort.

Then he establishes a movie production firm specializing in personalized films for weddings and bar mitzvahs.

Finally, he goes into pinball machine distribution.

But none of these endeavors is good enough, big enough, secure enough, or successful enough for the never satisfied, always frustrated Duddy, who nervously scratches and sweats his way through each one, making friends and enemies every step of the way.

The film moves so fast that it's almost impossible to fully appreciate all of its little bizarre, comic, and even tragic secondary characters and subplots: The bar mitzvah film he makes with the help of an alcoholic auteur (Denholm Elliott) is enough to make anyone want to convert; his girlfriend-partner Yvette (Micheline Lanctot) is as strong and honest as Duddy is unsure and cunning and, ultimately, is not a good match for him (although she has the kind of breasts Duddy

Canadian Club

In 1958 writer Mordecai Richler and director Ted Kotcheff sat on the floor of a French villa sipping cognac and vowed to turn Richler's book, *The Apprenticeship of Duddy Kravitz*, into a movie one day. But neither of them actually believed that they would succeed.

Richler and Kotcheff, both Canadians, were old friends and roommates. When Richler married for the second time, Kotcheff was his best man. But neither of them could interest a British or American film company in turning *Duddy Kravitz* into a movie. Then the Canadian Film Development Corporation (CFDC) came into existence as Canada's first organized attempt to build a major film industry. By this time, however, Richler and Kotcheff were busy with other projects.

Richler gave up, but Kotcheff persisted.

In 1972 Richler was in Cannes, writing a story about the famous annual French film festival for *Life* magazine. A Canadian producer, John Kemeny, and the head of the CFDC, Michael Spencer, were also there, and Kotcheff showed up as well. All agreed to try to have *Duddy Kravitz* made into a movie. But the CFDC didn't like the script, which a novice had written because Richler was still too busy. Richler then wrote the script himself, and that's the one that was used to finally make *The Apprenticeship of Duddy Kravitz*, sixteen years after that Kotcheff and Richler made their vow over a glass of cognac.

Richler's script was nominated for an Academy Award as best adapted screenplay.

worships); a friend he picks up along the way, the epileptic Virgil (Randy Quaid), is a victim both of his own malady and Duddy's self-absorption.

And then there's Uncle Benjy (Joseph Wiseman). "I wish I had more time for you, Duddy," he says, with just a tinge of regret. "I wish I saw what your grandfather saw."

But Zaida has *not* seen how his little Duddy has grown up. He is not aware that Duddy used the non-Jewish Yvette prima-

Richard Dreyfuss hustles with chutzpah *in* The Apprenticeship of Duddy Kravitz.

We know it won't last anyway. We know he'll have another brainstorm soon. He'll try something. And he'll give everything he's got to make it work—even if he has to scratch himself to death.

Jewish film director Paul Mazursky recently published a book of memoirs but neglected in its pages to answer one very important question: When he moved out of his family's apartment as a struggling young actor, did he stand in the street, look up at the building he was moving into, and confess, "Oh boy, am I guilty!"

By most accounts, Mazursky is Larry Lapinsky, the central character in *Next Stop, Greenwich Village*, the 1976 movie he wrote and directed. So he very well may have shouted like that. And he very well may have had a smothering Jewish mother who cried when he finally left home and who, for spite, would not even let him kiss her goodbye. And he very well may not have been sure where he stood with his new friends in Greenwich Village, some of whom were trustworthy, others disloyal.

If *Next Stop, Greenwich Village* is indeed to be thought of as a reflection of Paul Mazursky's first step toward his Hollywood career, it can be assumed that Larry Lapinsky, played by Lenny Baker, goes on to great success in the movies after the story ends. Baker,

rily to close a land deal that could not have been closed by a Jew. He is not aware of Duddy's decision to have pinball machines delivered almost at the cost of Virgil's life. This isn't the Duddy that Zaida would be proud of. And when he is finally told about one of Duddy's more flagrant misdeeds, concerning a forged check, he tells his grandson that he doesn't want the land after all. It must break Duddy's heart. As it should.

Director Kotcheff did a good job of making a quirky and cohesive film out of a strange and convoluted year in the life of Duddy Kravitz. Duddy may be a "little Jewboy in the making," but at least he's mature enough to accept a job driving a cab at the end of the story, something he once vowed never to do, when he realizes it may he the only sure way of getting back on his feet.

unfortunately, didn't fare as well; he died of cancer at the age of only thirty-six, a few years after *Next Stop, Greenwich Village* was released.

But the road to Hollywood is paved with some unusual and quirky stepping-stones, and that's what this movie is about. Mazursky's skill as a writer and director is in taking what could be very annoying people and frustrating situations and turning them into enjoyable slices of life at a special time in a special place. Greenwich Village in 1953 was a place where many wannabees could live with almost endless hope, given the atmosphere of the times, the spaces in which to learn and emote, and the camaraderie of all the Village people who stood behind you in your endeavors.

"I never wanted to be a cop or a fireman or a pilot," Larry says to his girlfriend Sarah (Ellen Greene). "For a brief time there I wanted to be a war hero. But I always wanted to be a star." Lapinsky or Mazursky speaking? Undoubtedly both.

It makes one wonder what Larry's mother, played by Shelley Winters in one of her several Jewish mother roles, would have done had Larry decided to become a cop instead. She doesn't even want him to leave home. But to leave home with a nightstick and a gun? Forget it. One thing Mazursky *does* mention in his memoirs is that he was able to create cinematic parents like those in *Next Stop* "without fear," because his own were both deceased by the time the movie was made—although he felt his mother was watching while it was being filmed.

"You call this an apartment?" she says to

Final Cut

It's not the kind of event most people would actually pay money to see, but the Jewish circumcision ceremony, the *brit milah*, has been featured in one way or another in more than a dozen movies, including *The Plot Against Harry, Hanna K., The Apprenticeship of Duddy Kravitz, King David, Crossing Delancey, The First Wives Club, A Price Above Rubies,* and others.

Because of the emotions involved, it is usually not the baby who becomes the center of attention in *brit* scenes. In *The Plot Against Harry,* the hapless ex-con played by Martin Priest goes to a *brit* where the father almost knocks over a tower of duck-shaped chopped liver in order to photograph the blessed event. In *The Apprenticeship of Duddy Kravitz,* Duddy produces a bar mitzvah movie for a client in which a close-up of the bar mitzvah boy's *brit,* juxtaposed with primitive African customs, is shown to an unsuspecting and shocked audience.

In *Crossing Delancey,* Amy Irving attends the *brit* of a friend's new baby at which the mother stays in the bedroom, the father becomes nauseated, another guest faints, and the *mohel,* or ritual circumciser, explains to all, with a minimum of sensitivity, precisely why the baby cries. And in *A Price Above Rubies,* Renée Zellweger plays a repressed Hasidic woman who glares murderously at the men handling her new son at his *brit* and yells, "Don't any one of you dare drop him."

And, of course, there's always a lot of food.

Larry on her first visit to Greenwich Village from Brooklyn. "I don't call this an apartment. An apartment has furniture." His father, in a perfectly droll performance by Mike Kellin, is as ineffectual as his mother is demonstrative. Leaving mom and pop behind, Larry is able to live the way he wants to live, working in a small deli making vegetable juice during the day, going to auditions and taking acting classes in Manhattan after hours. Being free of his parents also gives him more of a chance to make love at will to Sarah, his "ravishing Semitic beauty,"

"Boy, am I guilty!" Lenny Baker as Paul Mazursky's alter ego in Next Stop, Greenwich Village.

They don't, primarily because they don't show up all that often to begin with—only when Larry is having a wild party or when he and Sarah are snuggled together in the apartment in their underwear. Talk about timing.

"At least you're a Jewish girl," Larry's mother says to Sarah when she sees the two together in a compromising position.

His mother doesn't even have to be around to influence Larry's life. She shows up in a nightmare fantasy in his acting class and even does a scene with him.

"You can't be here!" Larry yells to the apparition.

"You think I'm your standard Jewish mother?" she responds. "I'm a funny lady who just shrieks and shrieks and wails? Am I not blessed, am I not a human being with feelings?"

"Oh God!" Larry screams toward the ceiling, "help a poor Jewish boy."

Still, Larry's enthusiasm, persistence, and manic energy get him through the nightmares, the fantasies, the abortion, the suicide of another friend, and several other Greenwich Village challenges. He has a dream *and* the confidence to see it through. He wants to be an actor, and nothing will stop him. Not even a Jewish mother.

At an audition for a movie, the casting agent says to Larry, "You got a real street look," apparently noticing Larry's overburdened demeanor.

"I live in Greenwich Village," he answers.

"You're not a *faigele* [homosexual], are you?"

"No, I'm Jewish."

Maybe that's burden enough.

as described by one of their new friends in the Village. The friend is Bernstein Chandler, a black homosexual who says he was named after the wonderful woman his mother worked for as a maid. Larry makes love to Sarah with an abandon he could only have dreamed of in Brooklyn.

"We should do a comedy act," Larry says to Sarah after one such session.

"We just did a comedy act together," she responds in perfect timing.

But that's one act without a happy ending, for it ends in her pregnancy, which they decide to abort. Just another daily challenge in Larry's new life. As long as mom and pop don't find out . . .

Enter *Kvetching*

In many of her Jewish roles, Shelley Winters acted as if she always gave people indigestion. In many of his Jewish roles, Lou Jacobi acted as if he always *had* indigestion.

Their characters were married to each other only once, but Winters and Jacobi were in three Jewish movies together: *The Diary of Anne Frank*, *The Magician of Lublin*, and *Next Stop, Greenwich Village*.

In *The Diary of Anne Frank* they were the bickering Mr. and Mrs. Van Daan, making life more miserable for each other than it already was under the circumstances.

Jacobi, a Canadian Jew born in 1913, added ethnic delight to many movies, notably as the permanently upset Uncle Gabriel in *Avalon* and as Benjy's exuberant Uncle Morty in *My Favorite Year*. Jacobi was also one of the featured actors on the famous 1960s comedy album, *You Don't Have to Be Jewish*.

Winters, born Shirley Schrift in 1922, has been one of cinema's most enduring Jewish mothers, appearing in *Enter Laughing* as the concerned mother Mrs. Kolowitz, *The Poseidon Adventure* as Belle Rosen, *Next Stop, Greenwich Village* as Mrs. Lapinsky, and *Over the Brooklyn Bridge* as Mrs. Sherman.

Winters won Academy Awards for best supporting actress in *The Diary of Anne Frank* and *A Patch of Blue*. And despite her unmatched status in concerned Jewish mother roles, Winters refused to be typecast: she also played Ma Barker in *Bloody Mama*, blasting her way through the Depression with her sons, including a young Robert De Niro.

When Joshua Shapiro was thirteen his mother did a striptease for his friends at his bar mitzvah. When he was fourteen his father, a small-time hood and gambler, taught him how to get a woman to want to make love to him. Maybe that's why Joshua as an adult says if he could change just one thing about his childhood, it would be to make a better world for himself.

It could also be because Joshua Shapiro, who eventually becomes a writer, was aimless and unsure of just what life was supposed to be.

Joshua, Then and Now was written and directed by the same team that made *The Apprenticeship of Duddy Kravitz*, Mordecai Richler and Ted Kotcheff. Like that movie, it was based on a Richler novel, and it was said to have been semiautobiographical. But instead of chasing money and land as Duddy does, Joshua is a conqueror who fights for bylines and women. Like Duddy, he must win at all costs.

James Woods as the grownup Joshua (the younger Joshua is played by Eric Kimmel) exudes the confidence and *chutzpah* Richler and Kotcheff needed for their main character. Joshua moves to England in 1954 to try to become an even more successful writer, but once there, female conquests become his main theme. Falling in love at first sight with a beautiful woman named Pauline (Gabrielle Lazure), who a fellow Canadian *thinks* belongs to him, Joshua woos her and wins her. Pauline is not Jewish, but she's so sure she wants to stay with the funny, impetuous Joshua that she asks him if he wants her to convert.

"You can learn to play tennis," he gently lectures, "but not how to be Jewish." It is one of the more reflective and restrained moments in a movie that is otherwise as frenetically paced as *Duddy Kravitz* was, but it is a moment that, regrettably, is not explored more deeply. The seed has been planted—we know that Joshua has feelings about Judaism, but the story is simply too caught up in his other pursuits to deal effectively with it. Not much is made of his writing career either, although his relationship with Pauline's family must fire his imagination, and thus his writing—not to mention his relationship with his own father, who is a pretty colorful character himself.

Pauline's father (Alexander Knox) is a Canadian senator who is put off by Joshua's family history, not to mention its present—Joshua's father, at the moment, is in jail for stealing a car. And Joshua's father is played by Alan Arkin, who gives a howl of a performance. Talking to Pauline's father about the marriage of their children, Arkin reminds the senator that it is against Jewish law to marry outside the religion, even though Esther married a gentile king and nobody complained. "Therefore," he tells the very proper senator, "my interpretation is that you are not to marry outside the faith, unless you happen to marry into a very, very good family."

Joshua's relationship with Pauline, too, is an element of his life that must give him rich stuff to write about. After Joshua and Pauline are married for a while and have children, personal and legal problems on Pauline's side of the family cause a major rift that seems nearly to rip the family apart. Pauline accuses him of marrying her only as "a golden *shikse*," a prize to show to his friends.

James Woods, Gabrielle Lazure, and Alan Arkin take Joshua Then and Now *through the then and the now of a moving family love story.*

But that is simply not true. Unlike Duddy, Joshua is capable of deep and lasting love, and he suddenly knows that all his running and working and conquering means nothing without something real and true and honest to feel passionate about. He just never stopped long enough to realize it.

Joshua's dad, sitting with the grandkids at the end of the story—just as Joshua and Pauline stand a chance to reunite—tells them, in the way only he can, "The book of Job is more than another gambling story with a happy ending. It has a moral. The moral is, if you continue to have faith in God, or even your family, even if you're up shit's creek, it'll end up paying double at the window."

Take every Jewish comedian in the world who *kvetches* after all the sketches and you've got Buddy Young, Jr., the comic driven to succeed despite a serious lack of sensitivity and an inability to laugh at anyone else—even other comedians. To him, they are the enemy.

Buddy is the central figure in *Mr. Saturday Night*, Billy Crystal's ambitious 1992 biography of Buddy, a character he began developing in his television appearances. In addition to portraying Buddy, Crystal also directed the movie and coscripted it with Lowell Ganz and Babaloo Mandel. Crystal, Ganz, and Mandel had also worked together on *City Slickers* the previous year. It is obvious that Crystal has made a lifelong practice of studying everyone from Jerry Lewis, Jackie Mason, and Jack Carter to Myron Cohen, Don Rickles, and Jackie Leonard because there are parts of them, and a dozen others, in Buddy Young, Jr. It makes you wonder just how many of *them* are equally nasty.

"I wanted to be the guy," Buddy says late in the picture, "who, when he walked into The Friars, everybody turned around and said, 'Why him, that lucky bastard? I'm funnier than him.' I wanted to be that guy. I still do." He says it to his brother and manager, Stan, who is brilliantly played by David Paymer. But Stan knew that already. Buddy should have been saying it all along to the other people he stepped on. Maybe they would have understood a little better before it was too late.

Mr. Saturday Night moves faster than Henny Youngman's act because Crystal wanted to tell a story that sprawls far longer than two hours would allow without acting like a Keystone Cop. That's part of the problem. There is so much content that some story elements seem annoyingly short-changed, particularly Buddy's role as a husband and father. For example, his daughter Susan was once involved in drugs and bad relationships, but we never find out too much about that. Buddy also has a son who is never seen and hardly ever mentioned.

What the movie does do well is to track this comic's career in a very believable way, from Buddy and Stan's family living room when they were kids, to Buddy's early Catskill dates and then his own television show, to his fading days when it becomes difficult for Buddy and Stan to round up enough people to fill a room for a show at a senior citizens' complex.

Buddy's humor, which he developed by making fun of his relatives, is Yiddish-flavored and comes from the same school as all the great old Jewish comics. One fateful day as a teenager, he bombs in front of the crowd at a vaudeville house and discovers that there are laughs in insults. "I want to show you something you haven't seen in a long time," he says to an overweight heckler, "—your feet." From that time on, Buddy is both aggressive and offensive at the same time.

Stanley, who started out working with Buddy as a duo, decides early on that it would make more sense to work *for* him. So Stan helps Buddy rise through the ranks, but at a steep price.

"Stanley," Buddy says to him after Stan insists he change a troubled monologue on his television show, "let's each do what we do best. I'll tell the jokes, you'll get me a soda when I'm through." It's a throwaway line to Buddy, but it cuts like a knife to Stan.

The story, too, cuts back and forth between the early days, the heyday career, and the elderly Buddy and Stanley, effectively

Billy Crystal is Mr. Saturday Night.

of comedy. There is no one he doesn't insult. "Don't get me started," he says to his audiences—before he starts in on just about everyone. Even his wife (Julie Warner) and daughter (Mary Mara) make it into the act, although not everyone thinks it's funny.

"I can't do this anymore—*schlep* work," Stan finally says to Buddy before retiring. He's had enough of his brother's insults and temper, which have cost Buddy important jobs in the past. Buddy is never unfunny (even at his mother's funeral he says, " My first thought was, did anyone get her recipe for kugel?") but he's unhappy because he never made it as big as he could have, and it's an endless source of grief.

Endless, too, are the arguments between Buddy and Stanley about their personal and professional relationship. "I didn't take your life, Stan," Buddy says to his brother after another quarrel. "I gave you one."

"Yeah," Stan says softly, "but you could have been nicer."

Buddy could have been nicer, and *Mr. Saturday Night* could have been just a bit longer to develop more of its story. But there's only so much nastiness you can take at one sitting. Even Don Rickles walks off the stage after an hour or so.

showing how words in one era impact feelings in another. Other than a poor makeup job and unconvincing acting by Crystal as the elderly Buddy (By contrast, Paymer's makeup and acting as the old Stan are phenomenal), each era is believable and interesting.

The world is Buddy's target, in the guise

Flattery

Paul Mazursky steals.

Mazursky, director of quite a few movies with Jewish characters and situations (*Next Stop, Greenwich Village*; *An Unmarried Woman*; *Enemies: A Love Story*), made four movies in the 1980s that were thematic loans: two from foreign films, one from a 1930s American film, and one from Shakespeare.

But in movies, stealing often is a legitimate way of creating something new and exciting that modern audiences might enjoy as much and sometimes more than the original works on which they are based..

Willie and Phil (1980), about two friends who fall in love with the same woman, is an Americanized version of François Truffaut's 1961 *Jules and Jim*. In fact, Willie (Michael Ontkean) and Phil (Ray Sharkey) meet after watching *Jules and Jim* at a neighborhood theater.

Tempest (1982), based on Shakespeare's *The Tempest*, is about a family (John Cassavetes, Gena Rowlands, and Molly Ringwald) in turmoil, whose individual experiences on a secluded Greek island are connected, by turns, with love, lust, and lunacy.

Down and Out in Beverly Hills (1986), about a bum (Nick Nolte) who makes the neurotic lives of the rich Whiteman family (Richard Dreyfuss and Bette Midler) even more neurotic, is a remake of a 1932 French film by Jean Renoir called *Boudu Saved from Drowning*. The original took over thirty-five years to be released in the United States, but when it was it received much praise from the critics.

And *Moon Over Parador* (1988), about an American actor (Richard Dreyfuss) recruited to imitate a deceased Latin American dictator, has almost exactly the same plot as *The Magnificent Fraud*, a 1939 film starring Akim Tamiroff.

14

Also Playing . . .

From Henry Street to Hollywood

The Jolson Story (1946)

In *The Jazz Singer*, Jolson more or less played Jolson because, while not exactly autobiographical, it reflected his own path into show business. Nineteen years later, Larry Parks played Jolson more or less playing Jolson in *The Jolson Story*. A classic primarily because it's about a legend who defined American music during that era, turning vaudeville into pop, this musical biography includes the songs (dubbed by Jolson) "April Showers," "You Made Me Love You," "My Mammy," and others. Three years later, in *Jolson Sings Again*, Parks as Jolson meets Parks as Parks, the actor hired to play him in *The Jolson Story*. The resemblance is uncanny. Directed by Alfred E. Green.

The Jazz Singer (1953)

A remake is one thing, but a remake of one of the most important films in history is another. Still, this Danny Thomas version (now the singer's name is Jerry Golding) holds up pretty well, with solid performances (Peggy Lee is the love interest) and serious direction (Michael Curtiz, who also made *Yankee Doodle Dandy*). One critic noted, "It wasn't much, but it played like *Citizen Kane* next to the 1980 Neil Diamond version." As long as no one tries to remake *Citizen Kane* . . .

Hello, Dolly! (1969)

Barbra Streisand made *Hello, Dolly!* even before *Funny Girl* opened. Everybody was convinced she would be a superstar who could carry *any* picture. Only Walter Matthau wasn't convinced. This $34 mil-

Barbra Streisand in Hello, Dolly!

lion Jerry Herman musical generated, among other things, a lot of work for a lot of dancers, seven Academy Award nominations, and much controversy about the casting of Streisand, whom many people considered too young for the role. Gene Kelly directed (but didn't choreograph) and bandleader Louis Armstrong appears as bandleader Louis Armstrong (who would have been minus two years old when the story takes place).

Funny Lady (1975)

James Caan makes Barbra Streisand an offer she can't refuse. As showman Billy Rose, he gives Fanny Brice a chance to bounce back from the heartbreak of her broken marriage to convicted gambler Nicky Arnstein with some love, laughs, and devotion. Well, at least she has some laughs. Caan is quite funny and effective as Rose, though Streisand's Fanny may now be a little too tiring to be a funny girl. But it does have

plenty of songs, routines, a brief return of Omar Sharif, and the extra added attraction of Ben Vereen as song and dance man Burt Robbins. Herbert Ross directed.

The Jazz Singer (1980)

The movie that persuaded Neil Diamond to stick to records. In this second remake of the classic tale, Diamond is Jesse Rabinowitz, and he heads west to have his singing career guided by agent Lucie Arnaz, with whom he falls in love, despite having a wife back east. His cantor father, Laurence Olivier, is against the whole thing—until he sees Neil and Lucie's new baby. Then he becomes an adoring Zaida as quickly and passionately as he drilled Dustin Hoffman's teeth in *Marathon Man*. Songs include "Love on the Rocks" and "America." Directed by Richard Fleisher.

License to *Kvell*

Boardwalk (1979)

A lot of talent came out of Coney Island. Two giant ones—Lee Strasberg and Ruth Gordon—went back in 1979 as David and Becky Rosen, an elderly Jewish couple trying to outlive their dying neighborhood. The film is filled with Jewish flavor, customs, traditions, sensitivities, and sensibilities. Unfortunately, it ends on a sour, violent note. Janet Leigh plays David and Becky's daughter. Directed by Steven Verona.

Tell Me a Riddle (1980)

The real riddle is why actress Lee Grant never really made it as a top-notch director. This, her feature directorial debut, was made for under $2 million and received fairly good reviews. Like *Boardwalk*, it's about an elderly Jewish couple, David and Eva, played by Melvyn Douglas and Lila Kedrova, who begin to question their love, only to rediscover it on a road trip. Though called depressing by some, the strong performances more than make up for the heaviness of the story. It's from a novella by Tillie Olson.

Falling in Love Again (1980)

How could the director know what falling in love was all about when he was all of twenty years old when this was made? Steven Paul also produced, wrote, and acted in the film, which was not very well received (although he was given *chutzpah* points for trying). Elliott Gould and Susannah York play a middle-aged Jewish couple who go on a trip back to New York, which makes poor Elliott remember happier, freer days. Michelle Pfeiffer made her debut in this one.

Down and Out in Beverly Hills (1986)

A nice Jewish family with a bum. Richard Dreyfuss and Bette Midler are Dave and Barbara Whiteman, and Nick Nolte is Jerry, the homeless man who finds a home, and then some, with the Whitemans and their maid, friends, neighbors, therapists, masseuses . . . Musician Little Richard plays their neighbor, and director Paul Mazursky wasn't able to film his scenes on Friday night or Saturday because Little Richard, he discovered, is a Jew who observes the Sabbath. Dave Whiteman wasn't always rich; he made his fortune in hangers. But the Whitemans were always Jewish; Dave sprinkles enough Yiddishisms throughout the movie to fill a closet.

Radio Days (1987)

In the 1940s, most families added another member to their actual numbers: the radio. There are many main characters in writer and director Woody Allen's nostalgic comedy: Joe (Seth Green), the little Jewish boy at the center of the family; his mother and father (Julie Kavner and Michael Tucker); all the actors and actresses who work on the radio shows the family listens to; and, of course, the radio itself. The family lives in Queens, New York, and the radio magic is spun in Manhattan, and sometimes there's a whole world between them. The supporting cast includes Mia Farrow, Josh Mostel, Dianne Wiest, Wallace Shawn (as The Masked Avenger), Jeff Daniels, Diane Keaton, and others.

Richard Dreyfuss and Bette Midler in Down and Out in Beverly Hills.

In the Face of Insanity

The Producers (1967)

Did you hear the one about the fat, obnoxious Jewish producer and his whiney, timid Jewish accountant who decided to let Mel Brooks make a movie about them? Brooks's classic satire about Max Bialystock and Leo Bloom won him a screenwriting Oscar and gave the world "Springtime for Hitler" (a play within the movie and its theme song). Zero Mostel and Gene Wilder play Max and Leo, whose scheme to put on a gigantic Broadway flop and escape with the investment money flops. Brooks also directed, which should give some clues to the *shtick* in store.

Zero Mostel, Kenneth Mars, and Gene Wilder in The Producers.

I Love You, Alice B. Toklas (1968)

Those special brownies come later. First, Peter Sellers is a quiet, conservative Jewish lawyer about to marry his nice, conservative Jewish secretary (Joyce Van Patten). Then he takes a casket with a dead neighbor in it to the cemetery in a psychedelic Volkswagen. Next, he becomes a hippie living in a pad with a groovy chick (Leigh Taylor-Young), while his poor mother (Jo Van Fleet) can't understand why her other son (David Arkin) is wearing a "*meshuggener* outfit" to the dead guy's funeral. There are also twin cantors at the wedding that almost was and various other *mushegaas*. Cowritten by Paul Mazursky (*Next Stop, Greenwich Village*) and directed by Hy Averback.

Private Benjamin (1980)

"All I want is a big house, nice clothes, two closets, a live-in maid, and a professional man for a husband," Judy Benjamin whispers to a friend when she is eight years old. When Judy grows up, she learns that she really hasn't grown up at all. First there's a wedding where she yells at her furniture man for not making her ottoman with upholstered balls instead of wheels, and things go downhill from there. Goldie Hawn, as Judy, joins the army and uses it to climb back up to self-respect. Goldie said she saw some realism behind the comedy and a little bit of her own life in the movie's sentiments. Prior to making it, she went through six weeks of actual basic training. Directed by Howard Zieff.

My Favorite Year (1982)

If Lou Jacobi is your uncle, you know things could get a little *meshugge*—espe-

Goldie Hawn as Private Benjamin.

cially if you bring a famous swashbuckling actor home for dinner. That's just one of the highlights in this affectionate send-up of live television, in which a young writer named Benjy Stone (Mark Linn-Baker) is charged with babysitting for the alcoholic Alan Swann, who is all set to appear on the television show where Benjy works. Peter O'Toole, as Swann, was nominated for an Academy Award as best supporting actor. This was the directorial debut of Richard Benjamin, who's played plenty of put-upon young Jewish men in his days as an actor. Lainie Kazan in all her *zaftig* yentishness is Benjy's mother.

The Outside Chance of Maximilian Glick (1988)

There must be something in the Canadian air that makes those northern Jews pick such long titles. With *The Apprenticeship*

of *Duddy Kravitz*, *Joshua Then and Now*, *Lies My Father Told Me*, and *The Outside Chance of Maximilian Glick*, Canada's distinctive role in Jewish moviedom is forever growing. Max (Noam Zylberman) is about to have his bar mitzvah, and as manhood approaches, he is forced to weigh his own dreams—which include getting to know a pretty, gentile piano player—against his family's Jewish traditions. The movie also features Saul Rubinek as a rather unorthodox Orthodox rabbi who wants to be a stand-up comedian. Directed by Alan A. Goldstein.

So It Was Written, So It Shall Be Filmed

The Ten Commandments (1923)

Thirty years before Cecil B. De Mille's quintessential Bible movie, there was Cecil B. De Mille's quintessential Bible movie. While the 1956 version is in a class of its own because of its all-star cast, special effects, and general epic proportions, his earlier one was enormously creative in its own way, particularly in its narrative. The story is in two parts, the first a retelling of the biblical story of Moses, the second about two modern brothers whose divergent lifestyles embrace or deride the words on the tablets the man in the first part brings down from the mountain. It also has special effects and a cast of thousands.

Samson and Delilah (1949)

Oy, has Samson got problems: He's got a nagging mother ("What did I tell you! He wants to marry a Philistine!"); an army that wants to kill him, which he defeats with chains, trees, swords, and the jawbone of

Russ Tamblyn and Victor Mature in Samson and Deliliah.

an ass; a beautiful woman who finds out the source of his strength and cuts it off ("You Philistine gutter rat!"); and a tragic ending ("He's lost everything but the love of his people"). Victor Mature as Samson looks and sounds like a biblical Rocky Balboa, and Heddy Lamarr as the seductive and destructive Delilah swings between desire and hate with the greatest of ease. Despite scenes right out of Jerry Springer (including midgets taunting the blinded Samson in an arena), Cecil B. De Mille's epic was a big success.

Ben-Hur (1959)

As if Moses weren't big enough, Charlton Heston got to play another larger-than-life figure in another huge, big-budget spectacle—although he almost didn't.

Rock Hudson, Marlon Brando, Burt Lancaster, and Cesare Danova were all seriously considered before Heston won the role. While not exactly a Bible story, it does concern a princely Jewish hunk in the time of Jesus who learns a thing or two about loyalty, oppression, and redemption, although by the end he pretty much ceases to be Jewish. The film won eleven Oscars, including best picture, director (William Wyler), actor, supporting actor (Hugh Griffith), music, editing, and special effects.

Sodom and Gomorrah (1963)

Very long, very fleshy. The set and costume designers must have had a ball as they dressed up the locations and undressed the cast. Naked statues abound, as do naked people drawn on hanging prints and barely clothed Sodomites roaming the city's alleyways. Actually the film received generally good reviews for its serious attempt to tell the amazing story without too many unintentional laughs. Stewart Granger as Lot, however, looks as if he has walked right off the set of *Dallas*. He himself gets a big laugh from the crowd when he tells them that Sodom will be reduced to dust (a bit of news he received from a higher authority). As everyone knows, he has the last laugh, in a manner of speaking. Directed by Robert Aldridge.

King David (1985)

Samuel brings David good news and bad news. "God has chosen you to unite His

Stewart Granger in Sodom and Gomorrah.

scattered tribes into one nation," the prophet says to him as a youngster. That's the good news. The bad news is that King Saul is insanely jealous, and the beautiful woman he sees bathing is married. Australian director Bruce Beresford (*Driving Miss Daisy*) is credited with making a serious and faithful adaptation of the sprawling story, but Richard Gere got only a tepid reception as David. Although there are certain plot devices and bits that seem borrowed from other movies, the film is entirely original, including a scene with David dancing orgasmically in his underwear at his coronation.

Mixed Doubles

Abie's Irish Rose (1946)

Bridget Loves Bernie, except in the 1940s and on the big screen. When a young Jewish boy named Abie (Richard Norris) decides to marry an Irish girl named Rosemary (Joanne Dru), all is not immediately peaceful at the Levy and Murphy homes. There are situations and opinions and little dramas and assorted silliness that, sooner or later, make everyone on both sides wake up and smell the Irish coffee. It was a Broadway play in the 1920s and there was an earlier movie version in 1929. In each one, Abie and Rosemary are married in three separate ceremonies (two religious, one civil). It was this film that prompted the creation of the Motion Picture Project, a group designed to work with studios in avoiding defamation of minority groups, particularly Jews. Directed by A. Edward Sutherland.

Hand in Hand (1960)

Small, sweet, and British. This little, easygoing, and heartwarming film tells the tale of a preteen Jewish girl and Catholic boy who become fast friends, despite (or maybe because of) their different heritages. Though barely more than an hour in length, *Hand in Hand* doesn't rush through its many episodes of discovery and total acceptance. At one point, the girl and boy even stick their fingers with a needle so that they can put them together, mix the blood, and become best friends forever and ever. Innocent days, innocent years, innocent feelings. Directed by Philip Leacock.

Minnie and Moskowitz (1971)

Can a pretty Protestant museum curator find happiness with a homely Jewish park-

Vincent Spano and Rosanna Arquette in Baby, It's You.

ing lot attendant? In director John Cassavetes' film, against all odds (not to mention their opinionated mothers), they do. Gena Rowlands (the real Mrs. Cassavetes) is Minnie Moore and Seymour Cassel is Seymour Moskowitz in what critic Leonard Maltin calls "one of Cassavetes' most likable films." Most Cassavetes films can be described as acquired tastes, including such fare as *Husbands*, *A Woman Under the Influence*, and *The Killing of a Chinese Bookie*. The director himself appeared in *Minnie and Moskowitz* as Minnie's soon-to-be-dumped married lover.

Just Tell Me What You Want (1980)

Want to see an obnoxious Jewish businessman get slugged by a fed-up *shikse* television producer in the middle of a crowded department store? Alan King is Max Herschel, and Ali MacGraw is Bones Burton, his mistress—until she's had enough of him and marries someone else. It's a sa-

tirical love story with sarcastic nods to the movie industry itself in which the Yiddish-spewing, self-martyred Max—who's almost like an overbearing Jewish mother—makes it his goal in life to get Bones back. King got consistently rave reviews for his performance. It was directed by Sidney Lumet, who also used King in *Bye, Bye Braverman* and *The Anderson Tapes*.

Baby, It's You (1983)

Desperately seeking Spano. Rosanna Arquette, a Jewish girl from middle-class Trenton, New Jersey, meets Vincent Spano, a Catholic boy from the working class end of town who calls himself the Sheik. They get together and attempt to have a meaningful relationship. From independent writer-producer John Sayles (*Brother from Another Planet, Return of the Secaucus Seven*), *Baby, It's You* is noted for its period detail (it takes place in the 1960s), true-to-life dialogue, and bright cast of up-and-coming actors, including Tracy Pollan, Matthew Modine, and Robert Downey, Jr.

Enduring the Darkness

Judgment at Nuremberg (1961)

As courtroom dramas go, this one is guilty of pulling out all the stops: top director and screenwriter (Stanley Kramer and Abby Mann), top cast (Spencer Tracy, Burt Lancaster, Richard Widmark, Marlene Dietrich, Judy Garland, Maximilian Schell, Montgomery Clift), and a juicy topic—an American judge presiding over a Nazi war crime trial. Schell won an Academy Award for best actor for his role as a German de-

Ida Kaminska in The Shop on Main Street.

fense attorney. Clift's character had been shattered by the Nazis, and in a bizarre twist of professional fate, his real-life heavy drinking lent his performance an air of realism that was highly touted. Unfortunately, he also had a real-life emotional breakdown at about the same time.

The Shop on Main Street (1965)

She's just a little old Jewish woman, and her shop sells nothing but buttons. But in the Nazi era, even little old Jewish button shop owners must be watched over, and this film is about the tenuous relationship between the owner and the man the Nazis assign to her. *The Shop on Main Street* was made in Czechoslovakia during what is known as the Czech Golden Age of Film (roughly 1962 to 1969), when Czech artists enjoyed a measure

of creative freedom they had rarely had before. This movie, directed by Jan Kadar, won an Academy Award as best foreign language film.

The Garden of the Finzi-Continis (1971)

Could they have been *that* ignorant, to think a garden wall would keep out the Nazis? This haunting, melancholy Italian movie, which won an Academy Award as best foreign language film, is about two families in the late 1930s—one rich, one not so rich, one spoiled, one not spoiled at all—and all the unrequited love, jealousies, illusions, and disillusions that unite and divide them. Director Vittorio De Sica said that he lived through the period and put all his own feelings into the picture.

Dominique Sanda and Lino Capolicchio in The Garden of the Finzi-Continis.

Marco Holschneider in Europa, Europa.

version of this one made in 1975), Robin Williams stars as a Jewish café owner in Poland who makes up radio news bulletins to keep up the spirits of his ghetto friends, neighbors, and customers. Despite starring a comic superstar, *Jakob the Liar* is an extremely dark and brutal film. It also stars Alan Arkin, Armin Mueller-Stahl, and Liev Schreiber, whose role as the husband in *A Walk on the Moon* earlier the same year gained a lot of well-deserved attention. Directed by Peter Kassovitz.

A Funny Kind of Elation

The House of Rothschild (1934)

Anti-Semitism, banking, sons, daughters, brothers, villains, Napoleon, love, war, the stock market, marriage… that's one busy house! And it's all served up in a lavish cinematic tour de force for George Arliss as both Nathan Rothschild and his son. The story concerns the famed banking family and their soap opera lives, with anti-Semitism providing a big chunk of the financial melodrama. It also features Boris Karloff, Loretta Young, Robert Young, and Florence Arliss as a woman who is asked to pretend she's Nathan's wife, which, of course, she was in real life. Directed by Alfred L. Werker.

Europa, Europa (1991)

If it wasn't autobiographical, it would be totally unreal. This is Solomon Perel's story of how, as a German Jew, he runs away to look for safety and, through a series of strange adventures, winds up as a young Nazi soldier. Further close-call episodes follow, including a love affair cut short, a few secrets uncovered, and the closest call of all at the end, when he's reunited with his lost brother at the last possible moment. The real Perel appears briefly at the conclusion. An amazing, harrowing, darkly humorous, and touching film by Polish director Agniezka Holland.

Jakob the Liar (1999)

Sometimes comic actor Robin Williams talks so fast you don't have time to figure out if he's telling the truth or not. In *Jakob the Liar*, the first of many quirky and original Holocaust films made after *Life Is Beautiful* (although there was an East German

Address Unknown (1944)

The Schultzes and the Eisensteins break up. Some war pictures depict the breakup of marriages, others of friends, some even of brothers (particularly Civil War movies). *Address Unknown* covers a different perspective: World War II's effect on two entire families in San Francisco, and how Nazi anti-Semitism affects their lives, loves, careers, and friendship. This was one of the first mainstream pictures to deal openly with the plight of Jews under Nazism. Paul Lukas and Morris Carnovsky were the heads of the Jewish families. William Cameron Menzies directed.

Tomorrow the World (1944)

Another unique perspective in a World War II story. This time an American couple adopt a German boy whose parents were killed and must then try to erase his Nazi indoctrination. Fredric March and Betty Field are the adoptive couple (they are the boy's uncle and aunt), and Skippy Homeier is the tough and almost maniacal twelve year old. Based on a Broadway play, *Tomorrow the World* was never a terribly popular movie. It was directed for the screen by Leslie Fenton.

The Young Lions (1958)

"A wartime *Grand Hotel*," quipped Pauline Kael. But she also liked it very much. From the Irwin Shaw novel, *The Young Lions* presents the point of view of some American soldiers, as well as a German officer who first embraces and then questions Hitler's policies. The Jewish soldier, Montgomery Clift, battles anti-Semitism and false accusations within his platoon—and then has to deal with more of the same stateside. Dean Martin is one of his pals, with problems of his own. The Nazi with a latent conscience is Marlon Brando. Also starring Maximilian Schell, Hope Lange, and Lee Van Cleef as an anti-Semitic sergeant. Directed by Edward Dmytryk, who also made *Crossfire*.

The Naked and the Dead (1958)

More young lions, with different names. Same year as the Clift-Brando film, similar all-star cast, same kind of journey to screen (this one from a Norman Mailer best-seller), and parallel themes. A bunch of soldiers in the Pacific during the Big One battle the enemy, and each other. This time Joey Bishop and Jerry Paris are the Jews who encounter anti-Semitism and treat it with various degrees of humor and muscle. Other members of this wartime *Grand Hotel* include Cliff Robertson, Raymond Massey, and Richard Jaeckel. Directed by Raoul Walsh.

The Old Jewish Neighbor Hoods

Murder, Inc. (1960)

He was a Jewish hoodlum without a raincoat eleven years before he became an Italian detective who never took it off. Peter

Barbara Rush and Dean Martin in The Young Lions.

Falk was nominated for best supporting actor as Abe Reles, the Jewish gangster who was part of the notorious Murder, Inc. gang in Brooklyn in the 1930s. Reles works for another bad Jew, Louis "Lepke" Buchalter (David J. Stewart), eventually squeals on him and the rest of the gang when things get just a little out of hand, and then pays the ultimate price. Columbo would never have been that dumb. Most of it was filmed on location and was considered an accurate portrayal of the era. Directed by Burt Balaban and Stuart Rosenberg.

No Way to Treat a Lady (1968)

A weary Jewish detective pursues a suspicious Irish priest, German handyman, middle-aged woman, Italian waiter, and homosexual hairdresser. The thing is, they're all the same person, and all played by Rod Steiger. The detective, Morris Brummel, is played by George Segal, and in addition to playing cat and mouse with the mass murderer, he has a new gentile girlfriend (Lee Remick) and a nagging mom (Eileen Heckart), who isn't even proud of him because she doesn't think a Jewish boy should be a detective. Steiger, by the way, also pretends to be a Jewish cop. Directed by Jack Smight.

The Big Fix (1978)

Richard Dreyfuss plays Moses. No, not *that* Moses, but an ex-radical named Moses Wine who becomes a private eye. His beloved 1960s return, in a way, when Moses is handed a case involving some shady radical dudes from the good old days. F. Murray Abraham (later an Academy Award winner for *Amadeus*) plays one of the shady dudes as a sort of fictional Abbie Hoffman, and Susan Anspach plays the onetime *shikse*

girlfriend who hands him the case in the first place. Dreyfuss, who produced, and director Jeremy Paul Kagan, the son of a rabbi, made the film partially because of the Jewish conscience that is part of Moses Wine's character.

Mobsters (1991)

The teen flick that thought it was an adult epic. Bugsy Siegel, Meyer Lansky, and some of their Jewish and Italian cohorts laugh, shoot, kibitz, grin, and connive their way through Prohibition. Young stars Christian Slater, Patrick Dempsey, and Richard Grieco try hard but are stuck in what most critics thought was a mediocre imitation of many similar films. F. Murray Abraham's in this one, too, as a gangster, adding a little style to the styleless proceedings. In England, *The Evil Empire* was added to the title to try to build more excitement. It didn't work. Directed by Michael Karbelnikoff.

Casino (1995)

He's handsome, Jewish, suave, well off, runs a big hotel and casino, and even talks of commandments and morality like a one-arm bandit rabbi. Robert De Niro plays Ace Rothstein in a movie about who really tosses the dice in Las Vegas. "Las Vegas washes away your sins," he says. "It's a morality car wash." The movie—almost a how-to film for people hoping to make a killing (so to speak) behind the scenes in Sin City—marked the return of De Niro, costar Joe Pesci, and director Martin Scorsese, all three of whom were involved in *GoodFellas* five years earlier. Sharon Stone also got some of her best notices for her role as De Niro's junkie wife.

Robert De Niro and Joe Pesci in Casino.

The Two-Thousand-Year-Old Patient

The Juggler (1953)

He cast a giant shadow a decade later, but Kirk Douglas cast a decidedly different one here as a European refugee going to Israel to try to put together the shattered pieces of his Holocaust-scarred life. The story takes him through many parts of Israel, where it was filmed, providing an almost documentary travelogue along with the sentimental melodrama. It was directed by Edward Dmytryk, whose *Crossfire* and *The Young Lions* also had significant Jewish content.

Judith (1966)

As if Israel didn't have enough bombs. In this unsuccessful effort, Sophia Loren plays a Holocaust survivor who goes to Israel to find and seek revenge on her Nazi husband, who has taken their little son. Peter Finch

plays her love interest. Since it takes place in 1948 and was actually filmed in Israel, there is a certain measure of visual interest (beyond Sophia herself) in seeing what the young nation must have looked like. The director, Daniel Mann, also did *Who's Been Sleeping in My Bed?* with Dean Martin and *Our Man Flint* with James Coburn close to the time he did *Judith*, which may indicate that Mann simply may not have been in a serious enough mood to handle the topic.

Hanna K. (1983)

So you have an American Jewish lawyer sleeping with an Israeli district attorney while vigorously defending a suspected Palestinian terrorist who may or may not be a terrorist and with whom the lawyer may or may not also be sleeping. But you want to call it a taut, political thriller when in actuality it's a silly ol' Middle Eastern soap opera. *Hanna K.* was directed by Costa-Gavras, who usually *does* do taut, political thrillers (*Z*, *Missing*). Jill Clayburgh is the lawyer, and she's always watchable. But there's a lot missing in *Hanna K.*, besides the rest of her last name.

The Little Drummer Girl (1984)

She's back!!! Well, in a way. It was widely speculated that the lead character in John Le Carré's story of a pro-Palestinian actress was modeled after Vanessa Redgrave, who had created an unnecessary and embarrassing stir at the Academy Awards seven years earlier. In the movie, Diane Keaton plays the actress, recruited by Israeli agents to help them in their fight against Palestinian terrorism. Klaus Kinski is one of the Israeli counterintelligence officers. The confused and muddled movie was directed by George Roy Hill, who fared much better with *Butch Cassidy and the Sundance Kid* and *The Sting*.

Goodbye, New York (1985)

This one's about a Jewish American princess—or more specifically, a Jewish Irish American princess—and her comic, eye-opening adventures in the Promised Land. Julie Hagerty is a New Yorker who falls asleep in an airplane at the airport in Paris and soon arrives in Israel by mistake, minus her luggage. Somehow she ends up on a kibbutz where she must adapt to many new ways and many new and interesting people, including a soldier played by Amos Kollek (son of longtime Jerusalem mayor Teddy Kollek), who also directed.

Between Two Worlds

Street Scene (1931)

It's almost as if playwright Elmer Rice and director King Vidor had taken the original Pulitzer Prize-winning play and plopped it in front of a movie camera, stage and all. But despite its static nature, this early black and white entry was lauded for being a deeply emotional and very accurate slice of New York tenement life and those who pray to get out of it. George Barnes's cinematography and Alfred Newman's score were particularly noted. Within the first few minutes, Jews on the street are told, "You people are the first to ask for help," and "We don't want no foreigners coming here to tell us how to run things." On top of that, it's hot as hell.

Molly (1950)

This is one family that got around, even though they hardly ever left the Bronx: They appeared on radio, on television, on stage, and—for the first time in 1950—in the movies. *Molly*, based on Gertrude Berg's famous family creation, the Goldbergs, is a gentle, sweet-natured ride through the lives of the extended family, which includes Philip Loeb as husband Jake and Eli Mintz as Uncle David, as they continue their very slow assimilation into American society—Bronx division. Because of her wisdom, strength, and affection, you don't have to be Jewish to love Molly. You don't have to be Jewish to *need* a Molly, either. Directed by Walter Hart.

American Pop (1981)

"Ralph Bakshi is to Walt Disney what Mick Jagger is to Perry Como," said *People* magazine. This animated film is about four generations of a Jewish musical family, originally Russian immigrants, and their journey through the American musical scene, from vaudeville to punk rock. It has more ups and downs, highs and lows, mobsters and drugs, love and despair, electricity and ethnicity than most movies with real people in them, and Bakshi is true to form. It must be remembered, though, that he also made the famous X-rated *Fritz the Cat*.

An American Tail (1986)

"In America," Papa Mousekewitz tells his family, "there are breadcrumbs on every floor." That may be true, but his cute little Russian family also believes that there are no cats in America, either. Have *they* got something coming to them! For all its appeal to young viewers, with little wide-eyed Fievel getting lost in the big bad city, *An*

American Tail (created by Don Bluth and a shop full of ex-Disneyites) is also a history lesson for people of all ages because of its scenes of nineteenth century immigrant life in New York—complete with sweatshops, peddlers, elevated trains, tenements, and plenty of Irish and Italian mice.

A Price Above Rubies (1998)

Basically, the only good thing Sonia does in this movie is say something to the rabbi that makes him incredibly amorous toward his wife. Unfortunately, he dies soon after. Other than that, this relatively sordid tale of a young, pretty, repressed, and miserable Hasidic woman does not have much going for it, not even the eminently watchable Renée Zellweger as Sonia. She connives, yells, allows herself to be seduced by her equally reprehensible brother-in-law, sleeps with a young Hispanic artist—and doesn't even seem to think she's doing anything wrong. She's supposed to be a woman of fortitude, whose worth is far above the price of rubies. Must be costume jewelry. Directed by Boaz Yakin.

In a Pickle

Marjorie Morningstar (1958)

Or, "Marjorie Morgenstern falls in love with a Jewish guy but ends up with Martin Milner." As played by Gene Kelly, Noel Airman (the Jewish guy) can't sing as well as he dances, but the problem is that he hardly dances in the movie at all. Natalie Wood is Marjorie, a New York City girl seeking summer romance and footlight glory in the Catskill Mountains in Herman Wouk's popular story. Ed Wynn plays her uncle, and he stays at the same resort as if

Fievel in An American Tail.

to sprinkle some of the Jewish values that Marjorie (and the screenwriter) got rid of as Wouk's story went from page, where it was a best-seller, to screen, where it bombed. Directed by Irving Rapper.

Bye, Bye Braverman (1968)

"You can't get a good egg cream anywhere," George Segal says to a couple of patient headstones in a cemetery that may or may not be the final resting place of Leslie Braverman, one of his writer friends. Segal and four other Jewish so-called intellectuals are on their way to the funeral but can't find the right chapel. What they find instead is Alan King as a sardonic rabbi and Godfrey Cambridge as a Yiddish-speaking cabbie. They also discover that they really have nothing significant to say to each other—even about their dead friend, although they'd like to believe they do. Directed by Sidney Lumet, who admitted that he took cemeteries much too seriously.

Vanessa Redgrave and Jane Fonda in Julia.

Julia (1977)

If only Vanessa Redgrave hadn't done such a wonderful job as Julia. Then she wouldn't have won an Academy Award for best supporting actress, and we would have been spared the infamous Oscar-night speech in which she called demonstrators against her pro-Palestinian politics "a small bunch of Zionist hoodlums. (She was later denounced by writer Paddy Chayefsky.) Other than that, *Julia* deserves its honors as a moving and evocative story of Jewish playwright Lillian Hellman (Jane Fonda), who becomes involved in the European resistance in the 1930s with her childhood friend Julia. Jason Robards won a best supporting actor Oscar as Dashiell Hammett, and Alvin Sargent won for his screenplay. Fred Zinnemann directed.

Girlfriends (1978)

Wanted: new best friend to be roommate; don't have to be Jewish, although maybe that would help you better understand . . . Melanie Mayron is the one who loses her roommate when the roommate moves out to get married. Melanie is then left to deal with life and all its warts on her own for the first time. *Girlfriends* had the misfortune of opening in New York during a newspaper strike, which meant that it was barely advertised and received very little press. So Mayron, along with costar Eli Wallach and director Claudia Weill, stood in front of the theater where it was playing and urged people to please go inside to see the movie.

Willie and Phil (1980)

Woody Allen and Al Pacino both love the same woman. Well, at least that was the way it was originally intended. But the roles eventually went to Michael Ontkean as Willie, a Jewish high school teacher, and Ray Sharkey as Phil, a Catholic fashion photographer. They meet at a movie theater after seeing *Jules and Jim* (which more or less becomes the outline for their lives and relationships) fall in love with Jeanette (Margot Kidder), and deal with each other's emotions over a nine-year period. It was directed by Paul Mazursky, who in his movies has always been familiar with Jewish sons, Jewish mothers, Jewish guilt, and all things Jewish. Woody Allen, by the way, would have played the Jew.

Wandering Jews

The Angel Levine (1970)

You'd have a devil of a time recognizing the story if you read Bernard Malamud's original. First of all, the real story features a middle-aged Jew named Manishevitz. In the movie it's an old Jew named Mishkin. Also, many plot elements were changed, and inner-city dialogue was added. Fortunately, the very basic idea is still there: a black angel (Harry Belafonte) is sent down to Earth to earn his wings by helping out class-A *kvetcher* Morris Mishkin (Zero Mostel). Directed by Jan Kadar and produced by Belafonte's company.

Romance of a Horsethief (1971)

The magnificent *menschen* ride again. Yul Brynner and Eli Wallach star in a joint American-Yugoslavian production about Jewish horse traders, led by Wallach, who use a little magic and a lot of *chutzpah* to try to outsmart and outdo the thieving Cossacks, led by Brynner, in a Polish village around 1900. Lainie Kazan is also on hand. Directed by Abraham Polansky.

Oh, God! (1977)

Okay, so he never really says he's Jewish in the movie—but God, played by George Burns, certainly gives that impression in this cheery, uplifting comedy-fantasy about His visit to Earth to let everyone know he's still around. He delivers that message through a grocery store manager played by John Denver. Given that his personality is closer to that of a Borscht Belt comic than the Almighty ("So sue me!"), it's a bit tough for Denver to believe that George is who He says He is. Of course, it helps that George has all the answers. Not to mention a cigar. Directed by Carl Reiner.

An American Werewolf in London (1981)

He should have stuck to Buckingham Palace, Stonehenge, and the West End. What's a nice Jewish boy doing in the English moors, where he can get a major hickey from an angry werewolf? But that's what happens to student David Kessler (David Naughton) in this horror film with a biting sense of humor and more Jewish jokes than you can sink your teeth into. Think of *Animal House*—directed, as was this movie, by John Landis— crossed with *I Was a Teenage Werewolf,* and extra dialogue supplied by Sheckey Greene.

Zelig (1984)

He'd even become, God forbid, a film critic if he were standing between two of them. But that's one thing Leonard Zelig didn't become in this metaphysical-comedy-drama about a human chameleon, written and directed by and starring Woody Allen. Zelig, the son of a Yiddish actor, with a Jewish identity that doesn't change nearly as much as he does, uses his inexplicable talent to be accepted, and in the process

David Naughton in An American Werewolf in London.

Neil Simon.

becomes a baseball player next to Babe Ruth, a Nazi listening to Hitler, even a Hasidic rabbi. All the while the world and one particular psychiatrist (Mia Farrow) are enraptured by him. Apparently so were the makers of *Forrest Gump*, who used the same kind of special effects ten years later.

Nu, What Else Is There?

Counsellor at Law (1933)

He worked hard for the money, but was it worth it? Now that he sees other parts of his life unfolding, successful Jewish lawyer George Simon may not think so. Some choices he and others in his life made along the way on his rise to the top threaten to break his spirit, just as they've already bro-ken his heart. John Barrymore as George lives up to the Barrymore legend and worked hard for the money—but he needed it badly because he reportedly drank his way through the entire production. Still, director William Wyler put up with Barrymore's excesses because he knew he could get that good old-fashioned great-ness out of him once more.

Body and Soul (1947)

A lawyer is one thing, but a boxer? Nice Jewish boys aren't supposed to box, but Charlie Davis does and becomes a champ. As Charlie, John Garfield won an Acad-emy Award nomination for taking this film the distance, to what most critics now re-gard as the best boxing movie ever made. Charlie has to decide just how far to go to get to the top—with some unwelcome in-trusions and temptations along the way. Heaven knows his mother (Anne Revere) would prefer him to do something else. Lilli Palmer is the girlfriend who helps him rise to the challenges. She's not Jewish, but mother doesn't mind. As always, mother knows best.

Enter Laughing (1967)

If Carl Reiner were really as dull as David Kolowitz, his alter ego in this semiauto-biographical story, we might never have had *The Dick Van Dyke Show, Oh, God!,* or the 2000-Year-Old Man comedy routines with Mel Brooks. Reiner wrote the book (on which Joseph Stein based his play on which Reiner and Stein based this movie) about a young Jewish machinist's apprentice who wants to be an actor, despite his mother and father's objections. The play made a star of Alan Arkin, but the movie's Reni Santoni doesn't measure up. There is an

Geoffrey Rush in Shine.

interesting supporting cast though: José Ferrer, Elaine May, Jack Gilford, Janet Margolin, David Opatoshu, Don Rickles, Richard Deacon (on loan from *The Dick Van Dyke Show*)—and one guess who plays the mother? Shelley Winters, of course. Reiner directed.

Biloxi Blues (1988)

Broadway bound by way of Biloxi. Eugene Jerome longs to leave Brighton Beach to become a writer, but Fort Biloxi, Mississippi, gets in the way at the end of World War II. The second in Neil Simon's semiautobiographical stage trilogy about the Jerome family, this one has a unique and affecting way of blending comedy with drama, as do *Brighton Beach Memoirs* and *Broadway Bound* in their different ways. Eugene learns about and comments on everything from his Jewish roots and his literary dreams to his sexual initiation and his Biloxi buddies. Christopher Walken (*Annie Hall, Next Stop, Greenwich Village*) plays the off-centered drill sergeant. Mike Nichols directed.

Shine (1996)

After a while you just want to smack his dad right in the smacker. Several times,

David Helfgott's father tells him that no one will ever love him as he does. Not five minutes later he screams at David, threatens him, and lays on the guilt thicker than his German accent. David, played to Oscar-winning perfection by Geoffrey Rush, is a piano prodigy, taught by his overly demanding father. Armin Mueller-Stahl, as the inexplicable old man, asks sternly after a competition, "Next time, what are you going to do?" "I'm going to win," David says, knowing it's the only answer that will suffice. Who ever said that every talented, close-knit Jewish family had to be warm? This one's not; David soon slides into a mental collapse. Although Rush won an Academy Award as best actor, the flashback Davids (Alex Rafalowicz and Noah Taylor) deserve just as much credit. Directed by Scott Hicks.

"Reel" Sources

The Internet is one of the newest and greatest friends for movie lovers looking to purchase or rent movies, Jewish and otherwise, that may be hard to find at local video stores. Several chains and on-line services make it easy today to research titles and order them without ever leaving your living room VCR. Many also have toll-free telephone numbers for additional help. In some cases, a title in the library of a retail chain may be located at a store out of town or out of state and sent by request to your local store, and then you can rent or purchase it there.

Blockbuster Video. Their web address is www.blockbuster.com and their toll-free number is 1-800-800-6767. If you would like to write to them they can be reached at:

Blockbuster Video
Customer Service Department
McKinney Headquarters
3000 Redbud Boulevard
McKinney, TX 75069

West Coast Video. Their web address is www.westcoastvideo.com and their telephone number is 215-497-5876. Write to them at:

West Coast Video
Customer Service Department
P.O. Box 1400
Newtown, PA 18940

Video Library

7157 Germantown Avenue
Philadelphia, PA 19119
Telephone: 800-669-7157
Web site: *www.vlibrary.com*

This is strictly an Internet service. They have no stores and do all their rentals on-line and through the mail—at competitive prices.

Critics Choice Video

Telephone: 800-993-6357
Web site: *www.ccvideo.com*

This is another online service with a massive library.

The Jewish Video Catalog

Ergo Media Inc.
668 American Legion Drive
P.O. Box 2037
Teaneck, NJ 07666-1437
Telephone: 800-695-3746
Web site: *www.jewishvideo.com*

The films in this catalog are available for purchase. Their list is obviously quite specialized and concentrates on documentaries, educational titles, the Holocaust, Jewish and Israeli culture, and Israeli film classics.

The Jewish Heritage Video Collection

Jewish Media Fund
Charles H. Revson Foundation
55 East 59th Street
New York, NY 10022
Telephone: 212-935-3340

The Jewish Media Fund, care of the Charles H. Revson Foundation, owns this extensive collection, which contains many mainstream Jewish movies as well as educational, documentary, and Israeli films.

The National Center for Jewish Film

Lown Building #102
Brandeis University
Waltham, MA 02254-9110
Telephone: 781-899-7044

This organization, based on the campus of Brandeis University, maintains an archive and library of many films related to the world Jewish experience.

Bibliography

Ausubel, Nathan (editor). *A Treasury of Jewish Folklore*. New York: Crown, 1948.

Barson, Michael. *The Illustrated Who's Who of Hollywood Directors*. New York: The Noonday Press, 1995.

Ben-Gurion, David. *Israel, a Personal History*. New York: Funk & Wagnalls, 1971.

Berg, A. Scott. *Goldwyn: A Biography*. New York: Riverhead Books, 1989.

Bleiler, David (editor). *TLA Film & Video Guide*. New York: St. Martin's Griffin, 1997.

Bly, Nellie. *Barbra Streisand: The Untold Story*. New York: Pinnacle Books, 1994.

Bjorkman, Stig, with Allen, Woody. *Woody Allen on Woody Allen*. New York: Grove Press, 1993.

Bokser, Ben Zion. *The Jewish Mystical Tradition*. New York: The Pilgrim Press, 1981.

Brown, Gene. *Movie Time*. New York: Macmillan, 1995.

Brown, Jared. *Zero Mostel, a Biography*. New York: Atheneum, 1989.

Brown, Julian (editor). *The Chronicle of the Movies*. New York: Crescent Books, 1991.

Carlson, Carole C. *Corrie ten Boom, Her Life, Her Faith*. Old Tappan: Fleming H. Revell Company, 1983.

Carnes, Mark C. (editor). *Past Imperfect: History According to the Movies*. New York: Henry Holt, 1995.

Clinch, Minty. *Burt Lancaster*. New York: Stein & Day, 1984.

Collier, James Lincoln. *Benny Goodman and the Swing Era*. New York: Oxford University Press, 1989.

Collins, Larry, and Lapierre, Dominique. *O Jerusalem*. New York: Simon & Schuster, 1972.

Curtis, Tony. *Tony Curtis, the Autobiography*. New York: William Morrow, 1993.

Bibliography

Custen, George Frederick. *Twentieth Century's Fox: Darryl F. Zanuck and the Culture of Hollywood.* New York: Basic Books, 1997.

Davis, Ronald. *The Glamour Factory.* Dallas: Southern Methodist University Press, 1993.

Deiser, David, and Friedman, Lester D. *American-Jewish Filmmakers.* Chicago: University of Illinois Press, 1993.

Douglas, Kirk. *Climbing the Mountain: My Search for Meaning.* New York: Simon & Schuster, 1997.

Ebert, Roger. *Roger Ebert's Video Companion.* Kansas City: Andrews McMeel Publishing, 1998.

Edelson, Edward. *Great Movie Spectaculars.* Garden City, New York: Doubleday, 1976.

Elley Derek, Editor. *Variety Movie Guide.* New York: Perigee, 1999.

Erens, Patricia. *The Jew in American Cinema.* Bloomington: Indiana University Press, 1984.

Fell, John L. *A History of Films.* New York: Holt, Rinehart & Winston, 1979.

Freedland, Michael. *Gregory Peck.* New York: William Morrow, 1980.

Friedman, Lester D. *The Jewish Image in American Film.* Secaucus, New Jersey: Citadel Press, 1987.

Gabler, Neal. *An Empire of Their Own: How the Jews Invented Hollywood.* New York: Crown, 1988.

Goldman, Eric A. *Visions, Images, and Dreams: Yiddish Film Past and Present.* Ann Arbor: UMI Research Press, 1979.

Golomb, Morris. *Know Jewish Living and Enjoy It.* New York: Shengold Publishers, 1981.

Gottfried, Martin. *Nobody's Fool: The Lives of Danny Kaye.* New York: Simon & Schuster, 1994.

Green, Stanley. *Hollywood Musicals Year by Year.* Milwaukee: Hal Leonard, 1990.

Griffin, Nancy, and Masters, Kim. *Hit and Run: How Jon Peters and Peter Guber Took Sony for a Ride in Hollywood.* New York: Simon & Schuster, 1996.

Griffith, Richard, and Mayer, Arthur. *The Movies.* New York: Simon & Schuster, 1970.

Guinness, Alec. *My Name Escapes Me: The Diary of a Retiring Actor.* New York: Viking Press, 1997.

Harris, Warren G. *Natalie and RJ: A Hollywood Love Story.* New York: Doubleday, 1988.

Hay, Peter. *Ordinary Heroes: Chana Szenes and the Dream of Zion.* New York: G. P. Putnam's Sons, 1986.

Herman, Jan. *A Talent for Trouble.* New York. G. P. Putnam's Sons, 1995.

Hersch, Foster. *Love, Sex, Death and the Meaning of Life: Woody Allen's Comedy.* New York: McGraw-Hill, 1981.

Hershinow, Sheldon J. *Bernard Malamud.* New York: Frederick Unger Publishing, 1980.

Heston, Charlton. *In the Arena.* New York: Boulevard Books, 1995.

Higham, Charles. *Cecil B. De Mille.* New York: Charles Scribner's Sons, 1973.

Hirschorn, Clive. *The Hollywood Musical.* New York: Portland House, 1991.

Hoberman, J. *Bridge of Light: Yiddish Film Between Two Worlds.* Philadelphia: Temple University Press, 1995.

Hopp, Glenn. *VideoHound's Epics.* Farmington Hills, Michigan: Visible Ink Press, 1999.

Howard, David M. Jr., (contributing writer). *Fascinating Bible Facts.*

Lincolnwood, Illinois: Publications International, 1992.

Insdorf, Annette. *Indelible Shadows: Film and the Holocaust.* New York: Random House, 1983.

Jenkins, Gary. *Harrison Ford, Imperfect Hero.* Secaucus, New Jersey: Citadel Press, 1999.

Jennings, Peter and Brewster, Todd. *The Century.* New York: Doubleday, 1998.

Kael, Pauline. *5001 Nights at the Movies.* New York: Holt, Rinehart & Winston, 1982.

———. *Deeper Into Movies.* New York: Atlantic Monthly Press, 1969.

———. *For Keeps.* New York: E. P. Dutton, 1994.

———. *Going Steady.* Boston: Little, Brown, 1968.

———. *Hooked.* New York: E. P. Dutton, 1985.

———. *I Lost It at the Movies.* New York: Atlantic Monthly Press, 1954.

———. *Reeling.* New York: Atlantic Monthly Press, 1972.

———. *State of the Art.* New York: E. P. Dutton, 1983.

———. *Taking It All In.* New York: Holt, Rinehart & Winston, 1980.

Kaminsky, Stuart. *John Huston, Maker of Magic.* Boston: Houghton Mifflin, 1978.

Karney, Robyn (Editor). *Chronicle of the Cinema.* New York: Dorling Kindersley, 1995.

Katcher, Leo. *Bankroll: The Life and Times of Arnold Rothstein.* New York: Da Capo Press, 1958.

Kimbrell, James. *Barbra, An Actress Who Sings.* Boston: Branden Publishing, 1989.

King, Alan with Chase, Chris. *Name-Dropping.* New York: Simon & Schuster, 1996.

Kresh, Paul. *Isaac Bashevis Singer: The Magician of West Eighty-Sixth Street.* New York: Dial Press, 1979.

Lally, Kevon. *Wilder Times: The Life of Billy Wilder.* New York: Henry Holt, 1996.

Lawrence, Jerome. *Actor: The Life and Times of Paul Muni.* New York: G. P. Putnam's Sons, 1974.

LeRoy, Mervyn, as told to Kleiner, Dick. *Mervyn LeRoy: Take One.* New York: Hawthorne Books, 1974.

Levinson, Barry. *Avalon, Tin Men and Diner: Three Screenplays by Barry Levinson.* New York: Atlantic Monthly Press, 1990.

Levy, Shawn. *King of Comedy: The Life and Art of Jerry Lewis.* New York: St. Martin's Press, 1996.

Lifson, David S. *The Yiddish Theatre in America.* New York: Thomas Yoseloff, 1965.

Lumet, Sidney. *Making Movies.* New York: Vintage Books, 1995.

Lyman, Darryl. *Great Jews on Stage and Screen.* Middle Village, New York: Jonathan David, 1994.

MacGraw, Ali. *Moving Pictures.* New York: Bantam Books, 1991

Mast, Gerald, and Bruce F. Kawin. *A Short History of the Movies*, sixth edition. Boston: Allyn & Bacon, 1996.

Maxford, Howard. *The A to Z of Horror Films.* Bloomington: Indiana University Press, 1997

Mazursky, Paul. *Show Me the Magic.* New York: Simon & Schuster, 1999.

McBride, Joseph. *Steven Spielberg, a Biography.* New York: Simon & Schuster, 1997.

McBride, Joseph. *The Book of Movie Lists.* Chicago: Contemporary Books, 1999.

McClelland, Doug (compiled by). *Star Speak: Hollywood on Everything.* Boston: Faber & Faber, 1987.

McDougal, Dennis. *The Last Mogul: Lew Wasserman, MCA, and the Hidden History of Hollywood.* New York: Random House, 1998.

Mordden, Ethan. *The Hollywood Musical.* New York: St. Martin's Press, 1981.

Morse, Arthur D. *While Six Million Died: A Chronicle of American Apathy.* New York: Random House, 1967.

Parker, John. *Warren Beatty: The Last Great Lover of Hollywood.* New York: Carroll & Graf, 1993.

Peters, Margot. *The House of Barrymore.* New York: Alfred A. Knopf, 1990.

Phillips, Julia. *You'll Never Eat Lunch in This Town Again.* New York: Random House, 1991.

Picon, Molly, with Grillo, Jean. *Molly! An Autobiography.* New York: Simon & Schuster, 1980.

Preminger, Otto. *Preminger, An Autobiography.* Garden City, New York: Doubleday, 1977.

Price, David (editor). *Anatomy of the Movies.* New York: Macmillan Publishing Company, 1981.

Quirk, Lawrence J. *Paul Newman.* Dallas: Taylor Publishing, 1996.

Rhode, Eric. *A History of Cinema from Its Origins to 1970.* New York: Hill & Wang, 1976.

Richler, Mordecai. *Home Sweet Home: My Canadian Album.* New York: Alfred A. Knopf, 1984.

Richman, Sidney. *Bernard Malamud.* New York: Twayne Publishers, 1966.

Roberts, Jeffrey. *Robert Mitchum, A Bio-Bibliography.* Westport, Connecticut: Greenwood Press, 1992

Robinson, David. *Chaplin: His Life and Art.* New York: Da Capo Press, 1994.

Rosenblum, Ralph, and Karen, Robert. *When the Shooting Stops . . . and Cutting Begins.* New York: Viking Press, 1979.

Roth, Philip. *The Facts.* New York: Farrar, Straus & Giroux, 1988.

Sanders, Ronald. *The Downtown Jews: Portraits of an Immigrant Generation.* New York: Harper & Row, 1969.

Shavelson, Melville. *How to Make a Jewish Movie.* Englewood Cliffs, New Jersey: Prentice-Hall, 1971.

Sikov, Ed. *On Sunset Boulevard: The Life and Times of Billy Wilder.* New York: Hyperion, 1998.

Silver, Alain, and Ward, Elizabeth. *Film Noir.* Woodstock, New York: Overlook Press, 1979.

Silverberg, Robert. *If I Forget Thee, O Jerusalem.* New York: William Morrow, 1970.

Simon, Neil. *Neil Simon Rewrites: A Memoir.* New York: Simon & Schuster, 1996.

Singer, Kurt. *The Danny Kaye Story.* New York: Thomas Nelson, 1958.

Sklar, Robert. *Movie-Made America.* New York: Vintage Books, 1975.

Spigness, Stephen J. *The Woody Allen Companion.* Kansas City, Missouri: Andrews and McMeel, 1992.

Spoto, Donald. *Laurence Olivier, a Biography.* New York: HarperCollins, 1992.

Strauss, David P., and Worth, Fred L. *Hollywood Trivia.* New York: Greenwich House, 1981.

Telushkin, Rabbi Joseph. *Jewish Literacy.* New York: William Morrow, 1991.

Thomas, Bob. *King Cohn: The Life and Times of Harry Cohn.* New York: G. P. Putnam's Sons, 1967.

Thompson, David, and Christie, Ian (editors). *Scorsese on Scorsese*. London: Faber & Faber, 1989.

Wagner, Walter (compiled by). *You Must Remember This*. New York: G. P. Putnam's Sons, 1975.

Walker, John (editor). *Halliwell's Film and Video Guide*. New York: HarperCollins, 1999.

———. (editor). *Halliwell's Filmgoer's and Video Viewer's Companion*, tenth edition. New York: HarperPerennial, 1993.

Warner, Cass, and Millner, Cork. *Hollywood Be Thy Name: The Warner Brothers Story*. Lexington: University Press of Kentucky, 1998.

Waskow, Arthur. *Down-to-Earth Judaism*. New York: William Morrow, 1995.

Wiley, Mason, and Bona, Damien. *Inside Oscar*. New York: Ballantine Books, 1996.

Winters, Shelley. *Shelley II: The Middle of My Century*. New York: Simon & Schuster, 1989.

Index

Index

Index

Index

About the Author

JOEL SAMBERG, author of *The Jewish Book of Lists*, has also written for *New Jersey Monthly*, the *New York Times*, the *Daily News Magazine, Moment*, the *Young Judaean, 3-2-1 Contact*, and many other publications. He has also been a humor and opinion columnist for several newspapers. Joel is a graduate of Hofstra University, where he studied drama and journalism, and has been involved in corporate communications and community theater. He lives in Verona, New Jersey, with his wife and three children.